IP Switching and Routing Essentials

Understanding RIP, OSPF, BGP, MPLS, CR-LDP, and RSVP-TE

Stephen A. Thomas

Wiley Computer Publishing
John Wiley & Sons, Inc.
New York • Chichester • Weinheim • Brisbane • Singapore • Toronto

Publisher: Robert Ipsen
Editor: Margaret Eldridge
Managing Editor: Penny Linskey
Text Design & Composition: Stephen Thomas

Library of Congress Cataloging-in-Publication Data:
Thomas, Stephen A., 1962-
    IP switching and routing essentials : understanding RIP, OSPF, BGP, MPLS, CR-LDP, and RSVP-TE / Stephen A. Thomas.
      p. cm.
    Includes index.
    ISBN 0-471-03466-5 (pbk. : alk. paper)
    1. Routers (Computer networks). 2. Telecommunication—Switching systems. 3. Computer network protocols. I. Title.
    TK5101.543.T48 2001
    004.6—dc21   2001046810

Printed in the United States of America.

10 9 8 7 6 5 4 3 2 1

CONTENTS

CHAPTER 1

Introduction

In 1997, David Isenberg published an influential essay titled "Rise of the Stupid Network."[1] The essay argued that the existing, dominant communications network—the international telephone system—would soon be insignificant compared to the Internet, the "stupid" network of the future. Isenberg chose the adjective "stupid" not to slight the Internet or its engineers but, rather, as a contrast to the latest telephony architecture, which is officially known as the Advanced Intelligent Network. In fact, Isenberg argued, the Internet will dominate precisely because it lacks intelligence. Instead of concentrating intelligence and control within the network as the telephone system does, the Internet pushes intelligence and innovation to the network's edges where end users can dictate its growth and success. The future telecommunications network, Isenberg concluded, will be one

---

[1] The full title is "Rise of the Stupid Network: Why the Intelligent Network was once a good idea, but isn't anymore. One telephone company nerd's odd perspective on the changing value proposition"; Isenberg's Web site, www.isen.com, includes links to the original essay. Isenberg and his views have been discussed not only in technical periodicals, but also in *Forbes*, *The Wall Street Journal*, and *USA Today*.

that does nothing more than transfer bits of data from one location to the other.

Isenberg makes it sound so easy. After all, how hard can it be to move a few bits around? Of course, as Isenberg understands, the Internet isn't really "stupid." In fact, the job of delivering data efficiently can be quite complex. The beauty of the Internet, though, is that delivering data is all the network has to do. The applications that users see as the Internet—electronic mail, Web browsing, multimedia, electronic commerce, etc.—are the responsibility of systems that use the Internet network; they are not really part of the network itself.

This text, therefore, is really about the heart of the Internet. It examines how the Internet carries out its main task: delivering data from one location to another.

This book may be conveniently thought of in thirds. The rest of this chapter introduces a few basic concepts that are critical to the Internet, including protocol layers, connectionless and connection-oriented data delivery, and network addresses. The following two chapters take a more in-depth look at the Internet Protocol (IP) itself and the UDP and TCP transport protocols. These first three chapters provide an in-depth background on IP and the Internet.

The second third of the book examines the Internet's three standard routing protocols—OSPF, RIP, and BGP. In each chapter we'll look at how those protocols are actually used in real networks, as well as their syntax and semantics. The final three chapters shift from IP routing to IP switching. Switching or, more precisely, Multi-Protocol Label Switching (MPLS) is a recent development for the Internet, and it promises much greater performance and flexibility for traffic engineering. Chapter 7 describes MPLS in full, while chapters 8 and 9 explore two common alternatives for exchanging label information: the Label Distribution Protocol (LDP), including its support for constraint-based routing, and the Resource Reservation Protocol (RSVP) with Traffic Engineering extensions.

Organizing with Layers and Hierarchies

Computer networks are complex undertakings, and ambitious networks like the Internet are especially complicated. To help manage that complexity, protocol designers rely heavily on two time-tested principles—layers and hierarchies. Layers organize effort, while hierarchies organize information.

Layers

A great many things must happen to make a network successful. Electromagnetic fields have to travel across wires, fibers, or air; those fields must be translated to and from digital information, and something must ensure that the information arrives intact; somehow the information has to travel across the right media to reach its intended destination; communicating systems must cooperate to make sure that the sender does not transmit more that the receiver can manage.

Engineers who design networks must deal with all of these issues and more. To do so effectively, they use a variation of the old-fashioned "divide and conquer" approach. Layering works by dividing all the functions of a network into groups and assigning those groups to *protocol layers*. Each protocol layer assumes responsibility for its own part of the entire network's total functionality, and when all layers operate together, they create a complete, functioning network.

Layering may sound a bit abstract, but it is actually a very familiar concept. Take audio compact discs (CDs), for example. By most definitions, the important part of the CD is the silvery disc itself. That is the part that goes in a CD player to produce music. The product as a whole, however, is more than a 130 mm disc. The other parts of the product act as layers around the disc, and each layer serves a particular function. For example, consumers want to store their discs conveniently, as well as protect them from damage. To solve those problems, the industry created the plastic jewel box. Jewel boxes provide easy storage, and they offer protection to CDs not in use.

Jewel boxes solve most of the problems facing CD consumers, but another level of problems exists at the retail music store. Especially when CDs first became available, most retail stores had display racks configured for long playing (LP) albums. A compact disc in a jewel box does not fit in those racks very well. In addition, the small size of the jewel box made it a tempting target for shoplifters.

Figure 1.1 ▼

Layers are common in many fields other than networking. An audio compact disc, for example, may be packaged in a jewel box, enclosed in a display package, and contained in a shipping carton. Each layer serves a special purpose in delivering the music content to its destination.

To address these problems, the product has another layer. That layer is a display package. Early CD display packages were cardboard boxes about 300×150×15 mm in size. These boxes fit in an LP display rack without being swallowed completely, and they were large enough to discourage shoplifting. From the layering standpoint, though, a display package is a separate entity from what is actually inside a jewel box. The jewel box effectively isolates the display package from the disc. Figure 1.1 shows these layers and one additional layer—the shipping carton that delivers groups of display packages to retailers.

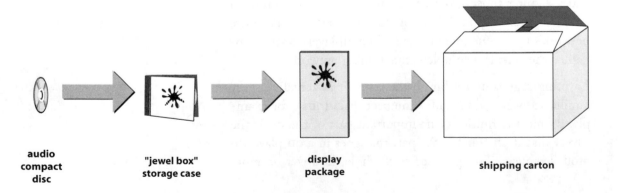

audio
compact
disc

"jewel box"
storage case

display
package

shipping carton

What benefits does layering provide the music industry? It splits up many of the various functions that contribute to a successful product, and it isolates those functions from each other. The manufacturers of the disks themselves need not worry about how those discs are packaged for shipment; they can focus their efforts on producing discs efficiently. Similarly, the freight company that delivers cartons to retailers does not care about the contents of those cartons.

This isolation, in turn, creates substantial flexibility. As LPs became less popular, music retailers could afford to reconfigure their display racks just for compact discs. At the same time, electronic inventory control devices became available to reduce shoplifting. These changes allowed the industry to replace its bulky display case with more compact packaging. And, because of layering, the move to compact display cases could happen without changing disc manufacturing or shipping methods. Imagine the problems if layering were not available. Any change to any function—shipping, display, storage, or disc manufacture—would require changes in every function. By making changes more costly, such an environment would stifle progress.

So how does this relate to computer networks? Actually, the practice is very similar. Suppose a user needs to transfer a file from one computer to another. The file itself is nothing but a series of digital bits, and computer networks transfer bits. It is not enough, however, to simply ship the bits across the cables; layering is essential. Figure 1.2 shows how a file transfer might be layered. Presumably, the file must be given a name on the remote computer. There may also be the question of a destination directory. This information can also be encoded as digital bits, and it can be added to the file's contents during the transfer. In computer communications, layers are usually added to the front of digital data, so figure 1.2 shows the file's name prepended to its contents.

The next problem facing network engineers is making the transfer reliable. It would not do for the file to acquire errors

Figure 1.2 ▶

This figure shows how layers apply to communications. Like the CD in figure 1.1, the content—in this case data for a file transfer—is enclosed in several layers. One layer provides essential identification (e.g. the name of the file), another makes the exchange reliable, and a third layer makes sure the data arrives at the right destination. The complete package, including the information of all layers, appears on the network link.

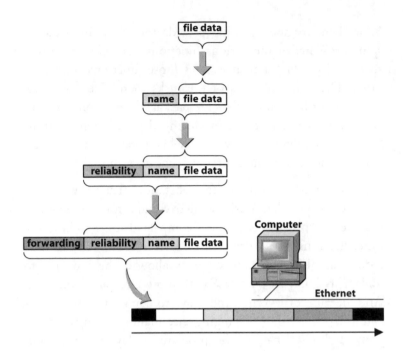

during its transfer. To provide this reliability, another layer of information may be added, resulting in more bits on the front of the data (which already includes the file name). These bits may include error detecting codes, and they may contain information necessary to retransmit the file, should an error occur.

Once the network has taken care of errors, it must get the file to the right place. After all, most networks have many possible destinations, and somehow the file must get to the right computer. This service requires correct forwarding and routing of the data, and they add another layer of information to the front of the data.

The figure's final protocol layer belongs to the specific network technology—in this case, Ethernet. The Ethernet protocol adds information before and after the data. That information, shown in black in the figure, serves to mark the beginning and end of the data as it crosses the network.

All this layering provides the same benefits to networks that it does to compact disc sales. First, it isolates the various services from one another. One group of engineers can go off and design a file transfer protocol without worrying about how the network forwards data. Another group can concentrate on reliable delivery, without concern for the type of data whose delivery they ensure.

The isolation give the Internet architecture flexibility. It makes it possible for protocol designers to upgrade the forwarding and routing services, without requiring massive changes to applications like file transfer. And, as new technologies are developed, other layers within the Internet architecture can immediately take advantage of them.

Hierarchies

Like layers, hierarchies are another abstract concept that helps organize computer networks. Hierarchies organize information and delegate responsibility. The effects of hierarchies are apparent in many aspects of everyday life. A common example is the global telephone system, which makes it possible to communicate between points anywhere in the world; it depends on a hierarchy. The hierarchy is that of telephone numbers themselves, and it makes sure that every telephone number is unique and unambiguous. Clearly this quality is important. Without it, there would be no way to guarantee whom callers would reach when they dial the phone.

It is possible to distribute unique phone numbers without establishing a hierarchy. The world could set up a singe master computer, for example, that assigned every phone number directly. When someone needed a phone number, he or she could apply to the master computer, which would search its massive database to find an available number.

Of course, the world does not assign phone numbers this way. The administrative burden would be too great. Instead,

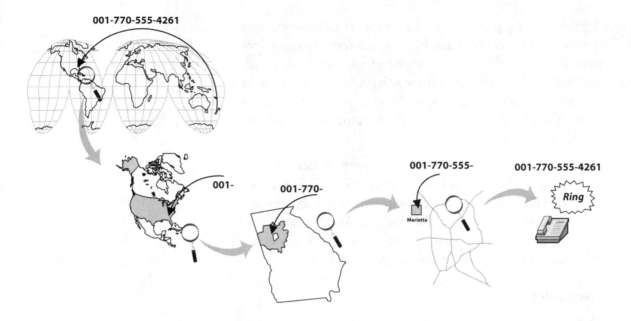

Figure 1.3 ▲

Hierarchies are another important quality of computer networks that other systems share. This example shows the hierarchy present in the worldwide telephone network. It highlights a phone call from New Zealand to the United States. Successive digits in the phone number narrow its scope, from country (001), to area (770), then to exchange (555) and finally to the specific circuit of the called party (4261).

a simple hierarchy exists. The hierarchy is based on geography. To reach the United States from New Zealand, for example, a caller can dial 001 770 555 4261. As figure 1.3 shows, each group of digits in this number indicates a successively more specific area of the world.

The benefits of this arrangement are obvious. If the local phone company in Marietta, Georgia wishes to assign a new phone number, it has to worry about only the last four digits. Everything else is preassigned and guaranteed to be unique, so there is no need for the local phone company to coordinate, for example, with its counterparts in New Zealand.

The IP-Based Internet

The discussion of layering and hierarchies may seem a bit abstract, but without these concepts, the worldwide, IP-based Internet would not be possible. The communication protocols themselves rely heavily on layering to organize their tasks, and the Internet naturally organizes its components into hierarchies. This organization creates two distinct roles for systems that make up the global network. Those roles—that of a host and that of a router—apply to all IP-based networks.

The Internet's Protocols

Readers who have experience with TCP/IP and the Internet probably know that it is much more than just two protocols. Indeed, TCP/IP standards define or reference over 1000 distinct communication protocols. With this many different protocols, a layered architecture is essential.

Unlike with some sets of communication protocols, IP's developers have not spent a great deal of effort formalizing its architecture. No precise definition of its layers exists, therefore. Most IP engineers would agree, though, that the IP architecture looks something like figure 1.4. This figure presents an abstract picture of how a networked computer organizes its protocols. As is common in such diagrams, it shows the layers of the architecture in a vertical stack. Applications reside at the top of stack. These are the protocols that actually organize the information the networks transfer. Example applications include file transfer, electronic mail, and Web browsing. They represent the innermost packaging of the architecture.

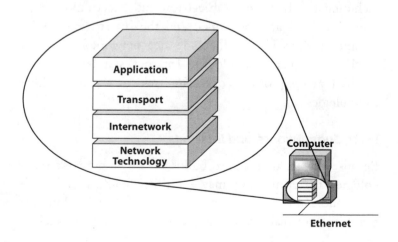

◀ **Figure 1.4**

Systems that communicate on the Internet use four different protocol layers for their communications. The application interfaces with a transport protocol, which interfaces with an internetwork protocol, which interfaces, in turn, with specific network technologies.

Immediately beneath the application is the transport layer. Transport layer protocols take the applications' information and deliver it to the destination. Transport protocols have the responsibility for distinguishing between multiple applications and for providing whatever reliability those applications require. The Transmission Control Protocol (TCP) is one transport protocol.

Transport protocols rely, in turn, on internetwork layer protocols. For the Internet, the primary internetwork protocol is the Internet Protocol, or IP. It makes sure that information travels through networks appropriately and reaches its destination, a process known as *forwarding*. To do that successfully, IP implementations have to understand the topology of the network; they need to know who is connected to whom. *Routing* is the process of discovering and distributing that information. The IP protocol suite includes many different protocols that assist in routing.

The lowest level in TCP/IP's protocol stack is the network technology itself, where systems connect to each other and actually exchange information. The Internet supports a diverse set of network technologies, ranging from simple dial-up modems to high-speed optical networks. Normally, the Internet standards do not concern themselves with the details of these technologies. Other standards organizations, including the Institute of Electrical and Electronics Engineers (for local area networks) and the International Telecommunications Union (for wide area networks), generally specify particular technologies. Internet standards merely specify how the protocols of the internetwork layer use those technologies.

Links, Subnetworks, and Internets

Because the IP architecture builds on other network technologies, its terminology may get a little confusing. A dial-up phone connection can properly be called a *link*, but that term does not really suit a simple local area network such as

Ethernet, much less a global frame relay infrastructure. The frame relay structure is clearly a *network*, but how does one distinguish a single frame relay network from an IP-based network made up of many frame relay networks?

Some IP engineers make this distinction by defining two types of networks. A *subnetwork* consists of all systems that can directly communicate with each other using homogeneous technologies. A single frame relay network forms a subnetwork. When IP joins several subnetworks together, the resulting collection is an *internetwork*, or *internet* for short. Figure 1.5 shows that internets consist of many subnets. Of course, the most important internet of all is the global Internet (generally written with an uppercase I.)

Unfortunately, a consistent use of these terms can become quite cumbersome, so this text, like much of the IP literature, will often simply use the term *network*. Only in cases where

▼ **Figure 1.5**

Even a small part of the Internet, like the example below, consists of many different subnetworks. Each subnetwork may be based on its own particular technology—Ethernet, frame relay, Token Ring, and others— but the Internet's communication protocols tie them together and allow all the different systems to communicate with each other.

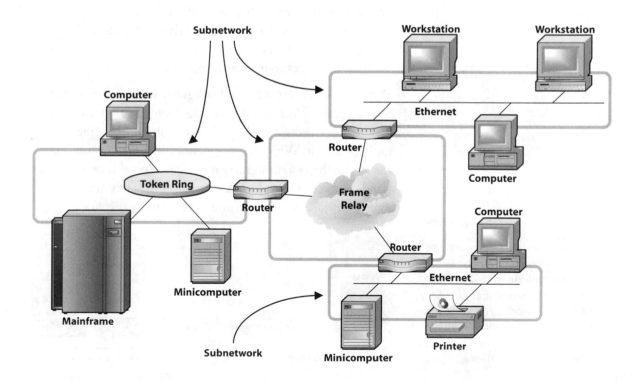

Real-World Routers

Despite the nice, clean definition, no pure routers actually exist. Commercial routers certainly focus on the internetwork layer and its routing and forwarding functions. Nonetheless, real routers do require some applications. They typically support remote login sessions for administration, file transfer applications to retrieve configuration data, and network management applications for operation and maintenance. Technically, therefore, these real products are both hosts and routers.

the distinction is important, and not otherwise clear from context, does it resort to the more precise terminology.

Hosts and Routers

The IP protocol architecture does more than just support various network technologies; it combines diverse technologies into a unified network. This unification highlights the distinction between the two roles that IP-based systems may play; IP-based systems may act as hosts, and they may act as routers. Systems that primarily send or receive messages are *hosts*; systems that relay those messages across networks are *routers*.

Figure 1.6 shows a simple network with two hosts and two routers. The personal computer and the server are the systems that exchange information. They do not share a common subnetwork, however. The PC connects to the left Ethernet, while the server resides on the right Ethernet. Fortunately, routers are active on both Ethernets, and the two routers can connect to each other using a dial-up link. These routers can accept messages from one host and relay them, through the other router, to the remote host.

Perhaps the easiest way to distinguish hosts from routers is to count the links and subnetworks to which they connect. If a system connects to a single link or subnet, then the system must be a host. With only one connection, there is no opportunity for the system to relay messages. Routers, on the other hand, connect multiple links or subnets. They accept messages from one connection and pass them to another.

Figure 1.6 ▶

Routers allow computers on different subnetworks to communicate with each other. They translate messages between different network technologies. In this example the routers translate from Ethernet to a dial-up phone line and back to Ethernet again.

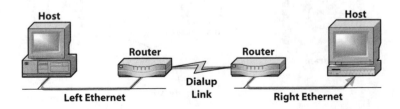

Based on this discussion, it is possible to distinguish the protocol layers within hosts and routers. Hosts necessarily include all of the IP architecture's protocol layers. Routers, on the other hand, mainly rely just on the internetwork layer. As long as a router is not originating or terminating traffic, it has no need for transport or application protocols. (But see the sidebar on the previous page.)

Figure 1.7 shows an abstract view of the message exchange from the previous figure. Each router accepts messages from a particular network technology, processes them in the internetwork layer, and forwards the message to another network technology.

Communication Services

Modern communication protocols give their users a great deal of flexibility. For example, Internet users who transfer files can choose from among at least six different protocols. Furthermore, the IP architecture does not confine this flexibility to the application layer. Various communication services are available from the transport layer, as well as from many network technologies. And on a lesser scale, IP itself supports several optional extensions.

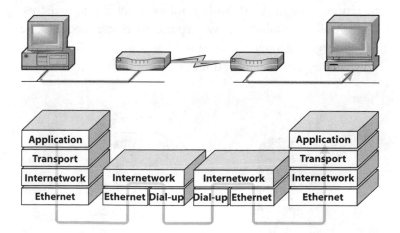

◀ Figure 1.7

The translation that figure 1.6 describes takes place in the internetwork layer of the routers. The internetwork layer protocol is common to all the systems, even though specific technologies may differ.

The most significant difference between communication services is how they deliver their messages. Network engineers classify delivery services as *connectionless* or as *connection-oriented*.

Connectionless Delivery

Connectionless delivery is the simplest service to provide. When a protocol provides this service, it treats every message independently. The protocol itself requires no interaction before accepting a message, nor does it provide a context for different messages in a conversation.

It may suffer from overuse, but the simplest example of connectionless service is regular postal mail. Users enclose each message in an envelope and give it to the postal service to deliver. The postal service does not require any negotiations before accepting a letter. Figure 1.8 highlights the similarities between postal mail and connectionless communication. The postal service accepts letters, and the communication network accepts messages. Each must be explicitly labeled with its destination. Like the postal service, the network treats each message independently, delivering it to its destination.

Even though the network views each message independently, connectionless services do allow users to interact with each other. Users themselves must take responsibility for that interaction, though. If an author mails a book proposal to a publisher, the publisher may respond to that proposal. The postal service, however, does not force a response. The same principle applies to connectionless communication. A system

Figure 1.8 ▼

Connectionless delivery is also what the postal service provides. The sender starts the message on its way—either by dropping an envelope in a mailbox or transmitting a message onto a network—and the network delivers it to the right destination. In both cases, the network doesn't know, or even care, that different messages may have any relationship to each other.

that receives a message may respond with its own message, That response is a separate message, and the delivery service treats it as such. Figure 1.9 illustrates this scenario. As the figure notes, the network does not know that the response message is a reply to the request message.

Connection-Oriented Delivery

Connection-oriented services represent a different philosophy. A protocol that provides such a service does more than simply transfer independent messages. It also establishes a context for those messages. Frequently, that context includes a guarantee of delivery. To provide this extra service, the protocol must do extra work. The work typically involves interaction with the recipient before data is transferred and periodic interaction as long as the conversation continues.

A convenient example of connection-oriented communication is a facsimile transmission, as shown in figure 1.10. Think about how sending a fax differs from sending a letter. With a letter, there is no preliminary interaction with the destination. The sender just drops the letter in the mailbox. With a fax, however, more involved interaction is necessary. The sender first dials the recipient's phone number and waits for an answer. Then the two fax machines negotiate the options they will use for the document. These steps establish the connection.

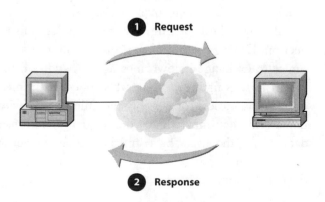

◀ Figure 1.9

As this example illustrates, systems can use connectionless delivery to carry on a conversation—just as etiquette often suggests answering a letter received in the mail. The network itself, however, (or the postal service) doesn't know the relationship between the messages.

Figure 1.10 ▶

A fax transmission represents connection-oriented communications. Here the network takes an active part in managing at least part of the dialog between the two systems. It rings the phone, conveys the answer, and hangs up, ending the call. The network establishes a connection that the two parties use to communicate.

Once the connection is established, the sender begins its transmission. Even during the transmission, though, the two fax machines interact. Depending on the options they have negotiated, the receiver may update the sender on the quality of the reception. If necessary, the sender can even retransmit part of the document. Finally, when the transmission is complete, the sending machine hangs up the phone, terminating the conversation.

Connection-oriented service works much the same way for data communications. Protocols that provide such service usually exchange their own messages before transmitting actual data. These preliminary messages establish the connection. During the life of the connection, the protocol continues to exchange its own messages in addition to any data it transfers, as figure 1.11 illustrates. These extra messages report on the success (or possibly the failure) of previous receptions, and they may trigger the sender to retransmit some data. Once the users have finished their conversation, the protocol can exchange more of its own messages to terminate the connection.

Combining Services

It might sound as though connectionless and connection-oriented services are totally incompatible. They do, after all, represent a considerable difference in philosophy. Despite that difference, however, many networks combine the services quite freely. One layer may offer one type, while a different layer offers the other. To see this process in action, consider the example network of figure 1.12, which shows two systems connected by an Asynchronous Transfer Mode (ATM) network. For this example, the personal computer wants to transfer a file to the server.

Communication begins when the PC's application program (a file transfer application) asks the transport layer protocol to

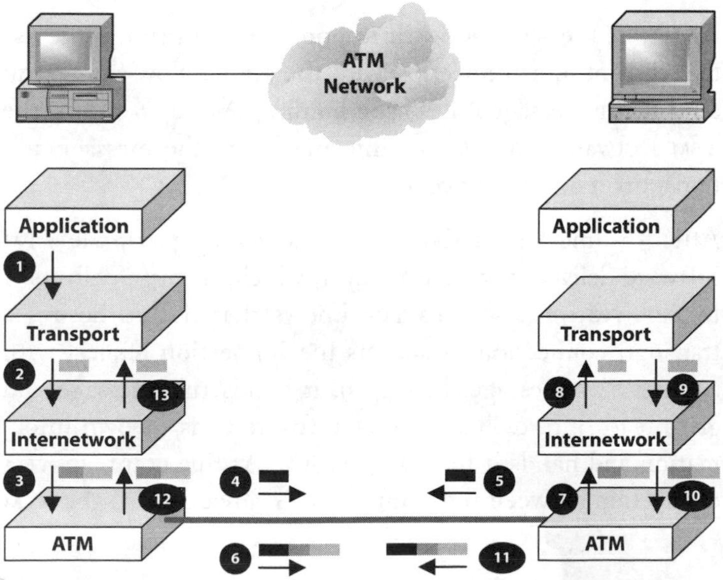

◀ **Figure 1.11**

With computer networks, connection-oriented communication establishes a context for the dialog between the systems. The network itself takes responsibility for associating a request with a response, and it ties the two together for the application.

◀ **Figure 1.12**

A computer network may combine connectionless and connection-oriented communications in a single exchange, with each protocol layer providing its own service. In this example, explained in more detail in the text, a connection-oriented transport layer protocol uses a connectionless internetwork layer protocol which, in turn, uses a connection-oriented network technology.

establish communications with the server. This action is step 1 in the figure. The application program uses TCP as a transport protocol, and TCP provides connection-oriented services. Its first action, therefore, is to send its own message to the server in order to begin establishing the connection. This first message carries no application data. At step 2, TCP builds this message and hands it to the internetwork layer protocol (IP) to deliver.

The Internet Protocol provides a connectionless service, so it treats the TCP message just like any other. It adds its own information and gives it to the ATM driver software to transmit (step 3). Because IP is connectionless, it does not establish a connection; it simply forwards TCP's message as soon as it gets it.

Like TCP, ATM provides a connection-oriented service. In order to deliver IP's message, the ATM driver software must establish its own connection to the destination. It builds an ATM-specific message and sends it to the network. This message (step 4) will establish the ATM connection. While the PC's ATM software waits for the connection, it holds the IP message.

At step 5, the ATM network responds by confirming the establishment of a connection with the server. Now the PC can send the IP message it has been holding. As step 6 shows, the ATM software adds its own information to the message and transmits it on the network.

After the message arrives at the server (step 7), the ATM software delivers it to the IP layer, which, in turn, delivers it to TCP. Now the server's TCP knows that the PC desires a transport connection. It accepts the connection request with another TCP message. In step 9, it builds this message and gives it to IP to deliver. The IP software adds its own information and hands it to ATM (step 10). At this point, an ATM connection between the computers already exists, so the ATM driver software can simply use that connection to deliver the response (step 11).

With steps 12 and 13, the PC receives the response and passes it to TCP. The transport connection is established, and the PC can finally begin sending its file. As the example shows, transferring the file relies on a combination of connections and connectionless service. The TCP and ATM software implementations each have to set up their own connections, while IP forwards messages in a connectionless manner.

Other combinations are possible at the transport and network technology layers. There are connectionless transport protocols (such as UDP) and connection network technologies (Ethernet, for example). The Internet's IP protocol, however, is always connectionless.

Network Addressing

This chapter's final topic answers a crucial question for any network architecture: How do systems identify each other? The issue is clearly critical; communications—remote logins, file transfers, mail exchanges, video conferences, and any others—succeed only if the right parties communicate. In order to communicate with the right system, other systems must be able to unambiguously identify it. Network addresses provide that unambiguous identification.

The Role of Network Addresses

If a network address provides identification, then it must identify something. In IP's case, the something is a little different from other network architectures. Technically, IP addresses identify interfaces, not systems. The distinction rarely matters for hosts. In most cases, hosts have but a single interface. Effectively, the system and the interface are equivalent. Informally at least, IP addresses are often thought to identify hosts rather than their interfaces.

Unlike hosts, routers usually support multiple interfaces. When they do, each of their interfaces may have a separate (and different) network address. Figure 1.13 shows a router attached to both an Ethernet and a Token Ring local area network. The router's Ethernet interface has the network address 1.2.3.4, while the Token Ring interface has address 5.6.7.8. Although both addresses belong to the same router, IP differentiates between the two when it delivers messages. Messages destined for address 1.2.3.4 arrive at the router from the Ethernet, while messages for address 5.6.7.8 arrive from the Token Ring.

In many cases, even this distinction remains unimportant. After all, both messages will reach the router. Particularly in an informal context, the router may be identified by the address of any of its interfaces.

Types of Addresses

The IP architecture supports three different types of network addresses; IP engineers names those types *unicast*, *multicast*, and *broadcast*.

Unicast messages are the most straightforward type of addresses. They refer to a single interface, and they do so unambiguously. When a system designates a unicast address as the destination of its message, it intends that the message reach a particular interface. The network takes responsibility for delivering the message to that interface.

Multicast addresses identify sets of interfaces. Most often, the set includes multiple interfaces that belong to different systems. When a message has a multicast destination

Figure 1.13 ▼

Network addresses identify subnetwork interfaces, as this example shows. The router in the center has to interfaces—a Token Ring and an Ethernet. Each interface has its own network address.

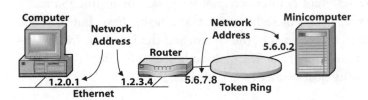

address, the network strives to deliver it to all interfaces in the set. This function lets a system generate a message once and have that message delivered to many different recipients.

Multicast addresses are obviously useful for multicast applications like video conferences. As Figure 1.14 shows, the messages that make up the conference are simultaneously delivered to all participants. Other IP-based protocols rely on multicast services for some of their internal functions. One router, for example, may need to quickly pass some information to all other routers. Instead of sending separate messages to each router one at a time, it can send the message once, but with a multicast destination address that identifies all other routers.

Broadcast addresses are a special case of multicast addresses. They identify to *all* interfaces on the network, rather than a set of interfaces. Since multicast addresses are more precise than broadcast addresses, the use of broadcast addresses is now discouraged.

IP Address Formats

Network addresses on today's Internet are 32 bits in size, and, as you've probably seen, have a somewhat unique notation. That notation is known as *dotted decimal*, and figure 1.15 illustrates how to interpret it. Each 8-bit byte in the 32-bit address is taken separately and expressed as a decimal number

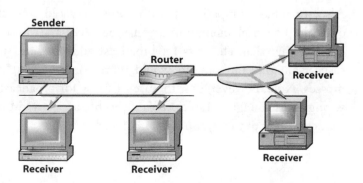

◀ **Figure 1.14**

Multicast addresses can identify several different interfaces simultaneously. Here the sender transmits one message destined for a multicast address; many interfaces receive a copy of that same message.

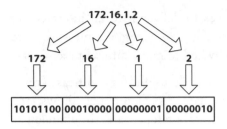

Figure 1.15 ▶

IP addresses are usually written in dotted decimal notation. The top of this example shows the address 172.16.1.2. As the figure illustrates, each of those four numbers represents a separate byte in the address, and each is expressed in decimal notation.

between 0 and 255. A decimal point (or period) separates each of these four bytes.

The address itself consists of two parts: a network prefix and a host identifier. The network prefix is a specific number of bits starting from the most significant bit, and it uniquely identifies an individual network or set of networks. For example, the notation "172.16.0.0/16" identifies a network prefix of 16 bits with the binary value 10101100 00010000. As Figure 1.16 shows, all systems on that network have the same prefix for their IP addresses.

Broadcast addresses are IP addresses that have a host identifier with all bits set to 1. Broadcasts are confined to single networks, and the network part of the IP address can indicate which network. For example, 172.16.255.255 represents all systems on the 172.16.0.0/16 network.

In some cases (e.g., during startup) a system may need to send a broadcast datagram before it knows the network address prefix for its interface. In those cases, the system can use an IP address that is nothing but 1 bits, 255.255.255.255. Also, to retain compatibility with some very old (but still operating) IP implementations, it may be necessary to use all 0 bits rather than all 1 bits for broadcast addresses. In such cases 172.16.0.0 and 0.0.0.0 would represent broadcast addresses. Note, however, that the use of zeros for broadcast is strongly discouraged. Table 1.1 lists the broadcast addresses that can apply to the 172.16.0.0/16 network.

Subnet Masks

Subnet masks are an earlier form of network prefixes and are still seen rather commonly in IP networks. A subnet mask, instead of counting the number of bits in a prefix, uses a 32-bit binary value to represent a network prefix. In the binary value, which is typically written in dotted decimal notation, a "1" represents bits that are included in the prefix, while a "0" represents bits that are not. For example, the network prefix 172.16.0.0/16 would be expressed as an address of 172.16.0.0 with a subnet mask of 255.255.0.0.

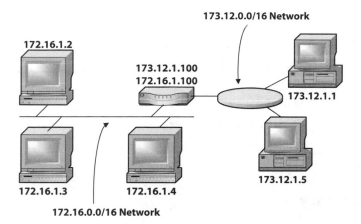

173.12.0.0/16 Network

172.16.1.2

173.12.1.100
172.16.1.100

173.12.1.1

172.16.1.3   172.16.1.4

173.12.1.5

172.16.0.0/16 Network

◀ **Figure 1.16**

This example shows two different subnetworks. Each subnetwork has its own IP address prefix, and all systems on a subnetwork have IP addresses that are part of that prefix.

Table 1.1 IP Broadcast Addresses for the 172.16.0.0/16 Network

Address	Scope
255.255.255.255	All systems on the local network
0.0.0.0	All systems on the local network (discouraged)
172.16.255.255	All systems on the 172.16.0.0/16 network
172.16.0.0	All systems on the 172.16.0.0/16 network (discouraged)

Although broadcast addresses are still used by many IP-based systems, multicast addresses are the preferred approach in the future. A range of IP addresses, 224.0.0.0 to 239.255.255.255, has been set aside just for multicast. None of these addresses can be used as a regular IP address. Most multicast addresses are designed to be used dynamically. That is, systems can create a specific multicast group for a particular application (a videoconference, for example) and then release that group once the application ends. A few multicast addresses, however, have been permanently defined. Table 1.2 lists some of those defined addresses.

Private IP Addresses

Although most legitimate IP addresses are designated for use on the public Internet, the Internet Assigned Numbers Authority has set aside three ranges of IP addresses for use on private networks. IANA guarantees that addresses from these ranges will never be assigned to systems on the real Internet, so private networks can use the ranges, safe in the knowledge that they will not create a conflict with legitimate Internet hosts. (There are no guarantees about conflicts with other private networks, however.) The private address ranges are 10.0.0.0/8, 172.16.0.0/12, and 192.168.0.0/16.

Table 1.2 Predefined IP Multicast Addresses

Address	Set of Systems
224.0.0.1	All systems on this subnet
224.0.0.2	All routers on this subnet
224.0.0.5	All OSPF routers
224.0.0.6	All OSPF designated routers
224.0.0.9	All RIP routers

Summary

This chapter introduces several concepts that underlie computer communications. The most pervasive of those concepts are layers and hierarchies. Networks use layers to divide their responsibilities into smaller, manageable pieces, and they use hierarchies to organize information. Both ideas appear throughout this text.

CHAPTER 2

IP—The Internet Protocol

Computer networks are built from a great variety of network technologies. The Internet itself includes everything from dial-up phone connections to high-speed fiber optic links. Such diversity naturally presents many challenges to network engineers, but ultimately it is the key to any network's success. Networks exist for communications; the more they communicate, the more value they provide.

To its credit, the Internet's architecture supports and encourages connection of nearly every network technology available. For Internet Protocol (IP) networks, it is IP itself that provides the common thread. The Internet Protocol unites disparate network technologies in a unified, global network

The Role of the Internet Protocol

The best indication of IP's importance is its name. It is *the* Internet Protocol, and it is the protocol that makes possible interconnected networks such as the Internet. Such networks require some independence from specific network technologies. The whole world cannot migrate to asynchronous transfer mode (for example) overnight. To provide that independence, IP isolates the transport and application protocols from the messy details of each network. Those protocols simply hand data to IP, and IP takes care of transferring the data across real networks.

Figure 2.1 illustrates this operation by showing the protocol layers involved in a communication exchange. The Internet Protocol resides above each particular network, whether that network is Token Ring, Ethernet, or a point-to-point link. It isolates the specifics of each network so that the transport protocol (TCP in the figure) and application (HTTP) protocols can ignore them.

Figure 2.2 highlights another major role for the Internet Protocol. Notice how every system in the figure relies on IP. All the systems shown—the computers and the routers—have a role in forwarding data packets between the workstation and server. The protocol responsible for packet forwarding is IP.

In general, a data packet's destination may be many networks away from its source. (In the figure, three different networks separate the two computers.) As packets travel from one to the other, IP in each system decides where to send it next. This decision is the very essence of forwarding.

Figure 2.1 ▼

The Internet Protocol isolates higher layer protocols from the specifics of particular network technologies. A transport protocol like TCP interfaces the same way with IP, whether the underlying subnetwork is Token Ring, Ethernet, or anything else. This architecture makes it easy for the Internet and other IP-based networks to accommodate technology advances. As new subnetworks appear, upper layer protocols continue to operate as before. They can take advantage of the new technology with themselves having to change.

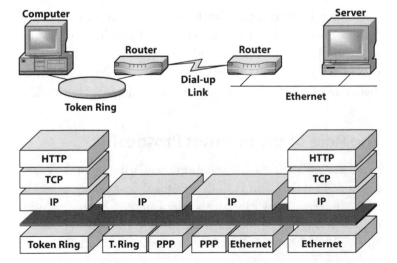

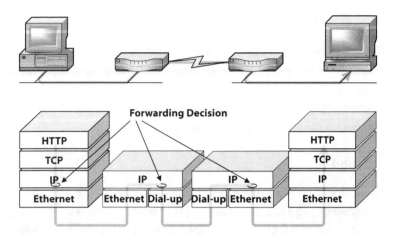

Forwarding Decision

◀ **Figure 2.2**

Each time IP needs to transmit a message, whether the message originated in the same system or is merely in transit through it, IP makes a forwarding decision. The forwarding decision tells IP where next to send the message.

Figure 2.2 highlights the path from the workstation to the server. It indicates the three different forwarding decisions along the way. The first forwarding decision occurs in the computer that originates the data. That PC must decide to send its traffic to the first router. Although the figure does not show it explicitly, this truly is a decision for the PC. Presumably, there are other systems on the Ethernet LAN, and the PC could just as easily send its messages to them. Instead, it sends them correctly to the first router.

As each message arrives at the first router, that router's IP must make a second forwarding decision. The router could send its messages to a system on the Ethernet (even, in theory, back to the sender), or the router could forward traffic across the point-to-point link. Clearly, the latter choice is the right decision, and, as the figure shows, the first router correctly makes it.

The final forwarding decision takes place in the second router. It eschews sending the data back across the point-to-point link or to an inappropriate system on the destination network. Instead, the second router delivers the data to its correct destination.

The IP Datagram

The Internet Protocol is a connectionless protocol. It treats each message independently, forwarding it through the network to its final destination. By convention, the packets that IP transfers are called *datagrams*. Each IP datagram begins with a common format, as shown in figure 2.3.

Version

The first four bits of each IP datagram contain the version number of the IP. The version that is most widely used today (and is the subject of this book) is version 4, so these bits carry the value 0100. Version 6, the presumed replacement for IP version 4, carries a small amount of traffic across the Internet. But the vast majority of IP systems—both today and in the near future—are IPv4 systems.

Header Length

The next four bits, which complete the IP header's first byte, indicate the total length of the IP header. Because only four bits are available, this field counts the number of 32-bit units that make up the header; it does *not* count the number of header bytes. As figure 2.3 illustrates, an IP header without any options is 20 bytes long. Such datagrams carry a header length value of 5.

Byte Order

Figure 2.3, like other figures in this text, organizes the packet into groups of 32 bits. As far as the underlying networks are concerned, however, an IP datagram is nothing but a series of bytes. Networks should order the bytes so that the top left byte is transmitted first. For IP datagrams, for example, the first byte transmitted is the combined versions and header length. Note that the transmission order of bits within each byte depends on the network technology. Ethernet, for example, sends the least significant bit first, while Token Ring stations begin their transmissions with the most significant bit.

Figure 2.3

Every IP datagram begins with an IP header. This example shows the standard 20-byte header, although systems may extend this header with options.

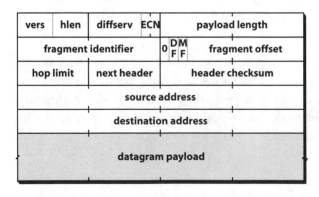

Because this field measure 32-bit units, all IP headers must be an even number of 32-bits in size. If desired options do not add up to an even multiple of 32 bits, then the sender must add extra dummy options to force the header size to an appropriate value.

Differentiated Service

The next six bits in the IP header identify the datagram's differentiated service, or *diffserv codepoint*, value. Note that only the six most significant bits of this byte actually carry a differentiated service value. The two least significant bits are not part of this field. Some networks are using these bits as an experiment to carry congestion information, but generally they are zero.

The diffserv codepoint signals routers to give the datagram special treatment. The special treatment may include expedited forwarding or extra protection from loss. A value of 0 indicates no special treatment is required. Most values for this field are not defined by the IP specification, Instead, it is up to individual networks to associate particular special treatments with particular diffserv values. The values that are explicitly defined (other than 0) are defined for historical reasons.

Originally, this byte in the IP header was known as the type of service field, and it was divided into two parts. The three most significant bits carried the relative precedence, or priority, of the datagram. The next three bits individually indicated a desire for low delay, high throughput, and high reliability. These three bits were used only very rarely on the Internet, and so the type of service field has been redefined to carry the diffserv codepoint.

To remain compatible with the precedence bits of older implementations, any codepoint values with the three least significant bits equal to zero are called class selector values. The class selector values are treated essentially the same as the original precedence; a higher value indicates higher relative priority. A class selector of 8 (001000_2), for example, is treated as a higher priority than the default diffserv codepoint of 0, while a class selector of 24 (011000_2) has a higher priority still.

Explicit Congestion Notification

The next two bits in the header contain the *explicit congestion notification* (ECN) field. The ECN field gives routers a way to signal hosts that their communication path is becoming congested. Well-behaved hosts can respond by reducing the amount of traffic they are sending.

Explicit congestion notification requires the cooperation of both hosts in a conversation as well as routers along the conversation's path. The general idea is a simple one. If a router notices that one of its links is becoming congested, it adds a special mark to datagrams that it forwards onto that link. The special mark doesn't change the contents of any datagram other than to indicate that, somewhere along its path, the datagram experienced congestion. When the destination host receives such a specially marked datagram, it sends a response to the sending application asking it to slow down. The original source slows down, and congestion at the router eases.

The place for the special congestion experienced mark is the ECN field of the datagram. As mentioned previously, however, these two bits are part of a byte that used to carry a type of service value. Because some older systems may still be using these bits for that purpose, routers cannot just add the congestion mark to any old datagram. They must first be sure that the hosts aren't using the old type of service field. Fortunately, older implementations will always set these two bits to 0. New implementations that support ECN, therefore, start by setting these bits to a different value, either 01 or 10. If a router wants to add a congestion mark to a datagram, it checks the ECN field. If the ECN value is 01 or 10, then the router is assured that the hosts support congestion notification. To actually add the mark, the router changes the ECN field to 11. Figure 2.4 illustrates this process.

Payload Length

Returning to the IP header of figure 2.3, the next two bytes contain the payload length. This value is the size of the datagram, not counting the datagram's IP header.

Fragmentation

The next four bytes in the IP header carry fragmentation information for the datagram. Fragmentation solves an important problem for the Internet Protocol: What if a datagram is too big for a particular network? Ethernet LANs, for example, can transfer frames no larger than 1514 bytes. A single IP datagram, on the other hand, may be much larger than that. Fragmentation lets a host or router divide a large datagram into several smaller pieces and send those pieces through the network. The receiving host puts them back together.

▼ **Figure 2.4**

Routers in the middle of a communication path can use the ECN bits to signal congestion to the communicating systems. These systems let the routers know they understand ECN by setting it to 01 or 10 in datagrams they originate. Routers change either of these values (but not 00) to 11 to indicate congestion on the path.

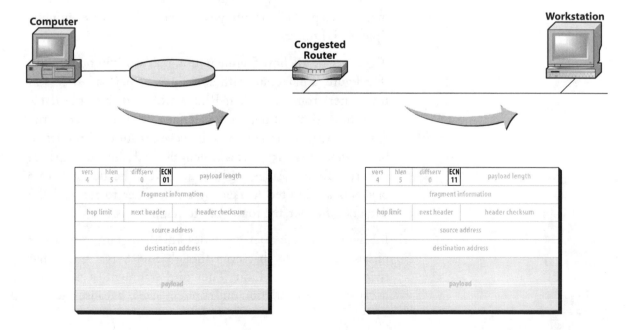

The first fragmentation field in figure 2.3's IP header is the *fragment identification*. This value unambiguously indicates the original datagram to which the fragment belongs. The sender picks this field's value, and it must be sure to pick a different value for every datagram that it sends. Note that the sender does this even if it has no intention of fragmenting the datagram because a router further along the path may have to fragment the datagram to pass it across a network.

The next three bits are individual flags for various aspects of fragmentation. Actually, the first bit is always zero and never used. The next bit is the *don't fragment* bit. A host can set this bit to tell routers not to fragment the datagram, even if that means they cannot deliver it. As we'll see in the section on ICMP, routers that encounter such a situation send an error message back to the sending host. The third bit is the *more fragments* bit. When any system fragments a datagram, it sets this bit on all fragments except the last.

The *fragment offset* specifies how far within the original datagram the first byte of the current piece belongs. Its value is in units of eight bytes. With this unit, IP must break all fragments (except the last) into pieces whose size is an even multiple of eight bytes.

Figure 2.5 shows how fragmentation may work in practice. In that figure, a datagram with 2918 bytes of payload arrives in the router from the Token Ring LAN. To deliver the datagram to its destination, the router must forward it across the Ethernet LAN. Ethernet LANs, however, require all frames to be no more than 1514 bytes in length (including the 14-byte Ethernet frame header). With a 40-byte IP header, Ethernet payloads are limited to 1460 bytes. In order to forward the datagram further, the router has to fragment it.

In figure 2.5, the router divides the datagram into three pieces. It must do that even though 2918 bytes is less that twice the 1460-byte limit. The third fragment is necessary because of IP's restriction on fragment sizes. Because the first

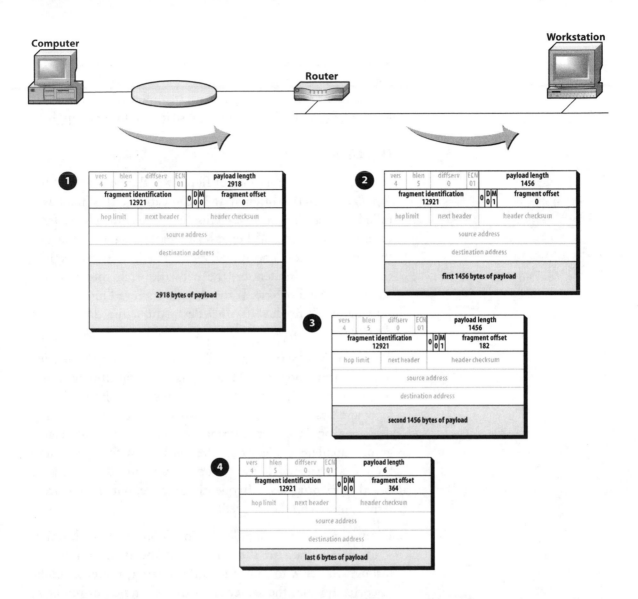

▲ Figure 2.5

If a router receives a datagram too big for the next subnetwork, it fragments the datagram into smaller pieces that do fit.

fragment must contain a multiple of eight bytes of payload, it cannot completely fill the 1514-byte frame. The closest the router can come is 1510. That value leaves room for only 1456 bytes of payload, which results in a fragment offset value of 182 in the next fragment.

The same restriction applies to the second fragment, so again only 1456 payload bytes are included. The final fragment contains the remaining six bytes of payload. Because there is no fragment offset for a following fragment (there is no following fragment), the eight-byte restriction does not apply.

Hop Limit

Returning to the IP header of figure 2.3, the next field is the *hop limit*. (In the original IP specifications, this field was called *time to live*, or *TTL*.) This field determines how far a datagram will travel. When a host creates a datagram, it sets the hop limit to some initial value. Then, as the datagram travels through routers on the network, each router decrements this field by one. If the datagram's hop limit becomes zero before it reaches its final destination, the datagram is discarded.

The hop limit serves one main purpose: It breaks *routing loops*. Routing loops should never occur in a healthy network, but, unfortunately, networks are not always healthy. When a loop appears, routers in the network base their forwarding decisions on incorrect information, and, as a result, datagrams circulate endlessly in the network without reaching their destination. (Routing loops should more properly be called *forwarding loops*; frequently they are, but the incorrect term is more commonly used.)

Figure 2.6 shows a simple routing loop. The workstation sends a datagram to the server, and the datagram travels through router A to router B. Unfortunately, router B thinks (incorrectly) that the server is on the other side of router A, so it sends the datagram back to router A. That router knows the true location of the laptop, and the only way to get there is through router B. Unfortunately, however, every time router A tries to send it through router B, router B stubbornly sends it right back to router A. A loop exists between these two routers, and datagrams for the laptop continue to circulate in this loop, never reaching their destination.

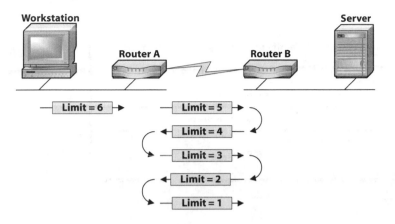

In this routing loop, router B mistakenly thinks the server is closer to router A. It forwards datagrams destined for the server back to router A, who sends them right back to B. Both routers, however, continue to decrement the datagram's hop limit as they should. Once the hop limit reaches zero, it is discarded. Although the datagram never reaches its destination, at least it doesn't circulate in the network and consume resources forever.

The Internet Protocol itself cannot correct the wrong information in router A, so it cannot get the datagram to its destination. With the hop limit, however, IP can prevent datagrams from circulating (and using network resources) forever. The workstation in figure 2.6 sets the initial hop limit of the datagram to 6. When router A forwards the datagram to router B, it decrements the hop limit to 5. Router B decrements the hop limit as well, and the routers continue doing so until the limit reaches zero. When it does, router B, rather than return the datagram once more to router A, discards it. The datagram never makes it to the server, but at least it eventually exits from the network.

Next Header

The *next header* field identifies the protocol one layer above IP in the datagram. It is also called the protocol field. Figure 2.7 highlights the fact that, although the next header field is part of the Internet Protocol, it signifies the protocol above IP in the stack. Table 2.1 lists some common next header values, though many more have been defined. Some of those protocols, including ICMP and IGMP, are intimately related to IP and are covered later in this chapter. Others are truly separate protocols; they merit their own chapters in the text.

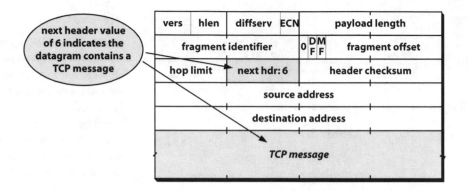

Figure 2.7 ▲

The next header field in the IP header identifies the protocol that the datagram's payload carries.

Table 2.1 IP Next Header Values

Value	Protocol
1	Internet Control Message Protocol (ICMP)
2	Internet Group Management Protocol (IGMP)
6	Transmission Control Protocol (TCP)
17	User Datagram Protocol (UDP)
46	Resource Reservation Protocol (RSVP)
89	Open Shortest Path First (OSPF)

Header Checksum

The 16-bit *header checksum* protects against corruption of the IP datagram's header while the datagram is in transit. Because it is such a visible feature of transport level protocols like TCP, it is easy to overlook the fact that other protocols such as IP can take advantage of a checksum's error-detecting properties.

Before forwarding an IP datagram, a system calculates the checksum to place in this field. The system starts with the complete IP header and then temporarily sets the checksum value to zero. The system then performs a 16-bit, one's complement addition on the header. It ignores any carries and places the 16-bit sum in the checksum field of the header, replacing the temporary zero value.

The IP Checksum

Because IP uses one's complement arithmetic for its checksum, systems cannot simply use standard arithmetic addition for this calculation. (Modern microprocessors normally use two's complement arithmetic.) RFC 1071 provides details on implementing the checksum efficiently in software, and RFC 1936 describes efficient hardware implementations.

When a system receives an IP datagram, it verifies the checksum before attempting to interpret the header. To verify the checksum, the system simply performs the same, 16-bit one's complement sum. If the result is $FFFF_{16}$, then the checksum is correct. If the result differs from $FFFF_{16}$, however, the checksum is incorrect, and the datagram is immediately discarded.

Addresses

The final two fields of the basic IP header are the source and destination IP addresses. Each one is a 32-bit network address. They identify the original source and ultimate destination for the datagram and do not change as the datagram traverses the network. Figure 2.8 clarifies this concept; it shows a single IP datagram as it travels across a network. The workstation originates the datagram and forwards it to router A over the Ethernet LAN. The datagram then crosses the ATM network in two separate cells. Finally, it reaches its destination when router B sends it across the Token Ring to the minicomputer.

Pay particular attention to the IP header, shown in white in the figure. Note that the source and destination IP addresses are always the workstation and minicomputer, respectively. This is true even though it passes through two intermediate systems along its path. To get it to or from the appropriate intermediate system, IP relies on the addressing of the underlying network technology.

The contrast is seen clearly at step 1, when the datagram travels from the workstation to router A. Note that the Ethernet header, shaded in the figure, specifies a destination address of router A. The IP header, however, lists the ultimate destination as the minicomputer.

Figure 2.8 ▲

A datagram's source and destination addresses do not change as the datagram travels through the network. Ethernet and other subnetwork addresses, however, change with each hop.

IP Options

In addition to the header fields we looked at in the previous section, IP defines several optional fields. These optional fields follow the addresses in the header. The header length field indicates whether options are present. If its value is more than 5 (which represent 40 bytes) the excess bytes are options. Figure 2.9 shows a datagram with an IP header of 28 bytes. Because a basic IP header contains only 20 bytes, the extra 8 bytes are options.

Each individual option in the header begins with a byte that identifies the option type. If the option is more than one byte in length, the next byte carries the size of the option data. This size includes the option type byte and the option size, as well as the option data. The remaining bytes of the option are the actual option data.

Table 2.2 lists all the defined IP options, although not all of them are commonly used today. The table includes the type value, the size, and an indication of whether the option is copied into fragments of the original datagram. If a router must fragment a datagram, those options that should be copied are placed in all fragments. Options that are not copied are preserved in the datagram's first fragment, but no others.

▼ **Figure 2.9**

The header length field in an IP datagram indicates the total length of the IP header, measured in 32-bit words. If its value is greater than 5, then IP options are present.

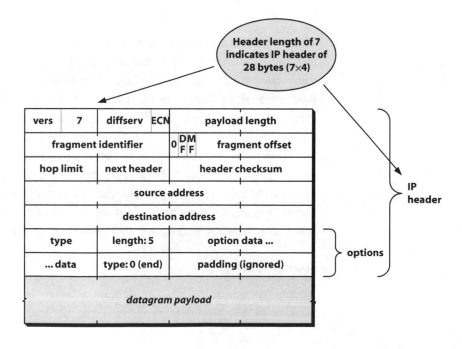

Practical IP Options

Two of the defined IP options, security information and stream identifier, are rarely used on today's Internet. Neither option is described in this text.

Table 2.2 IP Options

Type	Size	Copied	Use
0	1 byte	no	End of Options in Header
1	1 byte	no	Null Option
7	Varies	no	Record Route
68	Varies	no	Timestamp
82	12 bytes	no	Trace Route
130	11 bytes	yes	Security Information
131	Varies	yes	Loose Source Routing
136	4 bytes	yes	Stream Identifier
137	Varies	yes	Strict Source Routing
148	4 bytes	yes	Router Alert

The simplest option is the last. The *router alert* serves as a hint to intermediate routers that they ought to examine the datagram closely. It is typically used to flag datagrams carrying IGMP or RSVP traffic; its presence allows routers to quickly detect such traffic and optimize their processing accordingly. The option itself consists of the type byte (148), the length byte (4) and two bytes of zero.

The *end of options* and *null* option types allow systems to adjust the total size of the optional part of an IP header. Because the IP Header Length field indicates size in units of four bytes, all IP datagrams must have a header size that is an even multiple of four bytes. The basic header meets that criteria, but what if the desired options do not? In those cases, the system can add enough null options to force the length to an appropriate size. The system can also add an end of options indicator, and the rest of the IP header is simply ignored. Figure 2.9 uses an end of options indicator. Figure 2.10 shows how the null option can fill out an IP header.

Source Routing

Normally, the source of an IP datagram leaves it to the network to deliver that datagram to its destination. Sometimes,

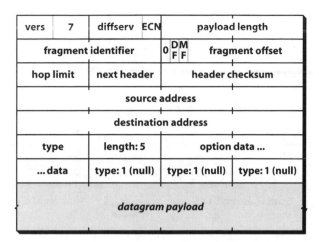

vers	7	diffserv	ECN	payload length	
fragment identifier			0 DM F F	fragment offset	
hop limit		next header		header checksum	
source address					
destination address					
type		length: 5		option data ...	
... data		type: 1 (null)	type: 1 (null)		type: 1 (null)
datagram payload					

◀ **Figure 2.10**

If the actual size of IP options doesn't match the header length—usually because the header length can only indicate units of four bytes—the null option can fill out the remainder of the IP header.

though, the sender wants more control over the datagram's path. The sender may wish to give the network hints as to the best path for the datagram, or it may wish to control the path to make sure the datagram does not travel through inappropriate routers. The source routing options give the sender this control. These options, combined with the destination address in the basic header, define a path through the network for the datagram.

Imagine the situation in figure 2.11. Giant Company needs to communicate with one of its suppliers. The natural communications path relies on the ATM network from Big Carrier, one of Giant's major competitors. For most traffic, this presents no problems; however, Giant is paranoid about particularly sensitive data. It wants to make sure that the sensitive traffic does not travel across its rival's network. Fortunately, an alternate path exists through the private network at the top of the figure. But that path relies on a relatively slow, point-to-point link. The trick is to make sure that sensitive traffic takes that alternate path and not the more efficient route through the high-speed ATM network. If the source workstation knows about this alternate path, it can, at least in theory, force its use with a source routing option. (See sidebar.)

Source Routing in Practice

The examples and discussion in this section present source routing as a tool for influencing the path of IP traffic. In fact, however, source routing is much less efficient than leaving forwarding decisions to the network's routers. For that reason, source routing is normally used only in special circumstances, such as, for example, while diagnosing network problems. The problem presented by figure 2.11, in particular, would normally be resolved by policy-based routing protocols using the techniques of chapter 6.

Figure 2.11 ▶

In this example, Giant company doesn't trust Big Carrier to carry communications with its supplier. The two parties would rather use the private network, even though Big Carrier might offer better performance.

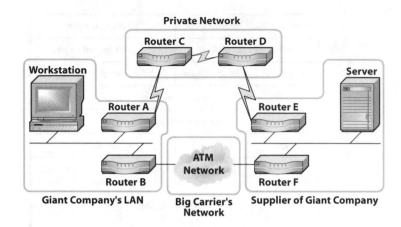

The two types of source route options—loose source route and strict source route—have the same format. Figure 2.12, a loose source route example, shows that the headers are mostly just a list of IP addresses. When the datagram leaves the source workstation, the basic IP header's destination address indicates the first hop on the desired path. Unlike a normal datagram, the destination address is not the ultimate destination for the datagram. The list of addresses in the source route option identifies subsequent hops along the desired path. As the datagram arrives at each hop, that system takes the next hop from the list and swaps it with the destination address. The datagram then continues on its journey.

The *pointer* byte in the option keeps track of the current position in the list. It indicates the beginning byte of the next address. Initially, the pointer value is 4 because the fourth byte of the option contains the first address in the list. At each stop on the list, the router adds 4 to this field, pointing it to the next destination in the list. When this value exceeds the size of the option, no further source route processing is required, and the datagram makes its way to its destination.

Figure 2.13 traces the results of this processing on a datagram from Giant Company. The datagram uses a source route option to avoid traversing Big Carrier's network. The figure

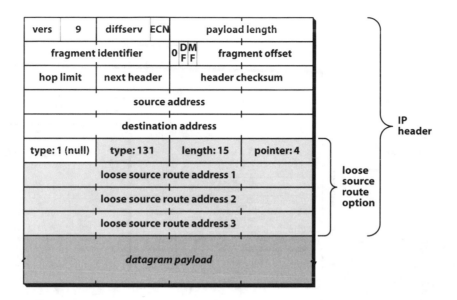

▲ **Figure 2.12**

The source route option lets a sender specify its own path through a network, possibly overriding the forwarding decisions that routers would normally make.

shows the relevant fields of the IP header at three places along its path.

The difference between strict source routes and loose source routes is the degree of discretion they give to routers along the path. Strict source routes give the routers no discretion at all. They must forward the datagram directly to the next IP address in the list; no intervening hops are allowed. Loose source routes, on the other hand, allow the datagram to pass through other intermediate routers on its way to the next listed destination. If a router finds it cannot satisfy a strict source route, it returns an ICMP error message to the datagram's source.

Recording Routes and Times

The source route options give the sender a great deal of control over the path a datagram takes through the network. Another IP option, the *record route* option, simply lets the end systems see the path that the routers choose for a datagram.

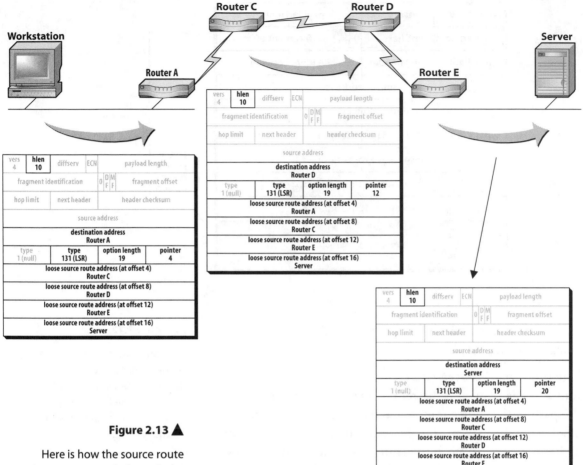

Figure 2.13 ▲

Here is how the source route option creates a path through the network. Notice that, at each step, the IP destination address is actually the next hop, not the ultimate destination. At each hop the router takes the next hop from the source route option and makes it the destination. It replaces that value in the option with its own IP address. When the datagram finally arrives, the source route option has recorded the actual path it took through the network.

As figure 2.14 shows, the format for a record route option is the same as for a source route option. The difference, however, is that the list of IP addresses is blank. Routers fill in the list and increment the pointer field as they process the datagram. Once the option is full, subsequent routers do not add their addresses.

The *timestamp* option is similar to record route. In addition to (or instead of) their IP addresses, intermediate routers record the time at which they process the datagram. As figure

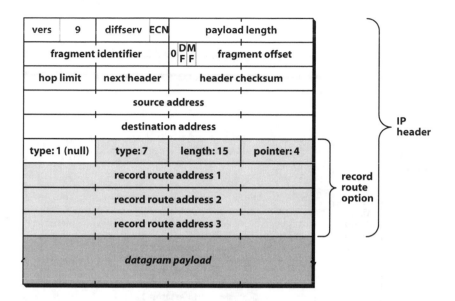

vers	9	diffserv	ECN	payload length		

(figure content)

▲ **Figure 2.14**

The record route option doesn't specify a path through the network, but it does ask routers to record the path that the datagram does take. Each router simply adds its IP address to the option.

2.15 shows, the timestamp option includes an overflow count and a format field. The overflow count is initially set to 0 and remains there as long as there is space in the option. When a router cannot insert its timestamp information because there isn't enough space in the option, it increments this counter.

The format field indicates whether routers should add just the 32-bit timestamp (format value of 0), the timestamp and their IP address together (format value of 1), or the timestamp only for prespecified addresses (format value of 3). In the latter case, the sending system fills in the IP addresses in advance but leaves the timestamp values blank.

For the timestamp option, the time value is the number of milliseconds since midnight UTC. If the router's clock is not synchronized to UTC, it sets the most significant bit of its timestamp to 1 to indicate a nonstandard time.

There is one important characteristic of both the record route and timestamp options: The source decides whether to use each option by putting it in the datagram, but only the destination sees the result. Using either option effectively,

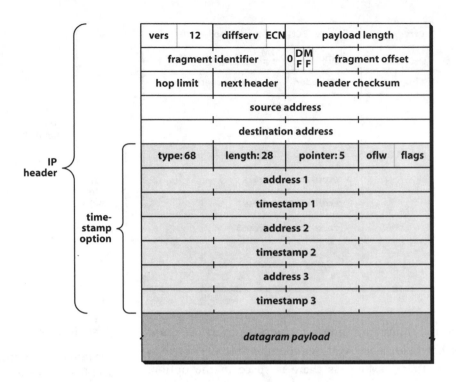

vers	12	diffserv	ECN	payload length		
fragment identifier			0 DF MF	fragment offset		
hop limit		next header		header checksum		
source address						
destination address						
type: 68		length: 28		pointer: 5	oflw	flags
address 1						
timestamp 1						
address 2						
timestamp 2						
address 3						
timestamp 3						
datagram payload						

IP header

time-stamp option

Figure 2.15 ▲

The timestamp option acts a lot like the record route. In addition to (or instead of) its IP address, however, each router records the time it processed the datagram in this option.

therefore, requires some coordination between the two end systems. An alternative to these messages that doesn't require this coordination is the combination of the ICMP trace route message with the IP trace route option. We'll see this operation in the following section on ICMP.

Internet Control Message Protocol

The Internet Protocol focuses on one major task—moving data from its source to its destination. Network layer protocol, though, must do more than simply move data. Systems rely on the network layer to coordinate many aspects of their operation. This coordination includes controlling address assignments, reporting errors, and providing diagnostic support. The IP architecture assigns these responsibilities to a separate network layer protocol, the Internet Control Message Protocol, or ICMP.

ICMP Message Format

Even though ICMP is a network layer protocol, it sends its messages inside IP datagrams. As figure 2.16 shows, the next header value of 1 identifies ICMP. The figure also shows the four-byte header that begins every ICMP message. The ICMP header consists of a type byte, a code byte, and a two-byte checksum.

The type and code bytes distinguish different kinds of ICMP messages. The type field provides the coarsest distinction. There are currently 16 different ICMP message types. Table 2.3 lists them, along with their type field values. The ICMP checksum uses the same algorithm as the checksum in the IP header. It is calculated using the entire ICMP message, beginning with the type field.

Table 2.3 ICMP Messages

Type	Message
0	Echo Reply
3	Destination Unreachable
4	Source Quench
5	Redirect
8	Echo Request
9	Router Advertisement
10	Router Solicitation
11	Time Exceeded
12	Parameter Problem
13	Timestamp Request
14	Timestamp Reply
15	Information Request
16	Information Reply
17	Address Mask Request
18	Address Mask Reply
30	Trace Route

ICMP in Practice

Several of the ICMP message types, Source Quench, Information Request and Reply, and Address Mask Request and Reply among them, are rarely used on today's IP networks. This text does not discuss them.

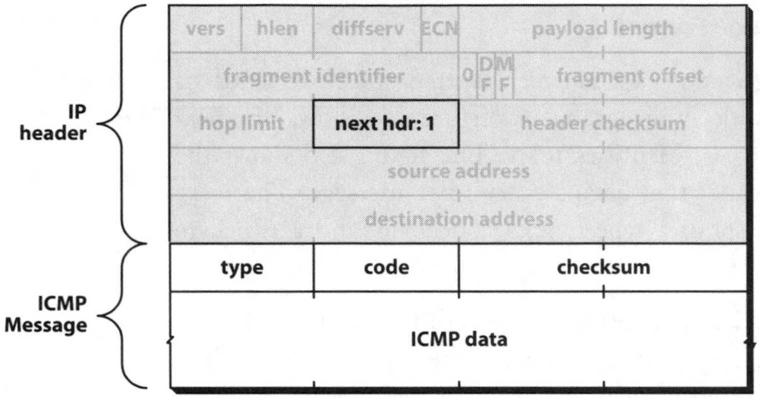
IP header
ICMP Message
vers
hlen
diffserv
ECN
payload length
fragment identifier
0
D F
M F
fragment offset
hop limit
next hdr: 1
header checksum
source address
destination address
type
code
checksum
ICMP data

Figure 2.16 ▲

IP treats ICMP messages like any other higher layer protocol. The IP next header value that indicates an ICMP payload is 1.

An important decision facing every system is selecting a source IP address for ICMP messages. Sometimes (e.g., if the system is a host with a single network interface and a single IP address), this decision is easy. In many cases, however, systems will have a choice, and it is important that they choose appropriately. There are four rules that determine the right answer.

The first two rules consider ICMP replies. The source address of the reply should be the same as the destination address of the original request. If the original message was sent to a multicast group, then the response should use as its source an IP address of the interface on which the request arrived.

The third rule applies to ICMP error messages. Such error messages are often generated by routers that are not the ultimate destination of the datagram in error. These messages, therefore, cannot use the original destination as the error's source. Instead, they should use a source address that provides the most information about the error being reported. For example, if the ICMP message indicates that a datagram needed to be fragmented but fragmentation was prohibited by the source, then the source address for the error message should be an IP address of the interface over which the original datagram would not fit.

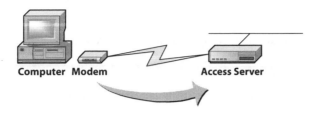

In this example the computer has only one place to send all its datagrams—across the dial-up link to the network access server. The PC knows implicitly that the access server is its next hop router.

Unsolicited ICMP messages, as well as those not covered previously, should follow the fourth rule. The source address for such messages should be an IP address of the link on which the message is transmitted.

Discovering Routers

One important function that ICMP provides is letting hosts discover routers. This function isn't important when the host has but a single point-to-point link, like the home PC of figure 2.17. In that case, the PC's IP layer has no choice: All datagrams are sent to the system at the other end of the dial-up link. Figure 2.18, however, is a different matter. There, the PC is part of a local area network. If the PC needs to send a datagram to a destination that's not on the same LAN, how does it find a router on the LAN that can accept the datagram?

Without ICMP, there are two ways that a host can discover routers on its local network. First, the administrator can manually configure that information for the host. A second

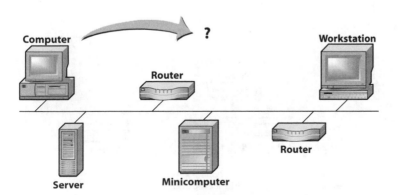

◀ **Figure 2.18**

Ethernet links, however, may have several systems connected to them. The computer in this example needs to find a router it can use to get the datagram to its destination.

alternative has the host listen for routing protocol messages and identify routers from those messages. Neither of these approaches is completely satisfactory, however. Manual configuration is error-prone and time-consuming, and it's difficult for network administrators to respond quickly when the network changes. Listening in on routing protocol exchanges, however, has its own risks. If the network administrator decides to switch routing protocols, for example, the host may suddenly be deprived of its information source.

Router discovery, a late addition to the functions of ICMP, solves the problem without the shortcomings of manual configuration or eavesdropping on routing protocols. The principle is quite simple. As figure 2.19 illustrates, routers on a network periodically advertise their presence. They do so by multicasting an ICMP *router advertisement* message to all systems on the network. (If multicast addresses are not available, routers can send this message to the broadcast address.)

Figure 2.20 shows a sample router advertisement message. As the figure shows, the message includes a count of the number of routers included in it, the size of each router address, and a *lifetime* field. The lifetime field carries the number of seconds that the router advertisement information should be considered valid. If a host fails to hear from a router for more than the specified lifetime, it should treat the information as expired.

Figure 2.19 ▶

If the computer listens long enough, it can hear each router announce its presence. Routers do that by multicasting a router advertisement to all systems on the subnetwork.

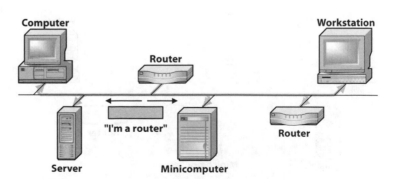

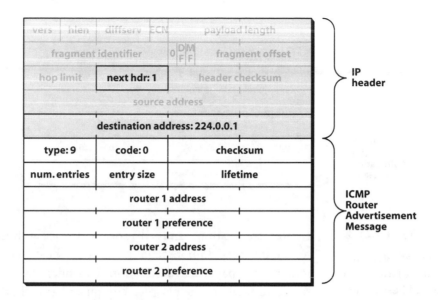

vers	hlen	diffserv	ECN	payload length	
fragment identifier			0 DMFF	fragment offset	
hop limit		next hdr: 1		header checksum	
source address					
destination address: 224.0.0.1					
type: 9		code: 0		checksum	
num. entries		entry size		lifetime	
router 1 address					
router 1 preference					
router 2 address					
router 2 preference					

IP header

ICMP Router Advertisement Message

The routers themselves are in the form of a list. Each entry in the list includes the IP address of the router and a relative preference value. When possible, hosts should select the router with the highest preference value.

The normal procedure is to have routers send a router advertisement message about once every 7 to 10 minutes. For that frequency, a typical lifetime is 1800 (30 minutes). A freshly restarted host may not wish to wait 7 to 10 minutes to find a router, however. To accommodate such impatient hosts, ICMP defines a *router solicitation* message. The router solicitation message, shown in figure 2.21, carries no information itself. It simply asks a router to respond directly to the host with a router advertisement message. The host generally sends this message to the all routers' multicast address, although it may send it to the broadcast address when multicasting is not available. Figure 2.22 shows the effect; all routers on the network receive the message. A router that receives a router solicitation message immediate responds with a router advertisement.

▲ **Figure 2.20**

The router advertisement is an ICMP message. Its destination is the all systems multicast address.

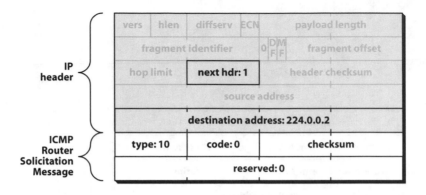

IP header

vers	hlen	diffserv	ECN	payload length

fragment identifier	0 DF MF	fragment offset

hop limit	next hdr: 1	header checksum

source address

destination address: 224.0.0.2

ICMP Router Solicitation Message

type: 10	code: 0	checksum

reserved: 0

Figure 2.21 ▲

Router solicitations are also ICMP messages. They have the all routers multicast address as their destination.

Router solicitations and advertisements let a host find a router, but they do not guarantee that the host finds the best router for a particular destination. Consider the network of figure 2.23, where the personal computer has a choice of two routers. Suppose that the PC needs to send traffic to the minicomputer. By comparing IP addresses, the PC knows that the minicomputer is not on its local Ethernet; reaching it requires the help of a router.

At this point the PC has a choice. It has heard advertisements from both routers. With nothing to guide its selection, the PC chooses to forward the datagram to the right router. Figure 2.24 shows the datagram's path through the network. As the figure shows, the PC has not made the most efficient choice. It could have forwarded the datagram directly to the top router. Still there is nothing illegal or improper in its choice, and the packet does reach its destination.

Figure 2.22 ▶

Here is how a host can use router solicitation. Instead of waiting for a router advertisement, the laptop multicasts a router solicitation as soon as it connects to the network.

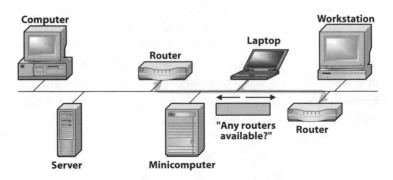

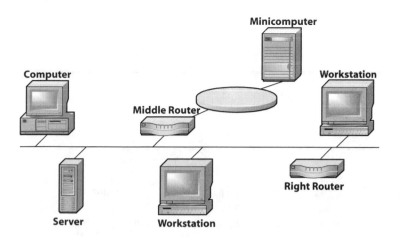

In this example, the personal computer wants to communicate with the minicomputer. It may have heard router advertisements from both routers, in which case it won't know which one is best for its particular traffic.

Of all the systems involved, the right router can most easily detect the inefficiency. It received the datagram from its Ethernet interface and then turned around and sent it right back out the same interface. This situation calls for an ICMP *redirect* message, which tells the host system of a better path to a particular destination.

After forwarding the PC's original datagram, the right router sends it a redirect message. Figure 2.25 shows this message. The redirect lets the original sender know about the better path. Figure 2.26 shows the message format. Its ICMP type is

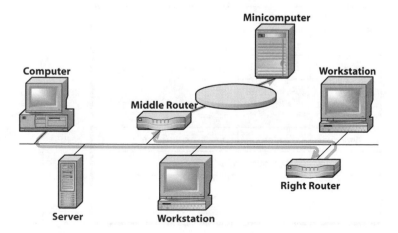

◀ **Figure 2.24**

If the PC guesses wrong and sends a datagram to the right router, that router will forward it to the middle router so it can reach its destination.

Figure 2.25 ▶

After the right router forwards the datagram, it can send the PC a redirect message. This message tells the PC of a better next hop for that particular destination.

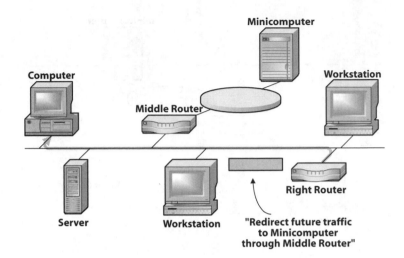

Figure 2.26 ▼

Redirect messages are carried as ICMP payloads. The message explicitly lists the better router to use, and it includes a copy of the datagram that triggered the message. This copy lets the PC know the particular destination to which it should apply the redirect.

5, and the code tells the host to redirect all messages to this host (code of 1) or to this network (code of 0). Code values of 4 and 3 specify redirection only for the original datagram's diffserv codepoint. Following the checksum is the IP address of the router to which further traffic should be redirected. The message concludes with the IP header and at least the first eight bytes of payload from the original datagram. This information lets the host know which datagram triggered the redirect.

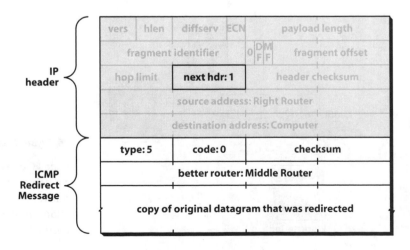

Reporting Errors

Another important service that ICMP provides is error reporting. When a host or router detects a problem with an IP datagram, it can report that problem to the original sender with an ICMP message. To make sure that error reporting doesn't get out of hand, though, ICMP places three restrictions on its use. First, error messages are never generated when the source or destination of a datagram is a multicast or broadcast address. Second, no ICMP error messages are generated when the original datagram itself carries an ICMP message. And third, ICMP errors are reported on only the first fragment (with a fragment offset of 0) of a datagram.

The most common ICMP error message is the *destination unreachable* message, shown in figure 2.27. Both hosts and routers can send this message when they recognize that a datagram cannot be delivered to its intended recipient.

The code byte gives further information about the reason for the error. Table 2.4 lists its possible values.

Like the redirect message, the ICMP destination unreachable message concludes with the IP header and the first eight bytes of payload from the original datagram. This information lets the host know which datagram triggered the error.

The Original Datagram

The official specification for ICMP requires that ICMP messages include the IP header and 8 bytes of payload from the original datagram that triggered the message. Later standards, notably RFC 1812, suggest including as much of the original datagram as possible. MPLS specifications that are currently still works in progress propose yet another approach: include 128 bytes (header and payload) of the original datagram.

▼ **Figure 2.27**

The destination unreachable message also carries a copy of the datagram that triggered it. This copy tells the recipient which specific destination cannot be reached.

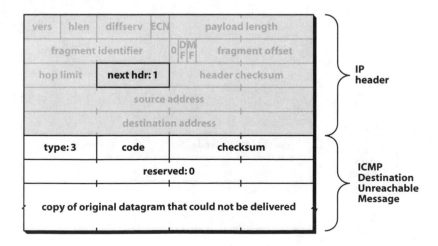

Table 2.4 ICMP Destination Unreachable Codes

Code	Meaning
0	Cannot reach the destination network.
1	Cannot reach the destination host.
2	The next header (protocol) is not available at the destination host.
3	The transport level port (e.g., the application) is not available at the destination host.
4	Fragmentation was required but was not allowed.
5	The specified source route could not be honored.

The *time exceeded* ICMP message, illustrated in figure 2.28, indicates one of two different errors, depending on the value of the code byte. A code byte of zero means that the datagram exceeded its hop limit before reaching its destination. Only routers should generate this error. A code byte of one, on the other hand, is created only by hosts. It means that the host gave up waiting for all of the fragments of the original datagram to arrive.

Figure 2.28 ▼

The time exceeded message has the same form as other ICMP error messages. It also includes a copy of the original datagram.

The final ICMP error message is the *parameter problem* error. Hosts and routers use this message to indicate that they could not interpret part of the original datagram. The pointer byte, shown in figure 2.29, indicates the specific byte at which the system first noticed a problem.

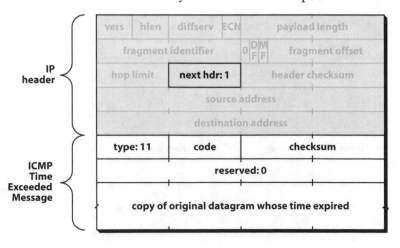

IP header

ICMP Time Exceeded Message

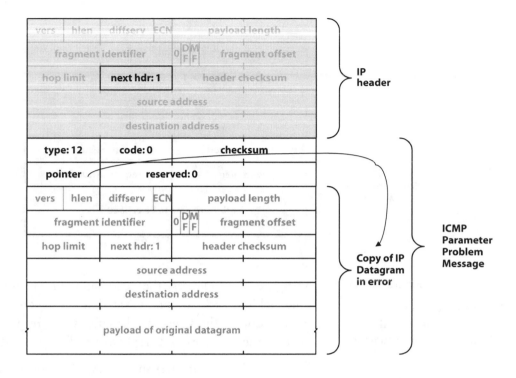

Diagnosing Network Level Problems

One of ICMP's simplest functions is network diagnostics. As users and administrators alike can attest, this is also one of its most appreciated functions. With its diagnostic messages, ICMP determines whether two systems can communicate with each other. It does this by sending an *echo request* message and waiting for an *echo reply*. Most operating systems invoke this service with the familiar `ping` command.

Figure 2.30 shows the echo request format. As the figure indicates, the message includes an identifier, a sequence number, and, optionally, extra data. The ICMP specification does not formally define the use of these fields, but they are intended to help the sender correlate any responses it receives with specific requests.

▲ **Figure 2.29**

The parameter problem message indicates that the sender couldn't understand part of the original datagram. The pointer field in the ICMP message notes the specific byte in the original datagram that caused the problem.

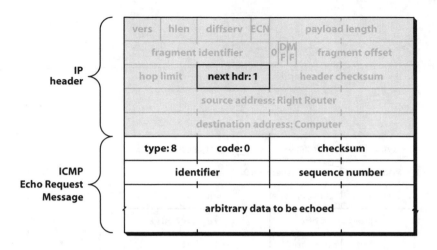

Figure 2.30 ▲

An ICMP echo request message can carry arbitrary data, an identifier, and sequence numbers.

Figure 2.31 ▼

The echo reply returns the same identifier, sequence number, and arbitrary data as the request.

As figure 2.31 indicates, the echo reply simply repeats the same fields. In the unusual event that the reverse direction doesn't support the same size datagrams, the responder may truncate the data port of its reply to avoid fragmentation.

The example of figure 2.32 shows the echo request and reply in operation. The figure highlights the fact that this message exchange simply confirms the ability of the two systems to communicate. It generally provides no details about the communication path.

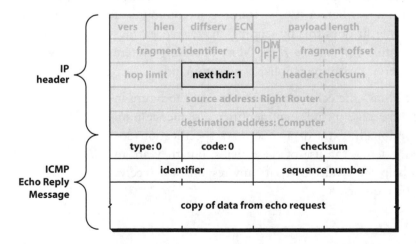

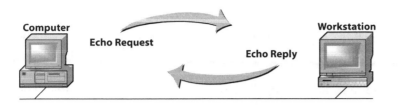

◀ **Figure 2.32**

Systems that receive echo requests immediate respond with echo replies. This reply assures the peer that the target is still operating.

An equally common, and more sophisticated, network diagnostic tool also relies on ICMP messages. That tool, known as `traceroute` (on Unix systems) or `tracert` (on Windows systems), displays the full network path between two hosts, listing all routers along that path. You can see the results of this command in the example output below.

```
> traceroute -n -q 1 www.waterscreek.com

traceroute to www.waterscreek.com (207.155.248.7),
  30 hops max, 40 byte packets

 1  66.20.92.1   101 ms
 2  209.149.96.65   20 ms
 3  205.152.37.248   30 ms
 4  157.130.72.53   31 ms
 5  146.188.233.210   30 ms
 6  146.188.232.90   20 ms
 7  146.188.141.42   120 ms
 8  152.63.15.85   130 ms
 9  152.63.65.169   120 ms
10  137.39.23.70   130 ms
11  64.220.0.177   120 ms
12  64.0.0.17   130 ms
13  64.0.0.130   111 ms
14  207.155.252.47   120 ms
>
```

To discover a network path, `traceroute` manipulates the IP header's hop limit field. When a user executes the command, the tool sends a datagram to the destination with a hop limit value of 1. The exact contents of the datagram aren't really important, but most Unix implementations send a UDP datagram with a nonexistent destination port, while Windows sends an ICMP echo request. When the datagram reaches the

Figure 2.33 ▼

Here is how a sequence of ICMP messages can reveal the path to a destination. At each stage the PC increases the initial hop limit by one, allowing the datagram to get one step further into the network before the limit expires.

first router in the path, the hop limit will expire and the router will return an ICMP time exceeded message. The command then sends the datagram again, but this time with a hop limit of 2. The second attempt will get past the first router, but its hop limit expires at the second router. The command repeats this process until it either hears from the destination host or reaches a configurable limit. Figure 2.33 illustrates the approach on a small-scale example. In it, the computer uses three exchanges to discover the path to the server.

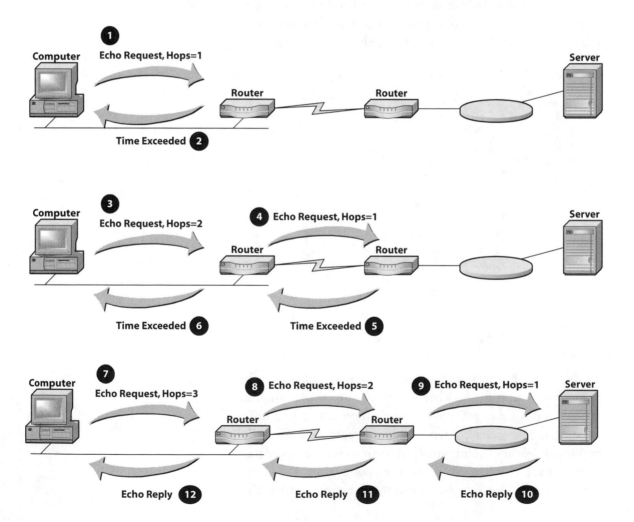

Internet Group Management Protocol

The Internet Group Management Protocol (IGMP) is another protocol like ICMP; although technically a separate protocol, it is an integral part of any IP implementation. Hosts use IGMP to announce (and later renounce) their membership in groups. Routers listen to these messages to track group membership on a link or network. They can then know how to forward datagrams addressed to groups.

All IGMP messages have the format of figure 2.34, though each message has its own type. Table 2.5 lists the IGMP types. The query message asks if a system belongs to a particular group. The report and termination messages allow systems to join or leave a group. Report messages also serve as the response to queries.

Table 2.5 IGMP Message Types

Value	Message Type
17	Membership query
22	Membership report
23	Membership termination
18	Old style membership report

In most cases, IGMP messages are sent to the group address in question. The destination IP address will then be the same as the multicast IP address in the message body. It is also

▼ **Figure 2.34**

IGMP messages are carried as the payload of IP datagrams. A next header value of 2 identifies IGMP.

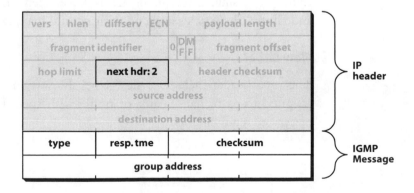

possible to query for membership in all groups. In such cases, the destination address is the all systems address, and the IP multicast address in the message body is set to zero.

The *maximum response time* field is used only in queries. It defines the maximum amount of time (in tenths of seconds) that a system may delay before responding to the query. To prevent every group member from responding simultaneously and swamping the network, each should delay a random amount of time before transmitting the response. That delay should range from zero to the maximum response delay time.

IP Version 6

So far this chapter has described version 4 of the Internet Protocol. That is the version of today's Internet, and it is likely to retain that prominence in the near future. Eventually, however, the supply of 32-bit IP addresses will be exhausted. To accommodate the expected growth of the Internet, and to streamline IP processing, the IETF has defined the next version of the Internet Protocol, IP version 6. Although we won't discuss IPv6 in detail in this text, here is a quick summary of the differences between the two versions.

Streamlined Header Format

The IPv6 header, shown in figure 2.35, is optimized for efficient processing. Superfluous fields have been eliminated, and all multibyte fields align on their natural boundaries.

Flow Label

The IPv6 header includes a flow label. Flow values may be assigned to particular streams of traffic with special quality-of-service requirements.

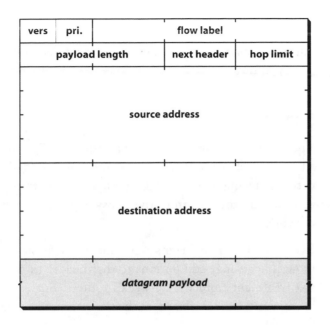

| vers | pri. | flow label | | |
| payload length | | next header | hop limit |

source address

destination address

datagram payload

◄ **Figure 2.35**

IP version 6 eliminates many header fields that are no longer useful—most notably fragmentation information and checksums. It significantly increases the size of the source and destination addresses, however, to accommodate 128-bit IPv6 values.

128-Bit Network Addresses

Perhaps the most drastic change, IPv6 addresses are 128 bits in size rather than 32.

Elimination of the Header Checksum

The IPv6 protocol does not include a checksum of its own header.

Fragmentation Only by Source Host

Intermediate routers cannot fragment an IPv6 datagram. Only the sending host can create fragments.

Extension Headers

Instead of including options in the IP header itself, IPv6 uses the next header field to add options (known as extensions) after the basic header.

Built-in Security

Support for both authentication and confidentiality is mandatory in IPv6.

Summary

The Internet Protocol is the key protocol of the Internet and all TCP/IP networks. It serves as a common foundation for all network technologies, isolating higher layer transport and application protocols from the idiosyncrasies of each type of network.

Every IP datagram begins with the same basic IP header, though hosts may add options to that header to request special treatment from the network's routers. Such options are infrequently used, however, as the basic IP header is sufficient for nearly all traffic.

Two companion protocols—ICMP and IGMP—are integral parts of any IP implementation. They provide router discovery, error reporting, network diagnostic, and group membership services to hosts and routers.

CHAPTER 3

Transport Protocols — An Overview of TCP and UDP

The protocols of the previous chapters move packets across networks. This chapter looks at transport protocols and shifts the focus to the systems on those networks. Just as the Internet Protocol uses the services of particular network technologies, transport protocols build on the services of IP. They rely on IP to deliver packets to the right place, and then they take over.

Transport protocols have two major responsibilities. First, they must distinguish the traffic of different applications within a system. The TCP/IP architecture contains a wide variety of applications. Frequently, several applications will be active in a system at the same time. Transport protocols sort out the various traffic streams, making sure to deliver exactly the right data to the right application.

The second obligation facing a transport protocol is reliability. Recall that IP cannot guarantee delivery of packets. Nor does it typically ensure that the data within those packets arrives free from corruption. Transport protocols compensate for these problems in different ways and to different degrees. Each provides a particular level of service to its applications.

Distinguishing Applications

One of the strengths of the TCP/IP protocol suite is the diversity of its applications. Its layered architecture makes it easy to develop and deploy application protocols for almost any purpose. As a consequence, IP-based systems often support many applications at the same time. Each application may simultaneously take part in conversations with peers across the network.

Consider the server at the top of figure 3.1. It is carrying on three conversations—network management, autoconfiguration, and a name query—at the same time. The transport protocol distinguishes the traffic for each application and, within the server's software, distributes the traffic to the right place. Figure 3.2 looks inside the server to illustrate this process.

Ports

To identify different applications, the IP architecture tags each packet with a number known as a *port*. Different applications use different values for port fields, and a transport protocol can use the port value to decide which application should receive a packet's data. In this way, the port value acts

Figure 3.1 ▶

A system like this server can carry on many conversations at once. It needs a convenient way to distinguish traffic for each of these applications.

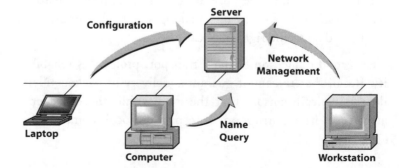

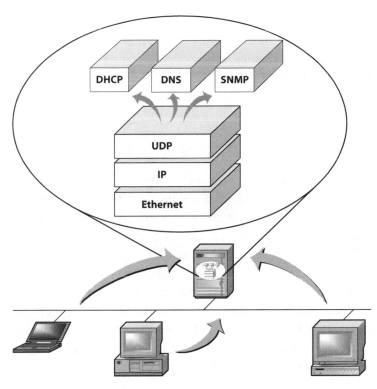

◀ Figure 3.2

Since many different applications may use the same transport layer protocol, it is up to that protocol to distinguish the applications. Both UDP and TCP have a port field that identifies applications.

like the IP next header field. The next header value distinguishes different transport protocols for IP, and the port value distinguishes different application protocol for a transport protocol.

Applications select a port in one of two ways. The two approaches correspond to the two roles that an application can play in a conversation. These roles correspond to a *client* and a *server*. Clients initiate most conversations by actively requesting information, while servers simply respond to such requests.

When a client application needs to make a request, it must know how to get that request to a server; it must know, in advance, which port value to use for the particular application. A server, on the other hand, doesn't have to know the port value to use for its response. It can have the client designate a port as part of its initial request.

This contrast occurs outside of network communications protocols. In the United States, for example, local phone systems provide directory assistance to translate names into phone numbers. In most cases, the caller (acting as a client) access this service by dialing 411. The client has to know this number in advance. The server, on the other hand, does not need to know the client's phone number. The operator simply responds on whatever line the call arrives.

The same principles apply to computer communications. Suppose that a client application needs SNMP network management information from a remote system. The client builds an SNMP request and sends it to the remote system. In order to ensure that the request reaches the SNMP application in that system, the client must specify a port value that it knows belongs to the SNMP protocol. The SNMP server, on the other hand, does not have to know the client's port in advance. When the server gets the request, it can examine the request to see which port the client has chosen to use. The server can return its response to that same port.

Port values that are predefined for specific applications are *well-known ports*. Table 3.1 lists the port values for several important applications.

Privileged Ports

Many computer systems restrict access to particular port values. Programs without adequate privileges (such as user programs) are allowed only a certain range of port values. This range does not include values typically assigned to server applications, and so the restriction prevents any user from running programs that act as servers. Using a server port requires special privileges from the operating system, and so the server port values are often known as *privileged ports*.

Table 3.1 Well-Known Port Values for Key Applications

Port(s)	Transport(s)	Application
20, 21	TCP	File Transfer Protocol
22, 23	TCP	Remote Login
25	TCP	Simple Mail Transfer Protocol
53	UDP, TCP	Domain Name Service
80	TCP	Hypertext Transfer Protocol
161, 162	UDP	Simple Network Management Protocol
179	TCP	Border Gateway Protocol
520	UDP	Routing Information Protocol

Sockets

By themselves, ports merely identify application protocols. They do not identify actual application programs running in real machines. By combining a port value with a network address, however, just such a distinction is possible. The combination is known as a *socket*.

Figure 3.3 shows two different conversations on a computer network. The server at the top exchanges management information with two other systems. As the figure shows, these two conversations use a total of four sockets. Sockets 1 and 2 define the conversation between the left and top hosts, while sockets 3 and 4 form the conversation between the top and right systems. As this example shows, different sockets can have the same values for both their port and network address. Sockets 2 and 3, for example, may both have the same network address (the top server) and the same port value (management traffic).

Datagram Delivery

Ports allow transport protocols to identify different applications. Of course, the reason for distinguishing applications is to deliver data to them, and the IP architecture provides two main types of transport service. The simplest transport service is datagram delivery. Datagram delivery is a connectionless service, which means that each unit of data (a

Stream Control Transmission Protocol

A third transport protocol for IP has recently been developed within the IETF. This protocol—the Stream Control Transmission Protocol (SCTP)—is relatively new and not yet widely deployed, but it provides critical services for certain new applications like telephony signaling. SCTP is a reliable transport protocol like TCP, but with greater reliability and better performance. SCTP gains reliability through *multihoming*, in which a system uses multiple IP addresses simultaneously. If the path to one of those addresses fails, traffic flow continues uninterrupted to another IP address. SCTP improves on TCP's performance with *multistreaming*, which multiplexes several independent traffic streams on a single connection in such a way that packet loss within one stream does not delay the other streams.

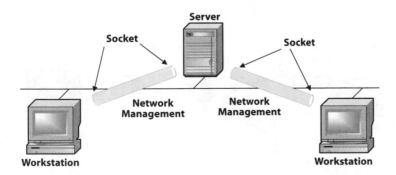

◀ **Figure 3.3**

A socket represents one endpoint in a communication exchange; it consists of an IP address and a transport port value. Two sockets—representing both endpoints—define a complete exchange.

datagram) exists entirely independently of all other datagrams, even other datagrams between the same two sockets. There is no reference to tie multiple datagrams together, and there is no reference that allows receives to acknowledge reception of a datagram. Finally, there is no reference that can establish a relative ordering of different datagrams.

In practice, datagram delivery is a best-effort service; that is, it does its best to transfer datagrams on behalf of applications, but it makes no guarantees. Datagrams may get reordered, even lost, in transit, and the applications must be prepared for such events.

Figure 3.4 illustrates how datagrams may get lost in transit. A personal computer sends four different datagrams to a server. While traversing the link between routers A and C, one of those datagrams (number 2) is damaged and discarded. Because router D never correctly receives datagram 2, it cannot forward it to the destination server. Datagram delivery provides no mechanism to recognize or recover from this loss. If the applications need either, they must provide it themselves.

Figure 3.4 ▼

Datagrams travel independently across a network and may, at this example shows, get lost in transit.

Figure 3.4 shows how datagrams may arrive out of order. In this example, router A sends every other datagram to router B. Router B, however, is slower than router C, and the datagrams it forwards experience a delay. Router D, therefore, receives datagrams 1 and 3 before datagrams 2 and 4. That is the same order in which router D delivers datagrams to the server, and so the server receives the datagrams out of order.

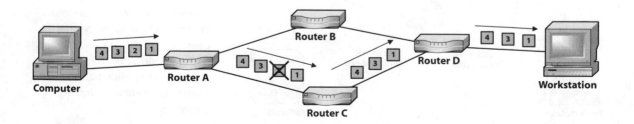

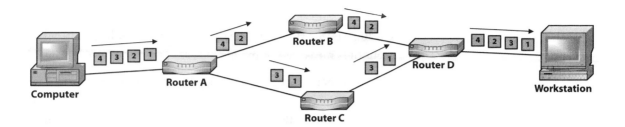

User Datagram Protocol

The transport protocol that provides a datagram delivery service is the User Datagram Protocol, or UDP. Because datagram delivery is such a simple service, UDP is a very simple protocol. Every UDP packet contains a fixed, eight-byte header followed by the application's data. Figure 3.6 shows a sample UDP datagram.

The port values identify the ports of the source and destination of the data. If the datagram carries a request for a server, then the destination port usually contains a well-known value. In such cases, the source port is often arbitrary. It normally indicates the port to which the server should address its reply. When the datagram carries a server's reply, the source port is typically well known, and the destination port identifies the requester.

▲ **Figure 3.5**

Datagrams may also arrive at their destination out of order.

▼ **Figure 3.6**

UDP datagrams are carried as the payload of an IP datagram with a next header value of 17. UDP has its own 8-byte header that precedes application data.

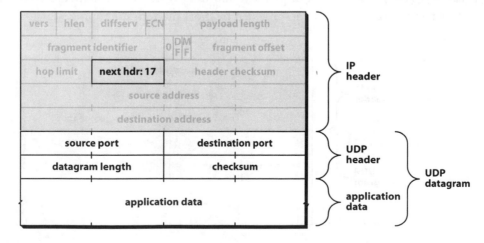

The datagram length is the total length of the datagram, including both the UDP header and the application data. Length is measured in bytes.

The final part of the UDP header is the checksum. This field provides a simple mechanism to detect errors introduced in the datagram while it traverses a network. The data that the checksum protects includes more than the UDP datagram. It also includes the source and destination network addresses, the IP next header value, and the datagram length. By including these fields, the checksum protects against datagrams that are not themselves corrupt but have been delivered to the wrong place. The Transmission Control Protocol (TCP), for example, uses the same checksum calculation. So if a system accidentally delivered a UDP datagram to the TCP software process, the inclusion of the next header field in the checksum would let the system detect the error.

Figure 3.7 shows how this additional data is added to the UDP datagram for purposes of checksum calculation. The added fields, shown in gray in the figure, are called a *pseudo header*.

Figure 3.7 ▼

Before calculating the UDP checksum a system "mentally" prepends a pseudo header to the actual datagram. The checksum can then detect errors in this information as well.

Table 3.2 summarizes the rules that a sender follows to construct the checksum. Note that the sum requires one's complement arithmetic. This operation is not the same as two's complement addition, which is the standard addition operation provided by most modern microprocessors.

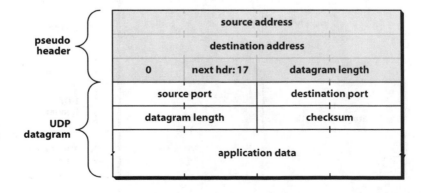

Table 3.2 Constructing the UDP Checksum

Step	Rule
1	Prepend the pseudo header to the UDP datagram.
2	If the application data contains an odd number of bytes, append a final byte of zero. (Do not increase the IP payload length or UDP datagram length fields to include this byte; it is not actually transmitted.)
3	Set the UDP checksum field to zero.
4	Calculate the sum of the resulting series of 16-bit values using one's complement arithmetic.
5	If the result of this summation is zero, set the checksum to be $FFFF_{16}$; otherwise, use the summation result as the checksum.

A receiver takes much the same approach. Table 3.3 lists its steps. If a receiver finds a checksum invalid, it discards the datagram without delivering it to an application.

Table 3.3 Validating the UDP Checksum

Step	Rule
1	If the checksum is zero, treat it as correct and skip the remaining steps. (See sidebar.)
2	Prepend the pseudo header to the UDP datagram.
3	If the application data contains an odd number of bytes, append a full byte of zero. (Do not include this byte in any data delivered to the application.)
4	Calculate the sum of the resulting series of 16-bit values, using one's complement arithmetic.
5	If the result of this summation is $FFFF_{16}$, the checksum is valid; otherwise, the checksum is invalid.

In some cases, applications may not even need the minimal error checking that the UDP checksum provides. To indicate that no checksum has been calculated, the sender sets the checksum field in the header to zero. If the actual calculation of a checksum results in a zero value, the sender changes that value to $FFFF_{16}$, which is equivalent to zero in one's complement arithmetic.

Why UDP?

The shortcomings of datagram delivery—loss and misordering—are not present in TCP, IP's connection-oriented transport protocol. And because TCP is widely available, it is reasonable to wonder why an application would use UDP instead of TCP. The answer lies in UDP's simplicity. Because UDP has no connections, applications do not have to establish or clear them. When an application has data to send, it just sends it. This approach makes things simpler for the application, and it can eliminate a substantial delay in the communication. UDP is also ideal for those systems that are so limited that they cannot afford to implement TCP. Regular computer systems do not usually suffer from this limitation, but special purpose devices (like uninterruptible power supplies) might.

The Transmission Control Protocol

The User Datagram Protocol represents the simplest transport protocol, but it is also the most limited. In particular, UDP adds little reliability to IP's connectionless service, and it makes no attempt to preserve the sequence of messages it delivers. Many applications cannot tolerate these limitations. They need assurance that their data actually makes it to the destination. In addition, their messages must often arrive in a particular order. These applications need reliable data delivery, and the Transmission Control Protocol (TCP) provides it for them.

Characteristics of Reliable Delivery

By providing reliable delivery, TCP offers a robust service to its applications. For TCP, reliability includes four major properties: error-free, assured delivery, in sequence, without duplication, from the sender all the way to the recipient.

The Transmission Control Protocol eliminates errors. Perhaps the most basic quality of reliable delivery is that it be free from errors. Data that TCP delivers to the recipient should be exactly the same data that the sender gave TCP originally. In a rigorous sense, this quality is impossible to attain. Even if TCP took the drastic step of sending a thousand copies of each message and comparing all of those copies in the destination system, undetected errors could still occur. Theoretically, after all, the exact same error could appear in all thousand copies. As a compromise, TCP actually provides a nearly error-free service; even if it cannot absolutely eliminate undetected errors, it can make them extremely rare.

The Transmission Control Protocol ensures delivery. When TCP accepts a message from an application, it also accepts responsibility for delivering that message; TCP guarantees that the data reaches its destination. Of course, successful delivery is not always possible. The recipient, for example,

TCP and Absolute Reliability

With the extensive service that TCP provides, it is sometimes easy to forget that TCP, by itself, cannot provide absolute reliability. When data reaches its destination, TCP can reliably deliver that data for an application protocol. TCP cannot, however, guarantee that the application protocol successfully processes the data. Consider a file transfer, for example. TCP can deliver data to the file transfer application. If the disk crashes, however, and the application is unable to write the data, then there is nothing TCP can do. If an application needs absolute reliability, then it must provide that itself.

may lose power before the data arrives. When TCP cannot honor its guarantee and actually deliver data, it informs the sender of the failure.

The Transmission Control Protocol delivers data in order. From TCP's perspective, reliable delivery means more than simply delivering data without errors. The protocol also endeavors to deliver data in sequence. This service ensures that the recipient receives the data in the same order that the sender sends it. Sometimes, it is easy to overlook the importance of in-sequence delivery. Does order really matter as long as the data actually arrives? The answer is definitely yes, as figure 3.8 illustrates. In the figure, the PC sends simple commands to the server. If those commands arrive out of order, the server deletes the old file before making a copy, clearly not what the user intended.

The Transmission Control Protocol eliminates duplication. Almost as a corollary to in-sequence delivery, TCP makes sure that data messages are delivered only once. Sometimes receiving many copies of a message is just as bad as (or even worse than) not receiving the message at all. Again, the clearest examples arise when the message contains commands as well as data. Imagine the consequences if a single request for a wire funds transfer arrives at a bank several times.

The Transmission Control Protocol operates end to end. All of these qualities of reliable delivery are part of a transport layer service. Transport protocols are end-to-end protocols,

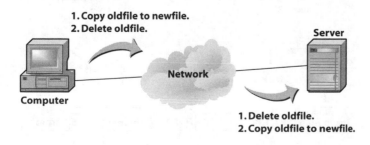

1. Copy oldfile to newfile.
2. Delete oldfile.

Server

Network

Computer

1. Delete oldfile.
2. Copy oldfile to newfile.

◀ **Figure 3.8**

If network messages arrive out of order unexpectedly, the results can be disastrous, as this example shows.

and TCP, like other transport protocols, operates only at the original source and ultimate destination of the data. As figure 3.9 shows, TCP does not participate at intermediate routers along the data's path. Only by operating at the communication endpoints can TCP provide a true delivery service to its users. After all, a user probably cares little if its message reaches the first router along the way to the destination; users want their messages to complete their journey.

The Need for Transport Protocols

The characteristics of TCP's reliable delivery—error-free, assured, in sequence, without duplication—are often characteristics of particular network technologies. Technologies such as ATM routinely provide these same qualities for the data that they transfer. Given this fact, why are transport protocols even needed? If a packet travels across several physical networks, each of which is reliable by itself, how could the overall path not be reliable?

Perhaps the most surprising failure of interconnected, reliable, networks is correctness. Even though physical networks themselves all provide error-free delivery, it may still be the case that a packet traveling through them does not arrive

Figure 3.9 ▶

Unlike IP, transport protocols like TCP are end-to-end protocols. Only endpoints—the traffic's original source and ultimate destination—use TCP. The routers in the middle don't know (or even care) that datagrams passing through them carry TCP messages.

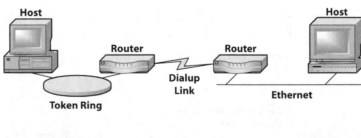

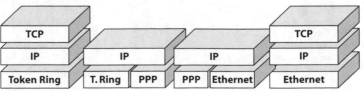

error-free. Of course, like TCP itself, network error-detection methods are not foolproof; they cannot detect every possible error. Most of them, however, are far better than TCP.

A more likely source of errors is not the networks, but the routers that connect the networks. Consider figure 3.10, which looks inside a router. In the figure, a packet arrives from the left network. The packet carries with it a frame check sequence (FCS) appended by the previous hop. The receiving router recalculates the FCS from the packet's data and compares the result with the actual FCS in the packet. If they match, the packet is accepted as error-free by the router. At this point, the left network has done its job and reliably delivered the packet through the network.

The important point is that (in most cases anyway) FCS checking is a job for hardware that actually interfaces to the

▼ Figure 3.10

Messages aren't completely safe from corruption even when subnetwork links are reliable. As this example shows, the messages may be vulnerable while they're queued in a router.

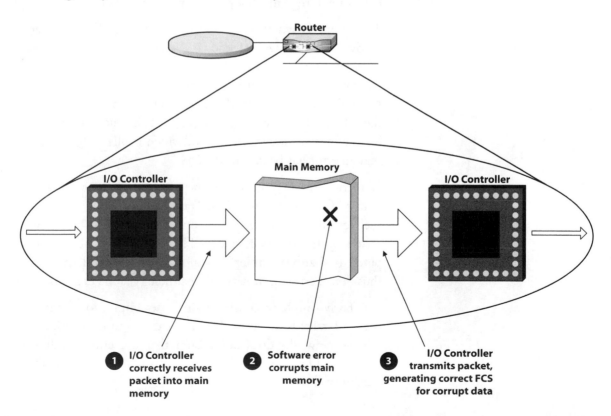

① **I/O Controller correctly receives packet into main memory**

② **Software error corrupts main memory**

③ **I/O Controller transmits packet, generating correct FCS for corrupt data**

network (such as the I/O controller in the figure). The router's software is not involved because software is generally not fast enough to perform the complex mathematical calculations required to check an FCS. For the same reason, the router's software cannot compute the FCS on packets that it forwards. That job, too, is left to the hardware that interfaces to the network. To see the consequences, follow the packet as it travels through the router.

Once the router receives the packet (successfully) from the left network, the router's software takes over. Suppose, however, that the software has a bug that causes the router to corrupt part of the packet while it sits in the router's memory. At this point (step 2 in the figure), the packet is no longer free from errors. Unaware of this problem, the router moves the packet to the right network. It asks the interface hardware to transmit the packet on that network.

This point is where things really go wrong. The interface hardware has no way of knowing that the packet now contains an error, and so the hardware happily calculates a new FCS for the packet as it transmits on the right network. This FCS will be correct for the data now in the packet, even though the data is wrong! The packet continues through the interconnected networks, each of which is blissfully unaware that an error has been introduced.

Detecting these types of errors requires work at the endpoints of the communication. Transport protocols can detect such errors because they rely on error-detection codes inserted by the original sender. These codes are not recomputed by hardware interfaces along the way, and they will thus detect errors that network technology alone can miss.

It is fairly simple to construct similar examples for other aspects of reliable delivery. In each case, a concatenation of reliable networks does not ensure that the entire path remains reliable. Transport level protocols like TCP provide that reliability.

Connection-Oriented Operation

For TCP, the basis for reliable delivery is a connection. Like transport protocols from other protocol suites, TCP relies on connection-oriented operation. For reliable delivery, connections are critical because they establish a context for the communications. This context allows TCP to relate different packets with each other, and with such a relationship TCP can identify a sequence of individual packets. The context also gives TCP a way to recognize duplicate packets, and it can determine when particular packets are missing. Together with a simple checksum, a connection's context gives TCP the tools it needs to deliver data reliably.

Identifying Connections

Most TCP implementations can simultaneously support many connections to many different systems. Figure 3.11 shows an example. The top server is supporting a remote login and two file transfer sessions, all at the same time.

Within the top server, TCP must differentiate three different connections. Conceptually, TCP acts as in figure 3.12. It distinguishes packets for each connection, manages each connection appropriately, and, of course, delivers data to the appropriate application.

To identify individual connections, TCP relies on socket pairs. Recall that a socket includes both an IP address (identifying

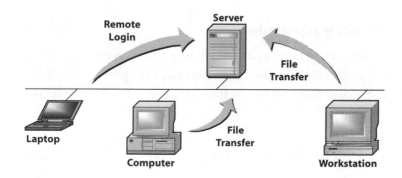

◀ Figure 3.11

A server can control many TCP connections simultaneously, just as it can carry on multiple UDP dialogs at the same time.

Figure 3.12 ▶

When a server controls multiple TCP connections at once, TCP is responsible for separating the traffic of each application. As with UDP, TCP relies on the destination port to distinguish particular applications.

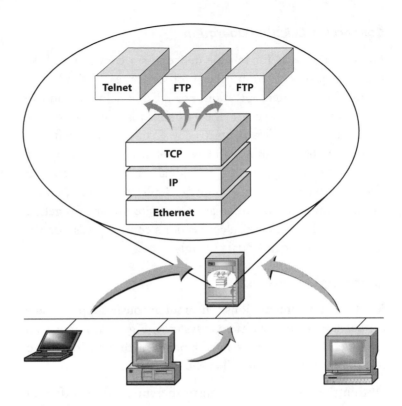

a particular system) and a port (identifying a particular application). A socket, therefore, is one endpoint of a connection. Because connections have two endpoints, a pair of sockets can uniquely identify a connection.

Many applications that use TCP depend on well-known ports for their servers. Table 3.1 includes some of the more important well-known port values on the Internet.

Establishing Connections

A TCP connection begins its life when two systems complete the connection establishment process. This process identifies the connection to both systems and prepares the connection for data transfer.

The procedure TCP uses to establish connections is known as a *three-way handshake*. Despite its name, the three-way handshake usually consists of four distinct events. Normally it proceeds as figure 3.13 shows. First, an application protocol in one system tells its local TCP that it is willing to accept a connection. This event is often called either a *listen* or a *passive connection request*. In the figure, the server performs this first step.

Next, an application in the second system asks TCP to actively establish a connection with the first application. This state is the *call*, or *active connection request*. To carry out its application's wishes, the client's TCP constructs a request packet and sends it to the server.

The third event in the handshake takes place when the server's TCP receives this packet. Because an application has previously issued a listen, TCP responds positively to the request packet. This confirmation is carried in the second packet of the connection establishment exchange.

As this point, the client's TCP knows that the connection establishment is complete. It has sent a request on behalf of its application, and it has received a positive response from the server. The server's TCP, however, is not quite as certain. Yes, it has responded to the request, but it does not have any assurance that the response has successfully reached the client. To provide that assurance, the client's TCP generates a third packet (and the fourth event of the establishment process).

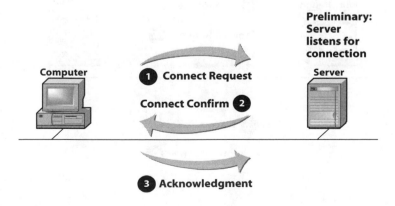

Preliminary: Server listens for connection

① **Connect Request**

Connect Confirm ②

③ **Acknowledgment**

Computer

Server

◀ **Figure 3.13**

Once the server prepares to listen for a connection, TCP begins its three-way handshake. The client starts the process with a connect request. The server responds with a connect confirm, and the client completes the handshake with an acknowledgment.

This third packet explicitly acknowledges receipt of the positive response. When it reaches the server, both systems know that connection establishment is complete. The term "three-way handshake" comes from the three distinct packets that the peer TCP implementations exchange.

Although connection establishment is part of TCP's responsibility, this example shows that application protocols must initiate it. An application in the server must indicate its willingness to accept connections, and an application in the client must actively seek such a connection. Without two agreeable applications, TCP cannot establish a connection.

This example shows the typical way that TCP establishes a connection. In it, one application makes a passive request and another application makes an active request. It is also possible for both applications to make active requests, in which case the connection establishment still succeeds. Figure 3.14 shows such an establishment. Both systems try to initiate a connection by sending connection request packets. Instead of sending positive connection responses, each system merely acknowledges the other's connection request.

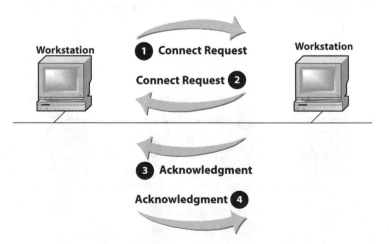

Figure 3.14 ▶

If two computers each try to start a TCP three-way handshake, each responds immediately with an acknowledgment. The connect confirm is unnecessary.

Transferring Data

Once TCP establishes a connection, it can begin to use it, which means transferring data across it. Of course, the whole point of connections is to make this data transfer reliable. The key to reliability is sequence numbers.

To transfer application data, TCP packages that data within a TCP packet. Most commonly, TCP packets are called *segments*. In addition to the data itself, segments contain sequence numbers. As figure 3.15 shows, the sequence numbers give every byte of application data its own number. When packets arrive at their destination, the receiving TCP can use these numbers to reconstruct the correct order for the data. If TCP receives data with the same sequence number, it recognizes that the data is duplicated, and it discards the extra copies. Similarly, if TCP finds gaps in the sequence numbers, it realizes that it is missing some data. It can then take appropriate steps to recover that missing data.

Note that sequence numbers are independent for each direction of data transfer in a connection. If, for example, a client is communicating with a server, the client uses its own sequence numbers for its requests while the server uses a separate set of sequence numbers for its responses. These two sets of sequence numbers have no relation to each other.

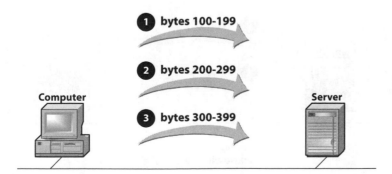

◀ Figure 3.15

Once a connection is established, the systems begin transferring data. TCP numbers every byte of data that it sends. This numbering lets the receiver detect missing bytes, as well as reorder any data that arrives out of order.

Acknowledgment

Sequence numbers alone let TCP recognize missing data. But TCP must do more than simply recognize when data is missing; it must recover that missing data. To recover missing data, the peer TCP implementations communicate directly with each other in a way that is transparent to the applications. After all, the receiver knows that data is missing, but it is the transmitter that has the data and needs to send another copy. To communicate this information, TCP uses acknowledgments. When one TCP sends a packet to another, it may include an acknowledgment number. By including an acknowledgment number, TCP says "I have successfully received all data up to (but not including) the data with this sequence number." To see this in action, consider figure 3.16.

In the figure, the client sends data in three different packets. The first packet contains bytes 100 to 199, the second packet has bytes 200 to 299, and the third packet has 300 through 399. After receiving the third packet, the server generates a packet with an acknowledgment number. Because the server next expects to receive byte number 400, the acknowledgment number in the packet is 400. When the client receives this acknowledgment, it knows that all of its data has successfully made it to its destination.

Figure 3.16 ▶

After the server receives data from the client, it sends an explicit acknowledgment. The acknowledgment identifies the next byte of data that the server expects and, implicitly, confirms receipt of all bytes up to that point.

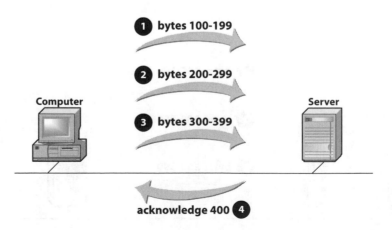

If data fails to reach the destination, clearly the destination system cannot acknowledge its arrival. Instead, the remote system can acknowledge only data prior to the missing bytes. Figure 3.17 illustrates this situation. The second packet containing bytes 200 to 299 never makes it to the server. Consequently, the server's acknowledgment contains the sequence number 200.

Note that the third packet (300 to 399) makes it safely across the network, but there is no way for the server to acknowledge it. Eventually, the client realizes that its second packet must not have arrived. In then retransmits the packet. With this second chance, the packet does make it, and the server promptly acknowledges data up to byte 400. As the example shows, there is no need for the client to retransmit the third packet (with bytes 300 to 399).

Flow Control

Sequence numbers also play a role in another important function—flow control. Flow control allows a receiver to

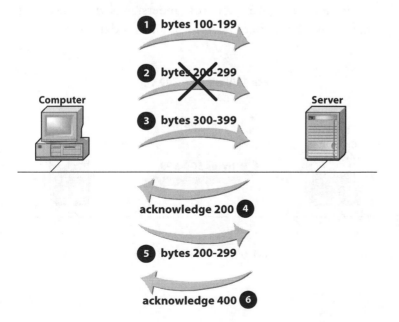

◀ Figure 3.17

If, as in this example, some data doesn't make it to the server, the server won't be able to acknowledge it. When the client sees what the server does acknowledge, it eventually realizes that some data didn't make it. As in the example, the client simply sends the missing data again. The server then acknowledges all data it has received.

limit the amount of data that the sender transmits. Such limits might be needed, for example, if the receiver has only a limited amount of memory in which to hold received data. Without flow control, the sender could transmit data without limit, overrunning the receiver's capacity.

Flow control is an ongoing part of every connection. As soon as TCP establishes a connection, and throughout the connection's life, each system tells the other how much data it can accept. It does this by specifying a window size. Figure 3.18 shows how window size limits the sender. In the figure, the server initially grants a window of 200 bytes. It does so with an acknowledgment packet. This packet says that the workstation next expects to receive byte number 400 and that it can accept an additional 200 bytes of data. The client then sends two packets, each with 100 bytes of data. At that point, however, the client must cease transmission. Because it has filled the allowable window, it has to wait before it can send any more data.

Urgent Data

In addition to regular data, TCP understands the concept of urgent data. Sometimes an application has data that it must

Figure 3.18 ▶

Along with each acknowledgment, the server indicates how much more data it is prepared to accept. In step 1 of this example, the server says it can accept 200 more bytes. After the clients sends those bytes, in steps 2 and 3, it has to pause and wait for further instructions from the server.

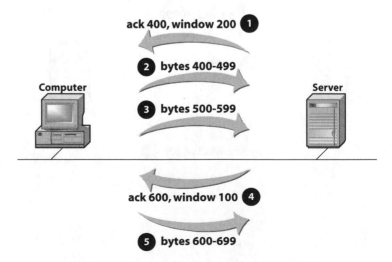

treat more urgently than regular data. If the application has already sent regular data on the connection, this urgent data will inevitably take its place behind less urgent data on the connection. As befits reliable operation, TCP delivers this data in sequence, and it cannot "jump" the urgent data ahead of regular data. It can, however, let the sending application tell its peer that urgent data follows. Presumably, when the receiver gets this indication, it will process the regular data as fast as possible in order to get to the urgent information.

Closing Connections

Of course, if TCP establishes connections for its applications, it will also close those connections once the applications are finished. As with connection establishment, TCP generally closes connections only when an application requests it.

Figure 3.19 shows the sequence of packets that the two systems exchange. When an application requests termination, its TCP sends a close indication packet. The peer acknowledges that packet, and data flow in one direction ceases. In the figure, this exchange corresponds to steps 1 and 2. After the exchange, the client no longer transmits data to the server.

To completely close the connection, TCP waits for the server's application to make its close request. When it does so, TCP

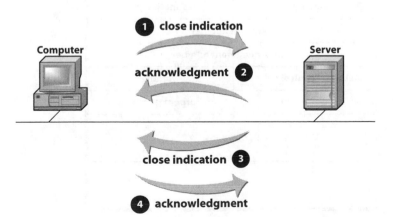

◀ Figure 3.19

When the two systems are finished with a connection, the send TCP close indications. Both system acknowledge each other's close message to complete the termination process.

repeats the exchange, but in the opposite direction. The server sends a close indication, and the client responds with an acknowledgment. After steps 3 and 4 of the figure, no data may flow in either direction, and the TCP connection ceases to exist.

TCP Packet Format

All TCP packets have the same basic format. The details of that format appear in figure 3.20. The header that precedes application data is the same for every type of TCP packet, from connection requests to user data. To distinguish packets with different functions, TCP uses different settings of the control field.

The TCP header starts off with source and destination ports. These fields indicate the port values for the sender and for the receiver.

Figure 3.20 ▼

A TCP message is carried in an IP datagram. The next header value of 6 indicates TCP. The TCP message, known as a segment, itself consists of a TCP header, including any options, and the application's data.

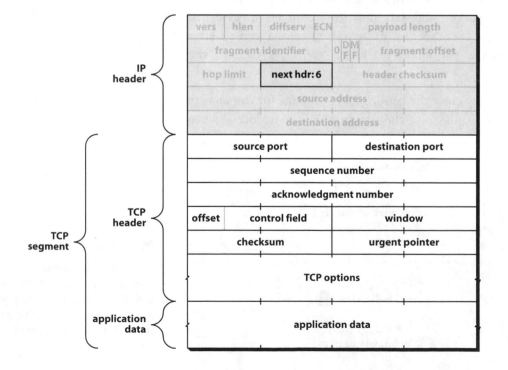

The 32-bit sequence number follows the ports. In most cases, this field is the sequence number for the first byte of application data in the packet. The exception occurs in packets with the SYN bit set. (See table 3.4.) In those packets, the sequence number field defines where the sender will start numbering its data. The data itself has the sequence number one greater than this field.

The next field is the 32-bit acknowledgment number. This field has meaning only if the ACK bit in the control field is set. When it is set, this value indicates the next sequence number the sender expects. It acknowledges receipt of all data up to (but not including) this value. Once TCP establishes a connection, it must include this field in every packet. (In other words, it should always set the ACK bit.)

The data offset indicates the number of 32-bit words in the TCP header. It tells the recipient where the application data begins. Data doesn't always begin at a fixed location in the packet because TCP may include a variable number of header options in each packet. The data offset field itself is 4 bits in size.

Following the data offset are 12 single-bit flags. The first four flags are currently undefined and should be zero. Table 3.4 lists the meaning of each bit. Note that some of the flag bits simply indicate whether another field in the header is significant. If the control field bit is clear, then the corresponding header field has no meaning. The header field is, however, still present in the packet.

Table 3.4 Defined Bits in the TCP Control Field

Bit	Meaning
CWR	Congestion Window Reduced.
ECE	Explicit Congestion Notification Echo.
URG	Urgent field is significant.
ACK	Acknowledgment field is significant.

continues...

Table 3.4 Defined Bits in the TCP Control Field (continued)

Bit	Meaning
PSH	Push function invoked.
RST	Reset the connection.
SYN	Synchronize sequence numbers.
FIN	Sender is finished with connection.

Following the control field is the 16-bit window. This number indicates how many bytes of data the sending system can accept. The first byte the system can accept is the one numbered by the acknowledgment field. Because the window value has significance only when combined with an acknowledgment number, this field is meaningful only when the acknowledgment field is valid. That is true when the ACK bit in the control field is set.

The next field in TCP's header is the checksum. It detects errors in the packet and allows TCP to provide error-free delivery. In fact, the TCP checksum covers more than just the TCP packet. It also includes the source and destination IP addresses, as well as the IP next header value. By including those fields, the checksum protects against packets that are not themselves corrupt but have been delivered to the wrong place.

The rules for constructing a checksum are identical to those for UDP. Because TCP does not permit the sender to omit checksums, there is no need to handle a checksum value of zero in any special manner.

The final required field for TCP headers is the urgent pointer. Unless the URG bit in the control field is set, this pointer has no meaning. When the field is valid, the packet indicates two things. First, the sender wants to send data that it considers urgent. Second, the pointer value itself identifies the end of the urgent data. If the receiver processes all data up to and including the urgent pointer, then it will have processed the urgent data.

Efficient Checksums

As is the case for UDP, a major factor in the performance of network implementations is their performance in calculating checksums. Several RFCs are devoted to the subject of maximizing this performance; the most thorough RFC on the topic is RFC 1071.

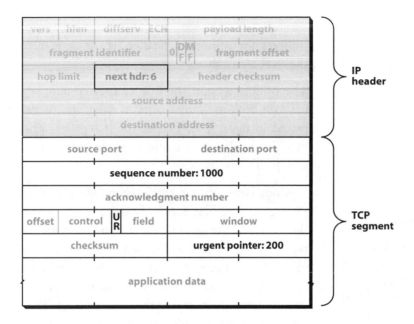

To see an example of urgent data, look at figure 3.21. There the TCP packet has a sequence number of 1000 and an urgent pointer of 200. With these values, the application data in the packet begins at byte number 1000. Urgent data extends up to and includes byte number 1200, and normal data resumes at byte 1201.

Two things are significant about the urgent pointer. First, it gives no indication of where the urgent data actually begins. If that is important, applications must determine it on their own. Second, the urgent data itself may not be included in a packet with an urgent pointer. If, in the example, the data packet contained only 100 bytes of application data, then the urgent data could conceivably be following in another packet.

For minimal TCP headers, the urgent pointer is the last TCP header field. Everything that follows is application data. If the data offset has a value greater than 5, however, then the packet includes TCP options, which precede application data.

▲ **Figure 3.21**

If TCP needs to send urgent data, it sets the URG bit in the control field and puts a value in the header's urgent pointer. The urgent pointer indicates the end of the urgent data. A system that receives a segment with URG set should immediately process data up to the urgent pointer as quickly as possible.

To determine the size of the options, TCP implementations subtract the minimum header size (five 32-bit words) from the data offset value.

The options area of the header may contain several individual TCP options. Those options take one of two forms, depicted in figure 3.22. The simplest type of option is a single byte option. It consists of a single byte that indicates its type and, implicitly, its value.

Options larger than a single byte take the second format in the figure. The first byte indicates the type of the option and the second byte counts the option's length (including the type and length bytes). The remaining bytes carry the option value. Note that TCP must know in advance which options are single byte and which are multiple bytes. Otherwise, it cannot correctly interpret the options field. Table 3.5 lists the official TCP options, plus one additional option (type 19) that, though not part of the official TCP standard, is commonly used for Border Gateway Protocol messages. (See chapter 6.)

Figure 3.22 ▼

If TCP needs to include options in its header, it adjusts the offset to indicate where the application data begins. The options themselves can either be a single byte or multiple bytes. Multi-byte options carry their size in their second byte.

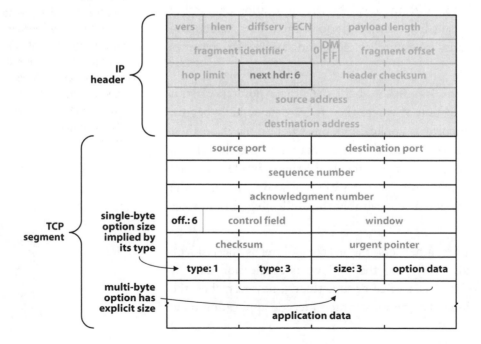

Table 3.5 TCP Options

Type	Length	Value
0	1	End of valid options in header.
1	1	No operation (ignore this byte).
2	4	Maximum segment size.
3	3	Window scale factor.
8	10	Timestamp.
19	18	Message digest of the packet.

The TCP State Machine

The Transmission Control Protocol uses its packets to establish, maintain, and close connections. Its operation is guided by a well-defined series of states, listed in table 3.6. Protocol implementations change states in response to application requests, received packets, and timer expirations. Figure 3.23 summarizes this behavior in a state transition diagram. The diagram uses arrows to indicate transitions between states. Each transition has a label that indicates which event triggers the transition and any actions that TCP takes that coincide with the transition. The events appear above the horizontal bar, and actions appear below it. Some transitions do not require that TCP take any action, and those transitions have nothing below their horizontal bars.

Table 3.6 TCP Connection States

Name	State
Closed	An imaginary state that represents a connection that does not exist.
Listen	Application has issued passive connect request.
SYN Sent	Application has issued active connect request.
SYN Rcvd	TCP has responded to a connect request.
Estab	Connection is established.
Close Wait	Peer has closed the connection.

continues…

Table 3.6 TCP Connection States (continued)

Name	State
Last ACK	Waiting for an acknowledgment of a close request.
FIN Wait-1	Application has requested a close of the connection.
FIN Wait-2	Waiting for peer to close the connection.
Closing	Waiting for peer to acknowledge closing the connection.
Time Wait	Waiting to ensure that no packets from the connection (that is now closed) remain in the network.

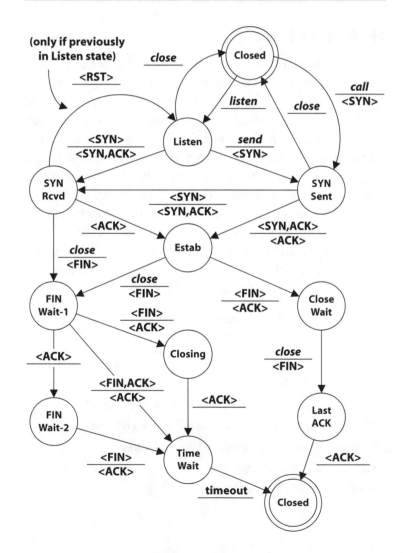

Figure 3.23 ▶

The TCP state machine completely specifies the behavior of systems using TCP.

Table 3.7 lists the events that cause state transitions. As the table shows, there are three different types of events. They include requests from the local application, packets received from the peer TCP, and timer expirations.

Table 3.7 Events in TCP State Transition Diagram

Name	Event
Listen	Application issues passive connect request.
Call	Application issues active connect request.
Send	Application provides data to transfer.
Close	Application requests closing the connection.
<SYN>	Connect request packet arrives from peer.
<SYN,ACK>	Connect response packet arrives from peer.
<RST>	Reset packet arrives from peer.
<ACK>	Acknowledgment packet arrives from peer.
<FIN>	Finish packet arrives from peer.
timeout	Timer expires.

The actions that the state transition diagram includes are packets that TCP sends to its peer. As table 3.8 shows, the state transition diagram considers only four possible packets as actions. Pure data packets that do not have acknowledgments are not the result of state transitions.

Table 3.8 Actions in TCP State Transition Diagram

Name	Action
<SYN>	Connect request packet.
<SYN,ACK>	Connect response packet.
<ACK>	Acknowledgment packet.
<FIN>	Finish packet.

Summary

The IP architecture includes two primary transport protocols—UDP and TCP. Application protocols choose between the two based on how much reliability they require. For the simple transfer of individual datagrams, UDP is efficient and effective. Applications that need a more robust transport service can rely on TCP to ensure the reliable, in-sequence, and error-free delivery of their data.

CHAPTER 4

Link State Routing and OSPF

As we've noted before, networks exist to deliver data. The data may take many forms, and it may serve many different transport and application protocols. For any network to be useful, however, data must reach its intended destination. Earlier chapters show how the Internet Protocol accepts data packets and moves them one step closer to their destination. With this chapter we'll see how IP knows which step is the next step and how, ultimately, IP knows where to route.

The Open Shortest Path First (OSPF) protocol is TCP/IP's primary routing protocol. Routers rely on OSPF to exchange information among themselves. That information gives each router a map of the network. By checking their maps, routers know how to move packets through the network to their destinations.

The OSPF protocol is an example of a particular type of routing protocol—a *link state* protocol. All link state protocols share the same basic principles, and this chapter begins by examining those principles. It then discusses the ways that OSPF organizes networks and how OSPF deals with unusual network topologies. It concludes with a detailed look at OSPF messages.

Link State Routing

Link state routing has a reputation for complexity. Certainly the size of the OSPF specification—currently 244 pages—does little to allay such concerns. Actually, however, link state routing relies on a few simple principles. It may take several words to describe those principles with the precision required by a protocol specification, but the principles themselves are easy to understand.

Routing protocols are the primary tool of routers, and routers have a simple goal. They want to understand how the network is put together so that they can tell how to get from one point to another. In a real sense, routers just want a map of the network, and routing protocols help them create such a map.

Link state protocols create the map in three distinct phases. First, each router meets its neighbors. In that phase the routers learn about their local neighborhood. In the second phase, routers share that information with all other routers on the network. During this phase, routers learn about every other neighborhood. In the final phase, routers combine the information about individual neighborhoods. This combination describes the entire network, and from it routers calculate routes.

With apologies to readers outside the United States, the U.S. interstate highway system provides a convenient example for discussing link state routing. Cities take the place of routers, and the roads between them act as links. Figure 4.1 shows the part of the system that the following text considers. (The figure sometimes combines several highways into one, and it distorts a few distances. Do not plan a family vacation using this map.)

◄ Figure 4.1

To understand link state routing, we can look at highways in the United States.

Meet Your Neighbors

Systems that participate in link state routing begin learning routes by meeting their neighbors. This phase could hardly be any easier. Each system simply sends a packet on all its links. That packet, called a *hello* packet, introduces the sender.

Referring to the example, Kansas City starts the process by sending a courier on all of its roads. The courier carries a message that says "Hello, I'm from Kansas City." All other systems take the same action, so Kansas City also receives couriers from its neighbors with their introductions. Figure 4.2 shows Kansas City introducing itself and its neighbors introducing themselves to Kansas City as well.

Once Kansas City receives hello packets from Dallas, Phoenix, and Salt Lake City, it knows the identity of its neighbors. Kansas City also knows the distance, or cost, to each neighbor.[1] Kansas City could summarize the information it has learned in a list like table 4.1. Of course, all the other cities take the same action as Kansas City. Each, therefore, quickly meets its neighbors, and each is able to construct a similar table.

---

[1] The highway analogy breaks down here. Highway distances are real, physical values. Short of building new roads, they do not change. Network costs, on the other hand, are arbitrary and set by network administrators. For this discussion, the distinction is not important.

Figure 4.2 ▶

To meet its neighbors, Kansas City sends messages down each of its highways. The cities at the other end of those highways also send greeting messages toward Kansas City.

Table 4.1 Kansas City Neighbor List

Neighbor	Highway	Distance
Salt Lake City	I-90	3150 km
Phoenix	I-40	2066 km
Dallas	I-20	1719 km

Share the Information

Once each city learns the identity of its neighbors, the second phase of link state routing takes over. In this phase, the cities share the information they have learned. Each city constructs a message containing its neighbor list, and it sends that packet to all other cities. These packets are *link state advertisements*, or LSAs. An LSA from Kansas City, for example, contains exactly the information in table 4.1.

Most link state advertisements, including OSPF, share neighbor information by *flooding* LSAs. Systems flood a packet by resending a copy of that packet to nearly every link. More precisely, when a system participates in flooding, it considers every LSA it receives a candidate to be flooded. The system makes sure that the candidate packet is new. If it is an old packet that the system has already seen, then it has already been flooded. The system can simply discard it.

If the candidate packet is a new one, the system remembers the information it contains (if, for no other reason, to ensure that it can recognize future, duplicate copies). The system

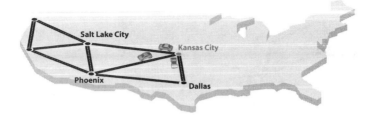

◀ **Figure 4.3**

To tell everyone about the neighbors it's met, Kansas City begins by sending a new message out all of its highways.

then transmits a copy of the packet on all links except the one from which it arrived.

Figures 4.3 , 4.4, and 4.5 show how flooding distributes Kansas City's link state advertisement across the network. Table 4.2.outlines the complete flooding procedure.

Table 4.2 Flooding Kansas City's Link State Advertisement

Step	Action
1	Kansas City transmits the LSA on all links: to Dallas, Phoenix, and Salt Lake City. (Figure 4.3.)
2a	Dallas receives the LSA from Kansas City and copies it to all other links, in this case to Phoenix. (Figure 4.4.)
2b	Phoenix receives the LSA from Kansas City and copies it to all other links: Dallas, San Francisco, and Salt Lake City. (Figure 4.4.)
2c	Salt Lake City receives the LSA from Kansas City and copies it to Seattle, San Francisco, and Phoenix. (Figure 4.4.)
3a	Dallas receives the LSA from Phoenix. Having already received it (from Kansas City), Dallas discards this copy. (Figure 4.5.)
3b	Phoenix receives the LSA from Dallas and from Salt Lake City. Already having seen this LSA, Phoenix discards it. (Figure 4.5.)
3c	Salt Lake City receives another copy from Phoenix and discards it. (Figure 4.5.)
3d	San Francisco receives the LSA from Phoenix and copies it to Seattle and Salt Lake City. (Figure 4.5.)
3e	San Francisco receives another copy of the LSA from Salt Lake City and discards it. (Figure 4.5.)
3f	Seattle receives the LSA from Salt Lake City and copies it to San Francisco. (Figure 4.5.)

Figure 4.4 ▶

When each of Kansas City's neighbors receives this new message, it turns around and sends a copy of the message to *its* neighbors.

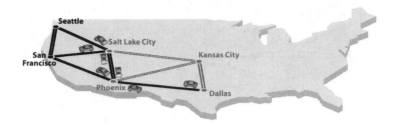

Flooding Efficiency

As this example clearly shows, flooding wastes. Systems receive multiple copies of the same LSA, and they end up discarding all but the first. In exchange for this bandwidth, however, flooding makes processing a lot simpler for the routers. Furthermore, any other approach is fraught with peril. Eliminating the duplicates would require some knowledge of the network's topology. But, of course, flooding LSAs is one step in determining that connectivity. Routers cannot share information more efficiently without knowing the topology, and they cannot easily learn that topology without flooding.

The example illustrates the most important feature of flooding. It ensures that all systems receive a copy of the LSA packet. Of course, in the sample network Kansas City is not alone in flooding LSAs. All other cities do the same. As a result, every system soon learns the neighbors of every other system. Each system has the view of the network that table 4.3 describes. That information makes up the *link state database* for the network.

Table 4.3 Example Link State Database

KC	Dallas	Phoenix	Salt Lake	San Fran	Seattle
Dallas 844	KC 844	KC 2066	KC 3150	Phoenix 1146	Salt Lake 1315
Phoenix 2066	Phoenix 1719	Dallas 1719	Phoenix 1083	Salt Lake 1175	San Fran. 1299
Salt Lake 3150		Salt Lake 1083	San Fran. 1175	Seattle 1299	
		San Fran. 1146	Seattle 1315		

Figure 4.5 ▶

Each city that receives the Kansas City message sends a new copy on any new highways. Eventually, Kansas City's information reaches all other cities on the network.

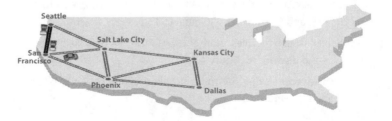

Calculate Routes

Once all systems have an up-to-date link state database, they can begin the final phase of link state routing—actually calculating routes. The technical details of this calculation are not a formal part of link state protocols. The protocols take care of distributing the information; systems then use that information to reach appropriate and consistent conclusions.

One particular algorithm is so much more efficient at determining routes, though, that nearly all link state implementations rely on it. The particular algorithm, originally proposed by Dijkstra[2], is so prevalent that most routing protocols assume its implementation and are optimized accordingly.

Dijkstra's algorithm constructs a directed graph, or tree, for the network. The tree's root is the system performing the calculations, and its branches are links to other systems. Table 4.4 describes the steps in the algorithm. To see Dijkstra's algorithm in action, consider how Kansas City would employ it. Figure 4.6 shows the computation; it is based on the link state database of table 4.3.

Table 4.4 Dijkstra's Algorithm

Step	Calculation
1	Start building the tree by creating its root—the local system. The distance to this system is zero.
2	For the system just added to the tree, examine the link state database. For each of its neighbors, compute the distance to that neighbor as the sum of the distances to the system just added and from that system to its neighbor. If the sum is less than any other path to the neighbor, tentatively add the path to the tree.
3	Search the tree for the nearest system that's still tentative. Add that system (and the path to it) to the tree permanently, and return to step 2. If there are no tentative entries remaining in the tree, the calculation is complete.

Shortest Path First

Dijkstra's algorithm is often called the shortest path first algorithm. Indeed, that is how the OSPF protocol gets its name. This name comes from the third step of the algorithm in table 4.4, where the system identifies the shortest path (nearest system) and treats it next.

[2] E. W. Dijkstra. "A Note on Two Problems in Connection with Graphs." *Numerische Mathematic* 1: 269-271, 1959.

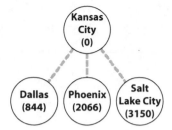

Steps 1 and 2: Add local Kansas City to tree and add its neighbors tentatively.

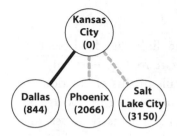

Steps 3 and 2: Add shortest tentative path (Dallas) permanently and its neighbors tentatively. (There are none.)

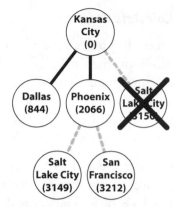

Steps 3 and 2: Add shortest tentative path (Phoenix) permanently and its neighbors (Salt Lake City and San Francisco) tentatively. Tentative addition of Salt Lake City replaces previous tentative path because new path is shorter (3149 vs. 3150).

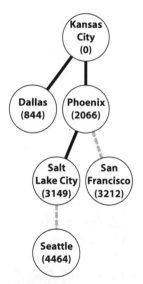

Steps 3 and 2: Add shortest tentative path (Salt Lake City) permanently and its neighbors (Seattle) tentatively.

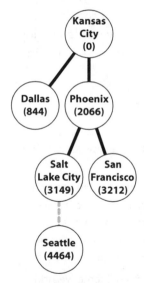

Steps 3 and 2: Add shortest tentative path (San Francisco) permanently and its neighbors tentatively. (There are none.)

Steps 3 and 2: Add shortest tentative path (Seattle) permanently and its neighbors tentatively. (There are none.) Because no more tentative paths exist, the calculation is complete.

▲ **Figure 4.6**

Dijkstra's algorithm tells routers how to use network information to calculate the optimum path to all destinations.

Once Dijkstra's calculation is complete, the system has a complete picture of routing in the network. To find the best path to any particular destination, the system need only find that system in the Dijkstra tree. Whichever path points to that system in the tree is the path to use to forward to that system across the network.

With figure 4.6 as an example, Kansas City would forward to Salt Lake City by way of Phoenix. Furthermore, Kansas City knows that Salt Lake City is 3149 km away.

Network Changes

The discussion so far has assumed a static network. Routers and links, once operational, remain operational indefinitely. Of course, real networks are not that stable. Routers restart, and links fail, yet the network must continue to function. In fact, one of the greatest strengths of IP is its resiliency in the face of unstable networks.

Fortunately, all the principles of the previous three subsections apply equally well to dynamic networks. The only difference is that all three phases happen in parallel, and they all take place continuously. Systems continuously introduce themselves to their neighbors, and they continue to receive neighborly introductions. When a system hears of a new neighbor, it updates its link state database and floods it again. The same thing happens if a system fails to hear from its neighbor. The flooding process updates everyone's link state database. A new database requires a new Dijkstra computation, so each router performs its calculations again. As the network changes, OSPF tracks these changes, and forwarding continues to function successfully.

To see this behavior in detail, consider how the sample network responds to a link failure. Suppose, as figure 4.7 illustrates, highway I-40 from Kansas City to Phoenix is closed. Eventually, both Kansas City and Phoenix recognize that the link is no longer available. If the cities can't detect the failure

Figure 4.7 ▶

In this example, the link between Phoenix and Kansas City has failed. Both cities will recognize the failure when they cease receiving hello messages from each other.

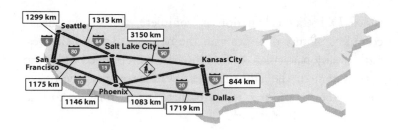

directly, they'll soon notice that they aren't receiving hello packets from their former neighbor. When recognition dawns, both cities update their link state advertisements and flood them across the network. Of course, this flooding takes place without the benefit of highway I-40. Once the flooding is complete, every system will have an up-to-date link state database as table 4.5 shows.

Table 4.5 Updated Link State Database

KC	Dallas	Phoenix	Salt Lake	San Fran	Seattle
Dallas 844	KC 844	Dallas 1719	KC 3150	Phoenix 1146	Salt Lake 1315
Salt Lake 3150	Phoenix 1719	Salt Lake 1083	Phoenix 1083	Salt Lake 1175	San Fran. 1299
		San Fran. 1146	San Fran. 1175	Seattle 1299	
		San Fran. 1146	Seattle 1315		

With the new link state database, each system must perform the Dijkstra calculations again. As figure 4.8 shows, that calculation changes how Kansas City routes to other destinations. Now, to reach Phoenix, it forwards packets to Dallas. In fact, all routes that used to go through Phoenix now take other paths.

This entire process—updating LSAs, flooding them across the network, and recomputing routes—typically takes less than a second or two. Link state protocols react quickly to network changes, and the network continues to function.

◀Figure 4.8

After Kansas City creates an updated link state database, it uses Dijkstra's algorithm to recalculate path's to the other destinations in the network. Notice that Kansas City can still reach Phoenix; it just has to go through Dallas as in intermediate hop along the way.

OSPF and Network Organization

The OSPF protocol employs all of the principles of a link state routing protocol. It meets neighbors, shares the information, and calculates routes. Of course, real networks introduce a few complications to these simple processes. One such complication is network organization.

In principle, OSPF could treat the entire Internet just like the U.S. highway example. Every router could exchange information with every other router. Unfortunately, that approach is not practical. There are just too many systems on the Internet. The required link state database would be enormous (far too large to store in any real system), and Dijkstra's calculations, even on high-performance supercomputers, would take hours. Even worst, the flooding of so many LSA packets would completely swamp the network, rendering it useless for actual user traffic.

To solve these problems of scale, OSPF establishes hierarchies within the network. Those hierarchies include autonomous systems, areas, backbones, stub areas, and not so stubby areas. This section looks at each of these divisions in turn.

Autonomous Systems

At the coarsest level, the Internet consists of many *autonomous systems*. That term is, perhaps, an unfortunate choice of name for this grouping. An autonomous system (AS) is actually a collection of many computer systems, routers, and other network devices. The equipment constituting an autonomous system shares a single administrative entity. That entity, which may be an educational institution, a business, a network provider, and so on, is responsible for all equipment within the AS.

Figure 4.9 shows the organization of three autonomous systems. (In order to fit the illustration on a page, these ASs are considerably smaller than most real autonomous systems.) Each AS forms a self-contained network, with its own administration and management. In most cases, though, networks provide more value when they connect more users. Increasing that connectivity means connecting autonomous systems. The figure shows such a connection through the ATM network in its center.

Autonomous systems define the limits of OSPF's interactions. Routers within an AS can exchange routing information using OSPF. They describe their links with LSA packets, and they can flood those packets throughout the autonomous system.

At the AS boundary, however, no OSPF traffic flows. The three routers in the center of figure 4.9, for example, can use OSPF within their respective autonomous systems, but they do not use OSPF to communicate with each other across the ATM network. Because they exist on the boundary of an AS, routers such as these three are *AS boundary routers*.

An AS boundary router can learn about the network beyond the autonomous system. It may learn information from

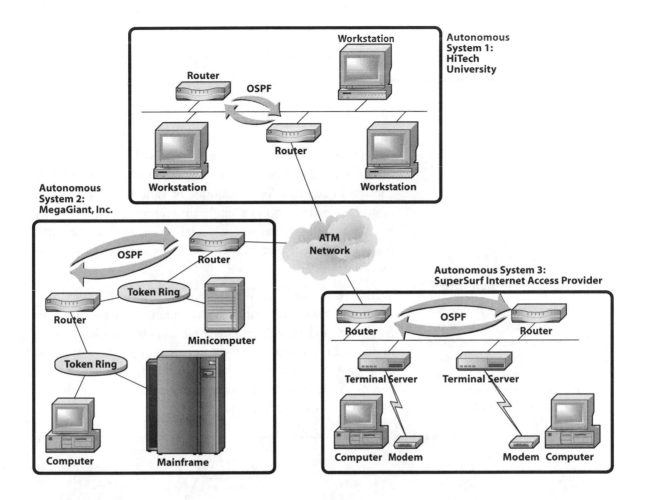

routing protocols other than OSPF, or it may learn from manual configuration. In either case, an AS boundary router can use OSPF to distribute that information within the autonomous system. It does so by building special link state advertisements. These special LSAs are *external LSAs*, so called because they describe topology external to the AS.

Areas

Autonomous systems provide some relief to a routing protocol such as OSPF. They limit the scope of the protocol's influence and reduce the memory, processor resources, and

▲ **Figure 4.9**

This example shows three autonomous systems. Routers within each autonomous system can use OSPF to exchange routing information. The figure doesn't show any communication between different autonomous systems. Such communication cannot use OSPF. Other routing protocols (such as BGP) coordinate that exchange.

network bandwidth the protocol requires. Sometimes, however, even an autonomous system by itself is too big and unwieldy. When such problems arise, OSPF offers another mechanism that provides additional hierarchy to its networks. That mechanism is the *area*.

Areas are arbitrary collections of networks, hosts, and routers. All systems within an area must be connected together, but otherwise OSPF places no restrictions on what is allowed in an area. As an example of various areas, consider figure 4.10, which shows a single autonomous system. The AS has three normal areas and a special area known as the *backbone*. The routers that connect different areas are known as *area border routers*.

Figure 4.10 ▼

Even within an autonomous system, OSPF can divide the network into smaller, more manageable pieces. These divisions are areas; a special area called the backbone connects directly with all other areas.

Within each area, OSPF functions normally. Routers construct and flood link state advertisements listing all of their neighbors, and they distribute these LSAs to all other routers in the area. At the boundary between areas, however, the OSPF protocol does not exchange simple LSAs. Instead, area border routers construct special LSAs that summarize the information within their areas.

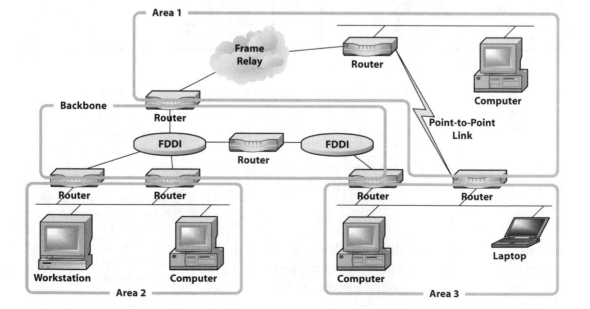

The router on the right side of the figure, for example, is an area border router connecting areas 1 and 3. It summarizes the topology of area 3 for area 1. To distribute that information, it floods *summary LSAs* into area 1. Similarly, the right router summarizes the topology of area 1 with LSAs that it floods into area 3.

The Backbone

The backbone is a special area within an autonomous system. It serves as the hub of the AS, and all other areas in the AS must connect to the backbone. As figure 4.10 shows, areas can also connect to each other directly, without going through the backbone.

Routers within the backbone are known as *backbone routers*. Figure 4.10 includes five backbone routers. Four of them are also area border routers; they connect the backbone to other areas. The exception is the router connecting the two FDDI ring networks. This router is still a backbone router because it resides in the backbone area, but it is not an area border router.

The OSPF protocol considers the backbone a particularly important area, and it provides special features to compensate for a break in the backbone connectivity. Consider figure 4.11, in which a backbone router is no longer operational. Without that router, the backbone is not completely connected. The two FDDI rings cannot communicate with each other.

The situation can be repaired by a network administrator. The administrator creates a virtual link between the two halves of the backbone. Figure 4.11 shows this virtual link winding through areas 1 and 3. Clearly, such a link is less efficient than the healthy backbone, particularly if the point-to-point link is not a high-speed link.

Nonetheless, virtual links do provide connectivity. By requiring manual configuration of virtual links, OSPF forces the

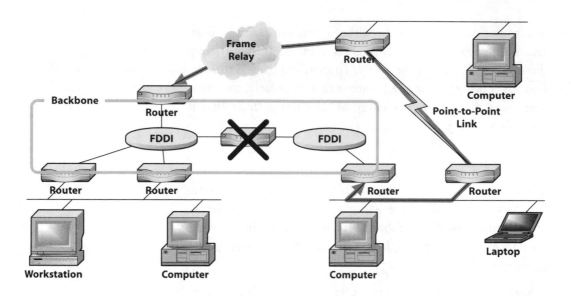

Figure 4.11 ▲

When different parts of the backbone area lose connectivity with each other, the backbone has become partitioned. This situation is serious; to compensate for the failure, the network administrator can create a virtual link that uses other areas to repair the partition. OSPF treats the virtual link like a direct connection between its two endpoints.

network administrator to recognize the seriousness of a broken backbone and the resulting loss in efficiency.

So far, we've discussed three different types of routers that OSPF defines. Table 4.6 summarizes these special types, along with the default *interior router*.

Table 4.6 Special OSPF Routers

Router Type	Characteristics
AS boundary router	A router with at least one interface outside of the OSPF autonomous system.
Area border router	A router with interfaces in at least two different OSPF areas.
Backbone router	A router within the OSPF backbone area.
Interior router	A router with all interfaces in a single OSPF area.

Stub Areas

The OSPF protocol relies on both autonomous systems and areas to reduce its traffic requirements. Destinations beyond the autonomous system are summarized in external link state advertisements, and destinations outside a single area are advertised in summary LSAs. In both cases, the detailed topology of the outside world is hidden. The LSAs simply indicate which destinations are reachable.

Even with such summaries, OSPF can still consume considerable network bandwidth. The Internet, for example, contains tens of thousands of destinations. An OSPF-based system must advertise each of these destinations in an external LSA, even if it does not need to detail the links necessary to reach them.

To avoid this overhead, OSPF defines a *stub area*. A stub area is a special OSPF area that has only one area border router; that is, there is only one way out of the area. (None of the areas of figure 4.10 qualifies as a stub area because each has at least two connections to other areas.)

Within the stub area, no summary or external LSAs circulate. They are not needed. Each router in the network learns only the location of the area's exit point—which is its area border router. Any packets for a destination outside the area are simply forwarded to that exit point. In effect, the area border router serves as the default router for packets that have nowhere else to go.

Stub areas are restricted in two ways. First, virtual links cannot pass through a stub area. A virtual link requires two separate connections into or out of the area, but a stub area can, by definition, have only one such connection point. The second restriction prohibits stub areas from containing an AS boundary router within them. This restriction also is natural. If the AS boundary router were within a stub area, it would not be able to advertise external LSAs. One characteristic of stub areas is that they do not flood external LSAs. Note, though, that the stub area's area border router can serve as an AS boundary router also. AS boundary routers are prohibited only inside a stub area.

Not So Stubby Areas

Stub areas are quite effective in reducing the burden on OSPF. Routers within a stub area learn about each other, and they learn how to get out of the area through the single area border router. In exchange, the routers forfeit the ability to exchange routes learned from any source other than OSPF. All such routes are classified as external routes, and OSPF does not propagate them within a stub area.

This restriction is sometimes too severe. It makes it difficult to coordinate additional routing protocols (such as the Routing Information Protocol detailed in chapter 5) within an area. A *not so stubby area*, more commonly known as an NSSA, provides most of the benefits of stub areas, but with a little more flexibility. In particular, an NSSA allows routers to exchange some information about routes learned from other sources, without incurring the cost of becoming a full OSPF area. An NSSA area allows the distribution of special NSSA link state advertisements. These NSSA LSAS are very similar to external LSAS; the only difference is how they are disseminated. External LSAS are not flooded in a not so stubby area, while NSSA LSAS are flooded within a single NSSA.

Special Networks

Until now, the discussion of OSPF has treated all subnetworks as if they were simple point-to-point links. Real networks, of course, consist of a variety of network technologies. Many of those networks require, or at least benefit from, special treatment by a routing protocol. In particular, OSPF makes special allowances for three special network types—broadcast networks, nonbroadcast networks, and demand networks.

Broadcast Networks

Broadcast networks provide an inherent broadcast or multicast capability, and they allow any system to communicate directly with any other system. By far, the most common type of broadcast network is a local area network such as Ethernet.

Broadcast networks merit special treatment because of their any-to-any flexibility. Consider, for example, the Token Ring LAN in figure 4.12. There are five routers attached to the network. Because each router can communicate with the other four, each would normally consider that it had four neighbors. Five routers, each with four neighbors, create a total of 20 entries in the link state database.

Twenty entries is not necessarily a great number of link state entries, but consider what happens as more routers attach to the LAN. As figure 4.13 highlights, the number of entries grows as the square of the number of routers. (The top trace in the graph shows this behavior.) On large networks, this growth represents a serious problem.

To help keep the size of link state databases manageable, OSPF treats broadcast networks a special way. It elects a special router from among those on the network. This router, known as the *designated router*, treats all routers on the network as neighbors, while the other routers consider only the designated router as their neighbor. As far as routing calculations are concerned, traffic between two such routers must pass through the designated router. (This restriction applies only to routing calculations; actual datagrams do not pass through the artificial designated router.)

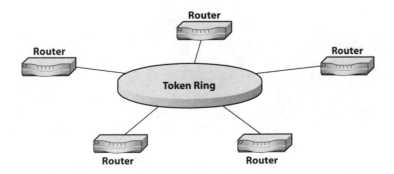

◀ **Figure 4.12**

In this example five routers share the same subnetwork. If each router considered every other router its neighbor, this simple network alone would create 20 entries in a link state database.

Figure 4.13 ▶

As the number of routers on a subnetwork increases, the size of the link state database grows as well. Without a designated router, database growth is proportional to the square of the number of routers. A designated router reduces the growth rate so that it is only linear, a much more scalable situation.

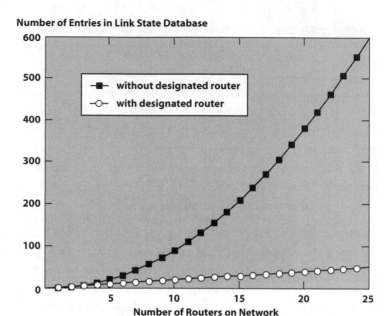

Number of Entries in Link State Database

Figure 4.14 shows the artificial topology OSPF creates. This topology is artificial because the designated router does not really exist. Instead, one of the other routers takes on the role of designated router in addition to its other responsibilities. Note from the figure that the designated router does not replace one of the normal routers. Rather, it is included in addition to those routers.

With a designated router elected, each true router on the network reports only the designated router as a neighbor.

Figure 4.14 ▶

The designated router is a virtual router that effectively serves as a placeholder in the link state database. All actual routers on the subnetwork are considered neighbors of the designated router.

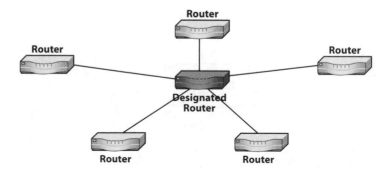

These links to the designated router are known as *network links*, to distinguish them from normal *router links*. (A detailed discussion of OSPF's different link types can be found later in the chapter.) The designated router, acting on behalf of the broadcast network, reports each true router as a neighbor.

With this construction there are only 10 entries in the link state database. Each of the five true routers lists one neighbor, and the designated router lists five. A glance at the bottom trace of figure 4.13 shows how the savings can grow and the network size increases.

In order to force a correct route calculation, all neighbors advertised by the designated router have a distance of zero. The distance between any two routers in the area is the sum of the distance to the designated router (which reflects the true distance) and the distance from the designated router (defined to be zero).

The OSPF protocol takes advantage of broadcast networks when it floods LSA packets. Instead of sending a copy of the LSA to every router on the network individually, the designated router transmits LSAs to a special multicast address. All OSPF routers listen to this address, and they all receive the flooded LSA packet. Because the designated router sends LSAs to all routers on the network, regular routers do not worry about flooding LSAs. Instead, they simply send LSAs to the designated router.

Clearly, the designated router plays a key role in OSPF's operation on a broadcast network. That importance could make networks vulnerable to failures of the designated routers. To reduce this vulnerability, OSPF elects a *backup designated router* the same time it elects a designated router. The backup keeps track of the same information as the designated router, but it normally remains silent, neither flooding LSAs nor inserting itself in the network topology. If the backup detects a failure of the designated router, however, the backup designated router becomes active immediately.

Nonbroadcast Multi-Access Networks

The designers of OSPF originally developed the designated router concept for local area networks, all of which feature a broadcast or multicast capability. The same approach—electing a special router to reduce OSPF overhead—can also work effectively on other networks. How many entries in the link state database, for example, does the network in figure 4.15 produce?

The figure shows an ATM network in which each of the four routers can communicate with all the others. Such a network is known as a *nonbroadcast multi-access* (NBMA) network. Four routers, each with three neighbors, results in 12 entries in the link state database. The same formula applies here as it does with LANs, and OSPF can handle the scaling problem in the same way—with a designated router.

Figure 4.16 presents a logical view of the same network after the election of a designated router. Now each router has only the designated router as a neighbor. The designated router reduces the number of link state entries from 12 to 8, and, as with local area networks, the savings are even more significant as the network grows.

Figure 4.15 ▶

Even when the subnetwork isn't a broadcast LAN, it only takes a few routers to create a lot of neighbors and, consequently, a large link state database. Here, just four routers can create 12 database entries.

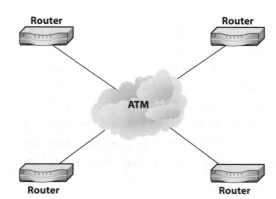

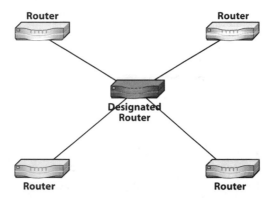

The designated router serves the same purpose with nonbroadcast networks as it does with LANs. This designated router reduces the link state database size by 50%.

There are only two real differences between OSPF's treatment of broadcast networks and NBMA networks. Most obviously, LSA flooding can use broadcast network services only on a broadcast network. On NBMA networks the designated router must transmit copies of LSA packets to each router singly. Nonbroadcast multi-access networks also have a more complicated process for electing a designated router.

Point-to-Multipoint Networks

The designated router concept works only for networks in which every router can communicate directly with every other router. Although that condition may hold on non-broadcast networks such as ATM or frame relay, it isn't a requirement for those networks. In fact, as the size of the network grows, provisioning a separate virtual circuit between every pair of routers can become both inefficient and expensive. An alternative topology connects only some of the routers directly to each other, as in the example of figure 4.17.

This configuration results in a *point-to-multipoint network*. Because OSPF cannot elect a designated router for such networks, it simply treats each individual connection in the network as a separate point-to-point link. In figure 4.17, the total number of link state entries is 10.

Figure 4.17 ▶

In this example, the routers can't all communicate directly with each other. There is data link connection between router A and router D. Because the frame relay network isn't fully connected, OSPF cannot use a designated router here.

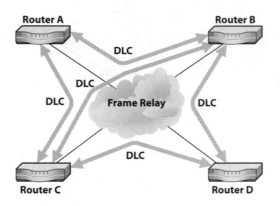

Demand Networks

Demand networks present another challenge to OSPF. These are networks whose expense is a direct function of usage. Narrowband ISDN links, for example, often incur charges based on the length of time they remain active. Such networks earn the name *demand* because, ideally at least, they should be active only when actual application traffic demands their use.

Unfortunately, OSPF normally counts on links remaining active indefinitely. Routers continually exchange hello packets to reassure each other of their health. Link state advertisements are also periodically reflooded through a network. Even without user traffic, these packets will consume bandwidth—and incur cost—on a demand network.

To cope with demand networks, OSPF makes two changes to its normal behavior. First, it eliminates the periodic hello packets used for neighbor greeting. Once a router learns the identity of its peer, it leaves the demand link inactive. Second, OSPF refrains from sending periodic LSA packets across demand networks. Unless the LSA's contents have changed, routers block it from crossing a demand link. To support this type of operation, OSPF has to relax a requirement of the LSA packets themselves. Normal LSA packets include an age limit.

Once the packet has existed long enough to exceed this age limit, any router holding a copy discards it. Periodic reflooding of LSAs refreshes this age limit and keeps routers from prematurely discarding valid LSA data. If a router is going to block an LSA from periodic reflooding across a demand link, it must remove the age limit from that packet.

Multicast Routing

So far, this text has considered routing as a guide to forwarding normal unicast packets. The OSPF protocol also provides experimental support for multicast routing. Link state protocols, in fact, require only slight enhancements to support multicast. To understand the differences between unicast and multicast, consider the sample network of figure 4.18. Imagine that all the links have the same cost. This example focuses on router B, which connects the two Token Ring LANs.

Before examining the multicast case, consider how router B forwards a unicast packet from the personal computer to the server. In order to forward this packet correctly (to router A), router B must know where the server is located. Of course, this is the very information that the Dijkstra computation provides. Figure 4.19 shows the resulting shortest path tree,

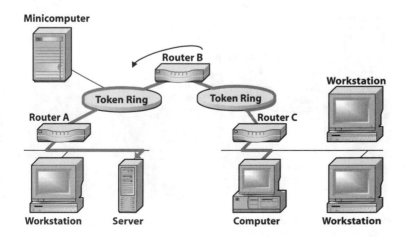

◄ Figure 4.18

A unicast message from the computer to the server passes through router B. Router B can look at the destination and, based on its routing information, forward the message appropriately.

Figure 4.19 ▶

Here is router B's Dijkstra tree. Each node in the tree is a potential destination and router B is the root. To find the path to a destination, router B sees which branch of the tree contains that destination; the next hop on that branch is the next hop for the destination's datagrams.

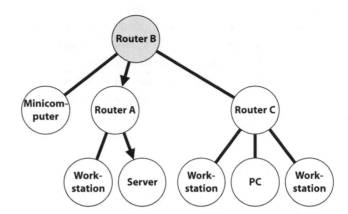

which clearly reveals the correct path to the destination. The packet's next hop is router A.

Note two important (and related) facts about unicast routing. First, the root of the shortest path tree is router B itself, the system performing the calculations. Second, it does not matter where the packet being routed originated. In this example, the source is the personal computer, but that information does not affect the forwarding decision that router B makes.

Now consider that the same PC sends a single multicast packet to all workstations on the network, as figure 4.20 illustrates. The packet travels through the network, eventually

Figure 4.20 ▶

When the computer sends a multicast message to all workstations, a copy of the message travels throughout the network. Once again, router B must forward that message towards its destination.

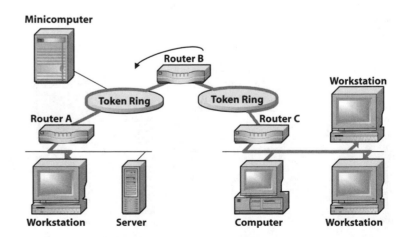

reaching every workstation. Imagine the packet arriving at router B. To decide how to forward the packet, router B must know the location of all workstations. For a multicast packet, however, the router cannot rely on its standard shortest path tree. It must construct a different tree, one like in figure 4.21. When shown as a diagram, the tree's structure clearly reveals how to forward the packet. Once again, the packet goes to router A next.

There is a major difference between the multicast tree and the unicast tree; the two trees have different roots. With the multicast tree, the root is the source of the packet, regardless of which system performs the calculation. Another difference is that there may be many destinations on the multicast tree, one for each system in the multicast group.

To see why the source of the packet makes a difference, consider what happens when the minicomputer sends a multicast packet. Again assume it is destined for all workstations

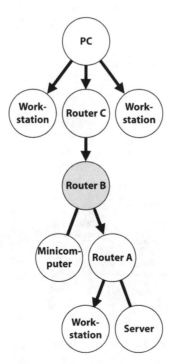

◀ **Figure 4.21**

Router B must use a different Dijkstra tree to forward multicast traffic. Here, the router itself is in the middle of the tree, not its root. The root for multicast trees is the sender of the message. This fact is very important for routing protocols like OSPF. For unicast messages, the router can use a single Dijkstra tree. Multicast routing, however, may require a separate tree for every possible source on the network.

on the network. A quick glance at the network in figure 4.22 shows what router B should do with such a packet. It should forward it to router C. This next hop differs from the last case, even though both have the same group destination.

Fortunately, a correct shortest path tree leads to the right forwarding decision. Figure 4.23 shows the tree for multicast packets from the minicomputer. It is clearly different from figure 4.21, as the minicomputer now serves as the tree's root. The figure also shows that the new tree correctly points to router C as the next hop.

As these examples prove, multicast routing can present a significant problem for OSPF routers. Those routers must calculate a different shortest path tree for each source system. Unfortunately, Dijkstra's calculation can be very computationally intensive, particularly with large networks.

To limit the burden on routers, OSPF strongly recommends that routers calculate multicast trees only when a multicast packet arrives for forwarding. They should then cache the results of those calculations. If the source sends additional packets to the multicast group, the routers can look at the cache instead of calculating the tree all over again.

Figure 4.22 ▼

To appreciate how routers must treat multicast traffic differently, consider this example. As in figure 4.20, the destination is all workstations. The sender in this example, however, is the minicomputer instead of the personal computer. This change completely reverses the forwarding decision of router B. Rather than send the message to router A, it must send it instead to router C. Unlike the case for unicast traffic, multicast routing depends on the source as well as the destination.

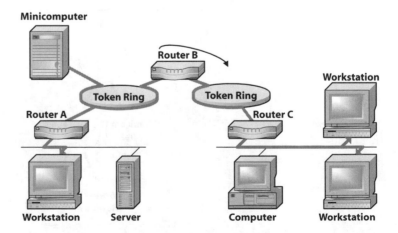

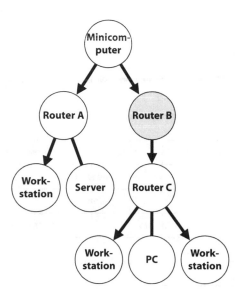

◀Figure 4.23

This multicast Dijkstra tree explains router B's decision. Given a tree rooted at the minicomputer, router C is the appropriate next hop. As in figure 4.21, the destination systems are the tree's leaves, and router B lies in the middle. The change of root, however, completely changes the tree's shape.

OSPF Message Format

Like ICMP, UDP, and TCP, Open Shortest Path First protocol packets are themselves carried as the payload of IP datagrams. A specific next header value of 89 identifies the payload as OSPF. All OSPF packets begin with a common OSPF header. As figure 4.24 shows, the header includes eight fields. The first byte indicates the OSPF version number; the current version number is 2. The second byte of the header identifies the specific packet type. The OSPF protocol uses five different types of packets, listed in table 4.7. After the common OSPF header, each packet type has its own unique format.

Table 4.7 OSPF Packet Types

Value	Packet Type
1	Hello Packet
2	Database Description Packet
3	Link State Request Packet
4	Link State Update Packet
5	Link State Acknowledgment Packet

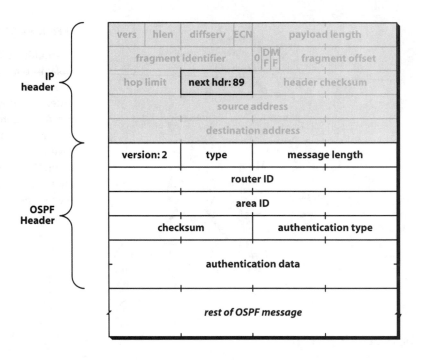

IP header

OSPF Header

Figure 4.24 ▲

OSPF messages are carried in IP datagrams. They begin with their own OSPF header.

The packet length field, naturally, indicates the size of the packet in bytes, and it includes the common header in its count. The next field uniquely and unambiguously identifies the router that originated the packet. Its value is one of the router's IP addresses.

The area identification indicates the area to which the packet applies. The OSPF protocol restricts most packets to a single area. A value of zero for this field signifies the backbone area. Packets traveling across the backbone directly and packets traversing a virtual link use this value.

The checksum field generally contains the one's complement sum of the entire packet, excluding the authentication field. When the packet uses cryptographic authentication, however, the checksum field is zero. The next two bytes indicate the type of authentication the packet uses, while the final eight bytes of the common header carry the authentication data itself.

Authenticating OSPF Messages

Table 4.8 lists the different types of authentication the OSPF specification defines. Routers are configured to use one of these authentication schemes on each of their interfaces, though they need not use the same type of authentication on all interfaces.

Table 4.8 OSPF Authentication Types

Value	Authentication Type
0	Null authentication
1	Password authentication
2	Cryptographic authentication

The null authentication scheme is the simplest of all. As the name implies, it's really no authentication at all. With this scheme, the 64-bit authentication data field may contain any value at all. It is never used or examined.

The password authentication scheme is only slightly less simple. With this scheme, the authentication data field carries a password shared by all the communicating routers. Password authentication doesn't really protect against malicious parties attacking an OSPF network. Because the password is transmitted—without encryption—in every OSPF packet on the network, an attacker need only eavesdrop on the network to discover the password and carry out an attack. Password authentication, however, does provide some protection against accidental misconfigurations. A router that is accidentally or inappropriately installed in an area will not be able to communicate unless it is given the network's password.

Cryptographic authentication offers the strongest possible authentication. It relies on a special mathematical function known as a *cryptographic digest*. The OSPF specification details support for a particular cryptographic digest: message digest 5 (MD5). Like other digest functions, the key property of the

Implementing MD5

The MD5 algorithm performs a set of convoluted calculations on its input and derives a 128-bit digest. The algorithm itself is moderately complicated, and it is certainly filled with various random and other magic numbers. Fortunately, RFC 1321 includes a complete implementation of MD5 in the C language.

MD5 algorithm is that it is easy to calculate but effectively impossible to reverse. In other words, it is a simple matter to take information and calculate its MD5 digest output. But starting with an MD5 digest and determining even part of the input used to generate it, however, is impractical.

Figure 4.25 shows how MD5 authenticates OSPF packets. Before sending its message, the router on the left appends a secret value to it and calculates the MD5 digest of the resulting combination. The router then removes the secret value

Figure 4.25 ▶

To calculate the authentication data for an OSPF message, a router starts with the message and a special shared secret known only to legitimate routers in the network. The sending router combines the message and the shared secret and computes a special digest. This digest becomes the authentication data carried in the OSPF message. When the message arrives at its destination, the receiving router performs the same digest calculation using the message (absent its authentication data) and the shared secret. If the digest results match, the message is assumed authentic.

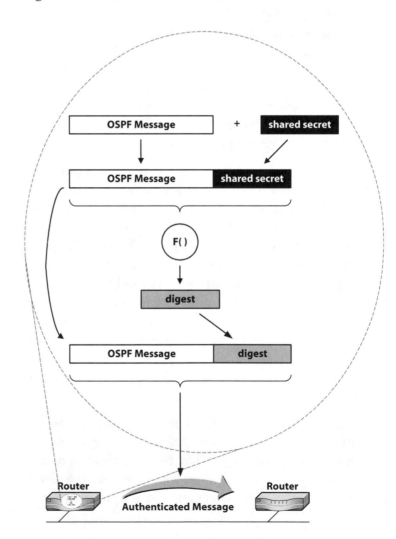

and adds the digest result to the packet. When the router on the right receives the packet, it also calculates a digest using the same secret value. If the digest results agree, the message is authentic. Notice that both systems rely on a shared secret, but (unlike the case for password authentication) the secret is never transmitted on the network. Cryptographic authentication, therefore, is not vulnerable to eavesdroppers.

When a packet uses cryptographic authentication, the authentication data area contains the four fields shown in figure 4.26. The first two bytes are reserved and always zero. The next byte contains a key identifier. This field tells the recipient which secret value was used to generate the digest, as well as the specific digest algorithm. (Although OSPF currently defines support only for the MD5 algorithm, other algorithms may be added in the future.) The fourth byte carries the size of the digest calculation, the results of which are appended to the OSPF message; for MD5 results are 16-byte values. The last four bytes contain a special sequence number that is incremented with every packet. This sequence

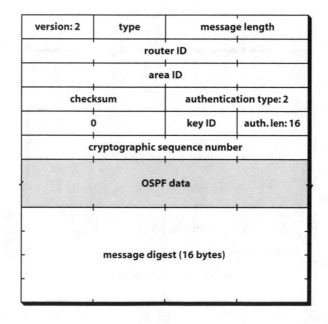

◀ Figure 4.26

OSPF's cryptographic authentication includes information in the OSPF header, but the digest results are appended to the message contents.

number ensures that no two OSPF messages (and, thus, their message digest values) will ever be identical, making it impossible for an eavesdropping attacker to capture a packet and replay it later.

Figure 4.27 ▼

To calculate the cryptographic digest, OSPF routers append the shared secret, extra bytes of padding, and a count of the number of bits of authenticated data. This information is replaced by the digest results when the message is transmitted on the network.

Figure 4.27 shows how routers calculate and verify the cryptographic digest. They append the shared secret, extra bytes known as *padding* that force the MD5 input to be an even multiple of 512 bits in length, and a 64-bit count of the input size. When the packet is actually transmitted on the link, the sender replaces this information with the digest result. Note that the digest result bytes are *not* included in the OSPF message length of the OSPF header. They are, however, counted in the IP datagram's payload length field.

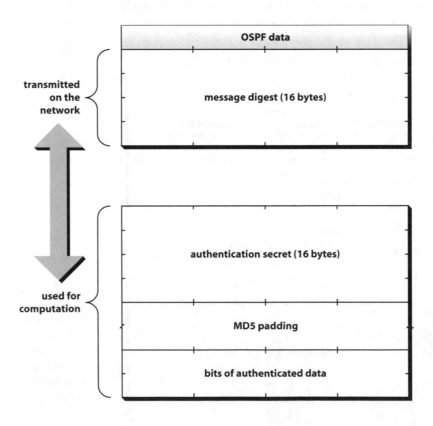

Meeting Neighbors

The OSPF protocol uses hello packets to meet neighbors, the first step in link state routing. Routers exchange hello packets across point-to-point and demand networks, and they send to multicast destinations on broadcast LANs. As you can see from figure 4.28, routers generate hello packets on all of their links and networks.

The hello packet itself, as figure 4.29 shows, contains more than the sender's identity. The first field after the common header, the network mask, indicates the sender's idea of the mask for the link or network. The hello interval tells how frequently the sender retransmits its hello packets; it is measured in seconds.

The options byte advertises the sender's OSPF capabilities. Individual bits indicate whether the router supports external LSAs, routing for multicast destinations, not so stubby areas (NSSAs), external attributes, and demand circuits. Receivers can use this information to adjust their interaction with the sender. They can, for example, avoid flooding certain types of LSAs to routers that don't support them, calculate paths "around" a router that doesn't have the necessary capabilities, or even refuse to peer with a neighbor that doesn't meet minimum standards.

The next byte defines the sender's willingness to become a designated router. Of all the routers on a network, the one with the highest priority gets the job; the second highest priority becomes the backup designated router. (In the case of ties, the prize goes to the router with the greatest numerical router ID.)

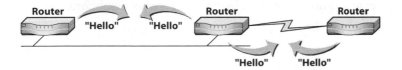

◀ **Figure 4.28**

OSPF routers periodically send hello messages on all their links.

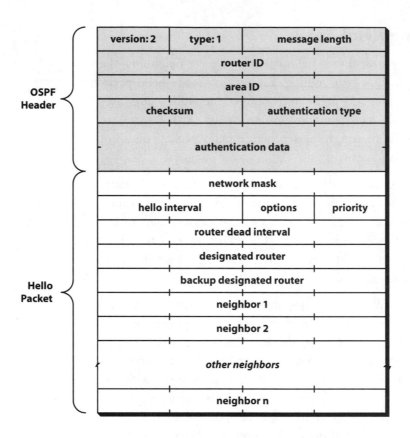

version: 2	type: 1	message length
router ID		
area ID		
checksum		authentication type
authentication data		
network mask		
hello interval	options	priority
router dead interval		
designated router		
backup designated router		
neighbor 1		
neighbor 2		
other neighbors		
neighbor n		

OSPF Header / **Hello Packet**

Figure 4.29 ▲

An OSPF hello message includes information about the link as well as a list of neighbors from whom the sending router has heard.

The router dead interval tells how long it takes to declare a router unavailable. If the router has not been heard from in this number of seconds, it is considered dead, and all routes are calculated around it.

The next two fields indicate the current designated router for the network and its backup. The final field, which is repeated as many times as necessary, lists neighbors that the sender has already met. This list establishes two-way communications between routers. Routers do not become neighbors just because they hear the other's hello message. They must receive a hello packet that lists themselves as neighbors.

Without this requirement, OSPF could end up calculating useless routes. For example, the left router in figure 4.30 can

By listing neighbors from whom they've heard, OSPF routers can detect failures that prevent only transmission or reception on a link, but not both.

transmit fine, but, due to a failure of its interface hardware, it cannot receive frames from the Ethernet. It will not, therefore, hear the right router's hello packets, and it will never list the right router as a neighbor. If the right router ignores this omission and considers the left router a neighbor, it, along with all other routers in the area, may calculate routers from right to left even when no such path actually exists.

Advertising Link States

Once a router meets its neighbors by exchanging hello packets, it distributes that information to the rest of the network. To do this, it floods link state advertisements throughout the network. The link state advertisement takes the form of a link state update packet, shown in figure 4.31. Note that its packet type is 4.

After the common OSPF header, the packet contains one 32-bit word with the number of individual advertisements in the packet. It is immediately followed by the advertisements themselves. Each advertisement has two parts. First is a generic link state header. All advertisements have a common header, which is sufficient to uniquely identify the particular advertisement.

Figure 4.32 details the link state header. The first 16 bits store the advertisement's age. This value starts at zero when the LSA is first issued, and it increments by one each second from that time forward. The age increases while the update packet traverses the network. Every router that retains a copy in its link state database also increments the age of that copy. When an advertisements' age reaches 3600 (one hour), it is always considered out of date.

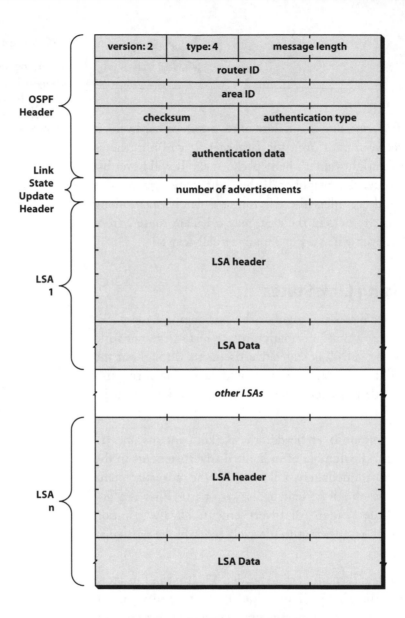

Figure 4.31 ▲

A link state update messages consists primarily of link state advertisements.

When an advertisement in any router's link state database expires, the router immediately refloods the expired advertisement through the network. Of course, the LSA should simultaneously expire in every router automatically, but in real life some routers have clocks that run faster or slower

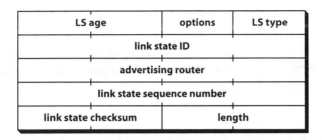

◀ **Figure 4.32**

A link state advertisement begins with an LSA header. The header provides enough information to unambiguously identify the full advertisement.

than others. Immediate reflooding makes sure that as soon as one router thinks an LSA has expired, all other routers will agree. This process keeps the link state database in all routers consistent, and it ensures that they all calculate consistent routes.

The options byte identifies the capabilities of the router that generated the LSA. It has the same format as the options field of the hello packet. The LS type byte distinguishes the various types of link state advertisements. The LSA header (figure 4.32) is the same for each type, but the data varies considerably. Table 4.9 lists the different types OSPF recognizes. The following subsections examine each type in detail.

Table 4.9 Link State Advertisement Types

Value	LSA Type
1	Router link
2	Network link
3	Summary link to network
4	Summary link to AS boundary router
5	External link
6	Group membership advertisement
7	NSSA link
9	Opaque link confined to a local network
10	Opaque link confined to an area
11	Opaque link for an entire autonomous system

Fletcher's Checksum

Fletcher's checksum was originally used by many protocols of the International Standards Organization. It is generally viewed as a compromise between a simple one's complement checksum (easy to compute but not very robust) and the cyclic redundancy checks of many link levels (very robust, but expensive to compute in software). Because the Fletcher checksum itself has become popular, several research papers have presented ways to implement it very efficiently. Anastase Nakassis provides perhaps the most comprehensive treatment in "Fletcher's Error Detection Algorithm: How to Implement It Efficiently and How to Avoid the Most Common Pitfalls" (*Computer Communications Review* 18.5 [October 1988], pp. 63–88.) His paper includes references to other major works on the subject.

The link state ID uniquely identifies each link, according to the advertising router. Usually, routers select the IP address (which they know is unique) of the link as its identification. The advertising router is, of course, the router ID of the system that originates the advertisement.

Because advertisements automatically expire after one hour, routers must reissue them more frequently than once an hour (assuming their data remains valid). The standard interval for reissuing LSAs is 30 minutes. To distinguish a reissued advertisement, routers use the link state sequence number. This field acts like a version number for the LSA. Each time the advertising router reissues an advertisement, it increments the sequence number.

The link state header concludes with a checksum and length field. The checksum is not TCP/IP's normal one's complement sum; it is a special error-detection code known as Fletcher's checksum. It covers the entire advertisement except the link state age field. The final length field indicates the size, in bytes, of the entire advertisement, including the 20-byte header.

Router Links

The simplest link type is a router link. It represents a normal link between two routers. Figure 4.33 shows the structure of a router link state advertisements, including both the link state header and its data.

The *route type* defines the type of router. The router may be an endpoint of a virtual link, an external (AS boundary router), or an area border router. Multicast-capable routers can also indicate if they wish to be "wildcard" routers and accept all multicast packets. After a reserved word that must be zero, the router link LSA contains a word that indicates the total number of individual links it contains. Note that a single link state update packet may include many LSAs, and each router LSA may include many individual links.

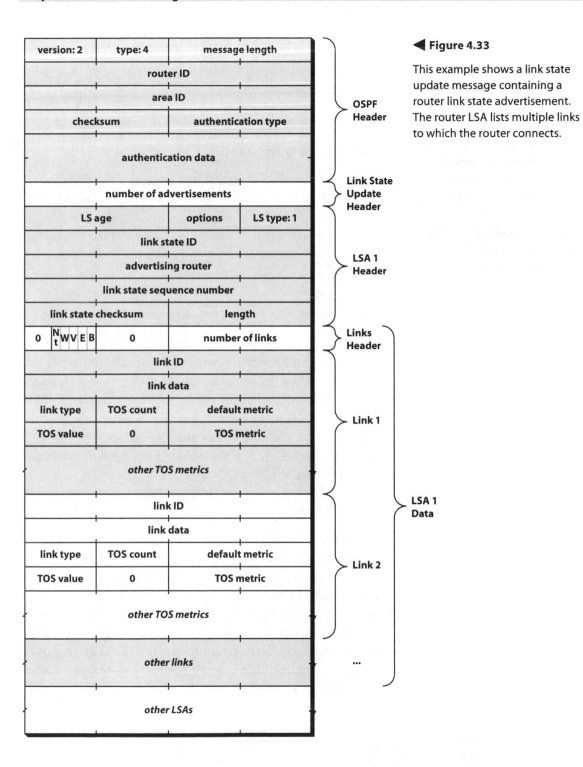

version: 2	type: 4	message length	
router ID			
area ID			
checksum		authentication type	
authentication data			
number of advertisements			
LS age		options	LS type: 1
link state ID			
advertising router			
link state sequence number			
link state checksum		length	
0	Nt WV E B	0	number of links
link ID			
link data			
link type	TOS count	default metric	
TOS value	0	TOS metric	
other TOS metrics			
link ID			
link data			
link type	TOS count	default metric	
TOS value	0	TOS metric	
other TOS metrics			
other links			
other LSAs			

OSPF Header

Link State Update Header

LSA 1 Header

Links Header

Link 1

Link 2

LSA 1 Data

◀ **Figure 4.33**

This example shows a link state update message containing a router link state advertisement. The router LSA lists multiple links to which the router connects.

TOS Forwarding

If a network uses different types of service, then the routers calculate separate Dijkstra trees for each TOS, and they forward packets according to their marked service type. Unfortunately, computing and maintaining multiple trees is a significant computational burden. That, combined with the fact that IP datagrams rarely use the TOS markings, means that TOS forwarding is rarely used today.

The *link ID* field identifies what lies at the other end of the link from the router, while the *link data* field further defines that object. Both fields depend on the value of the *link type* field that follows. Table 4.10 lists the different link types, as well as the values for link ID and link data that they imply.

Table 4.10 Link Types for Router Link Advertisements

Value	Type	Link ID	Link Data
1	Point-to-point link	Neighbor's router ID	Interface number
2	Connection to transit network	Designated router's IP address	Router's IP address on the network
3	Connection to stub network	IP address for network	Network's IP address mask
4	Virtual link	Neighbor's router ID	Router's IP address on network

Each link entry concludes with a list of metrics, which are the costs to use the link, based on different measurement systems. The measurement systems are known as *type of service* (TOS), and every router is required to support at least the default (0) TOS. If the router supports other TOS values, it lists them here. Other values include such measurements and delay and reliability.

Network Links

The second type of link state advertisement is the network LSA. Networks that have a designated router use the network LSA. As figure 4.34 shows, true routers use router LSAs to advertise links to the designated router, while the designated router uses network LSAs for its links to true routers. Figure 4.35 illustrates the network link state advertisement itself, header and data. As the figure shows, the LSA is quite simple. It includes the IP address mask for the network and then a list of routers attached to the network.

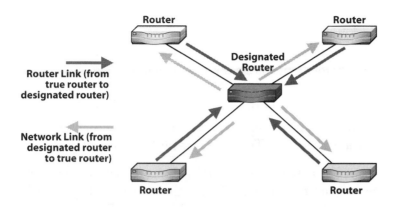

◄ Figure 4.34

When a network uses a designated router, router LSAs describe links *to* the designated router. A special network LSA describes links *from* the designated router.

Router Link (from true router to designated router)

Network Link (from designated router to true router)

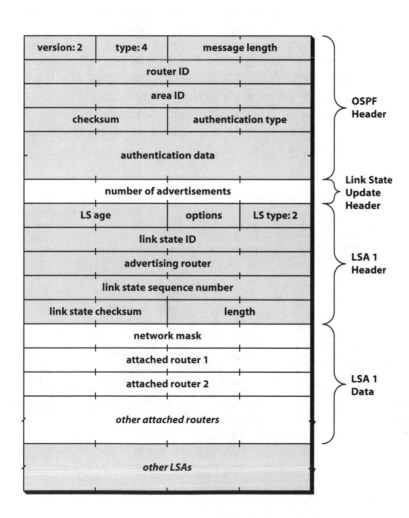

◄ Figure 4.35

This example shows a link state update that contains a network LSA. The LSA itself simply lists the neighboring routers.

Summary Links

The next two types of advertisements are summary LSAs. Area border routers distribute these within their areas to advertise destinations outside of the area. The different LSA types indicate what those destinations represent. Type 3 LSAs identify other networks within the autonomous system, yet outside of the area. Type 4 LSAs identify AS boundary routers.

Figure 4.36 shows an example network that requires both type 3 and type 4 LSAs. Router 0A is attached to the backbone and to a frame relay network in area 1. That makes it an area border router. (In fact, because one of its areas is the backbone, this router is also a backbone router.)

An as area border router, router 0A generates type 3 summary LSAs and floods them through each of its areas. The frame relay network lies in area 1, so the router floods LSAs describing that network into the backbone. In the same way, it generates LSAs describing the FDDI rings of the backbone and

Figure 4.36 ▼

This example network requires several summary LSAs. It has several routers that straddle multiple areas, and it has routers that connect outside of its autonomous system.

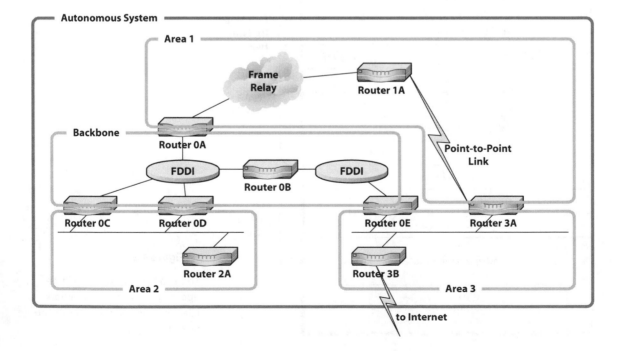

floods those LSAs throughout area 1. Type 3 LSAs teach the backbone routers about the frame relay network and the area 1 routers about the FDDI rings.

Now consider router OC. It receives the summary LSAs from router OA, and it adds the frame relay network to the networks it knows about. As an area border router, it also builds summary LSAs. It summarizes the backbone in the LSAs that it floods through area 2, and that summary includes the frame relay network as well as the FDDI rings. In fact, these LSAs also contain the Ethernet LAN in area 3, as the router learns of that network from router OE's advertisement.

Router 2A, strictly in area 2, receives summary LSAs from both router OC and OD. Through those advertisements it learns of the world outside its area. It is able to calculate routers to the FDDI rings, the frame relay network, and the LAN in area 3.

Figure 4.37 shows the format of a type 3 LSA. The network mask carries the IP address mask of the destination network. If the advertising router supports TOS routing, then it includes a metric for each TOS. All type 3 LSAs must include a metric for the default type of service. Recipients can determine the number of TOS values present from the LSA length in the link state header. This structure implies that a type 3 LSA can describe only a single network. To describe multiple networks, a link state update packet must include multiple type 3 LSAs.

Type 3 advertisements describe what is outside of an area, but they describe networks only within a single autonomous system. To route beyond the autonomous system, routers rely on type 4 advertisements.

Figure 4.36's networks have a single connection outside of the autonomous system. That connection is through router 3B, so router 3B is an AS boundary router. Router 3B tells other routers that it has a path to other ASs by issuing type 4 LSAs.

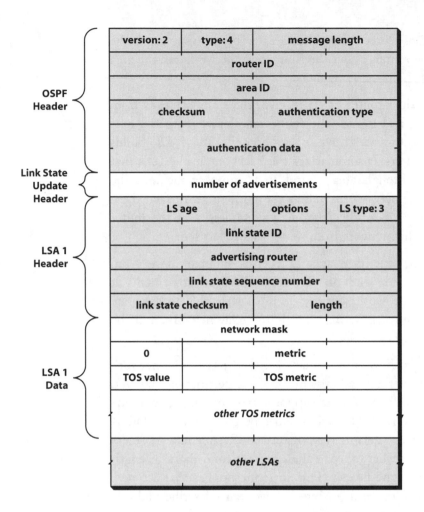

version: 2	type: 4	message length
router ID		
area ID		
checksum		authentication type
authentication data		
number of advertisements		
LS age		options	LS type: 3
link state ID		
advertising router		
link state sequence number		
link state checksum		length
network mask		
0		metric
TOS value		TOS metric
other TOS metrics		
other LSAs		

OSPF Header

Link State Update Header

LSA 1 Header

LSA 1 Data

Figure 4.37 ▲

This example shows a link state update message with a type 3 summary LSA.

As figure 4.38 shows, type 4 LSAs are identical to type 3 LSAs (except for the value of the LS type). The network mask, however, has no meaning for type 4 advertisements and must be zero. Indeed, the main purpose of a type 4 LSA is simply to announce the presence of an AS boundary router.

External Links

When the rest of the autonomous system receives type 4 LSAs, they learn how to reach the AS boundary router. That information alone does not tell them what destinations are

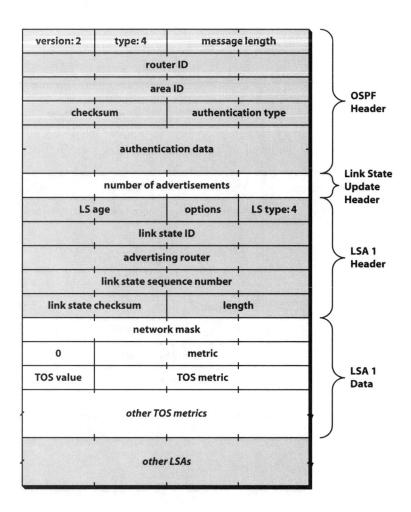

version: 2	type: 4	message length
router ID		
area ID		
checksum		authentication type
authentication data		
number of advertisements		
LS age	options	LS type: 4
link state ID		
advertising router		
link state sequence number		
link state checksum		length
network mask		
0	metric	
TOS value	TOS metric	
other TOS metrics		
other LSAs		

- OSPF Header
- Link State Update Header
- LSA 1 Header
- LSA 1 Data

▲ Figure 4.38

This example shows a link state update message with a type 4 summary LSA.

available beyond the AS. This is the job of an external (type 5) advertisement.

Figure 4.39 shows the structure of an external LSA. The advertisement includes a network mask and five other fields. The advertisement repeats these five fields for each type of service available. The default type of service is always available, so one set of fields is always present.

The first bit following the mask indicates whether the metric is external. If this E bit is set, the metric is external, and it is not directly comparable to any metrics for the same type of

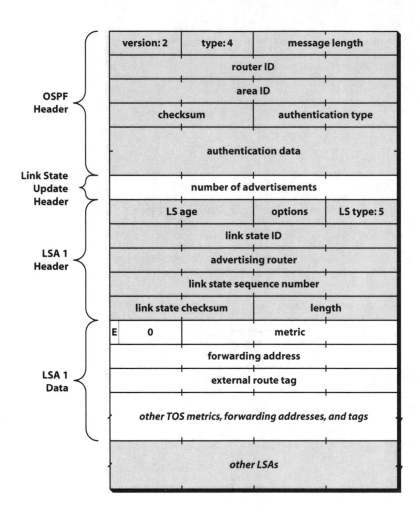

Figure 4.39 ▲

This example shows a link state update message with an external LSA.

service within the autonomous system. The next seven bits define the TOS value; they are followed by the metric value itself.

The *forwarding address* identifies the system to which packets should be forwarded. Often this is the same as the advertising router. A value of 0 indicates this equivalence explicitly.

The final field for each TOS, the *external route tag*, is not relevant to OSPF itself. Rather, OSPF routers merely distribute the value in their link state updates. Other routing protocols can put whatever information they wish in this field, and they are free to use it in any manner whatsoever.

Figure 4.40 shows how the different advertisements combine to define a path to a remote destination. In the figure, router 2A calculates a path to a destination on the Internet. That calculation requires three distinct stages. First, router 2A consults the link state database for the desired destination. The search reveals that router 3B, through its type 5 (external) advertisements, can reach the desired network. Second, router 2A must calculate the path to this AS boundary router. It finds type 4 summary advertisements from router 0D that indicate such a path. Note that those summary advertisements do not specify the detailed path between router 0D and router 3B, so they do not identify the FDDI rings, or routers 0B and 0E, or even area 3's Ethernet. Router 2A does find what it needs, though; router 0D has a path to router 3B.

The third stage is confined to area 2. Router 2A must find a path to router 0D. Because the routers share one broadcast

▼ **Figure 4.40**

The different types of LSAs combine to identify a complete forwarding path. Router 2A uses four different types of LSAs (all of which it receives from OSPF's flooding) to calculate a path to the Internet.

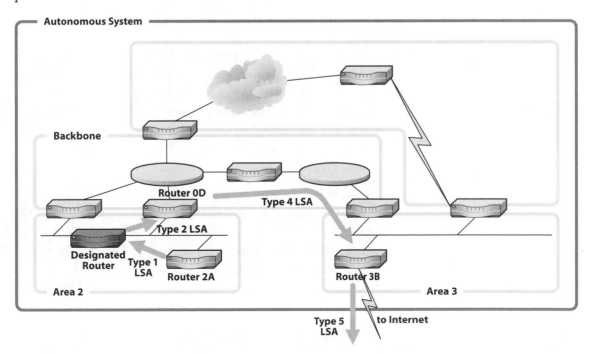

network, this path requires two steps. First a router (type 1) LSA identifies the path to the network's designated router. Then a network (type 2) LSA completes the path from the designated router to the area border router OD.

In summary, the path from router 2A to the external destination takes four steps. First, there is the router link from 2A to the designated router. Second, the network link connects the designated router to OD. Third, a summary link provides a path from OD to 3B. The last link, an external link, connects 3B to the destination.

Group Membership Advertisements

Group addresses require their own advertisement type, and designated routers originate it. Designated routers keep track of group membership in their networks. For each group that has any members, they build a type 6 advertisement. Such an LSA, shown in figure 4.41, uses the link ID field of the link state header to indicate the specific group address. It then lists one or more *vertices*; these are paths to members of the group.

Vertices may be one of two types. In the simplest case (vertex type 1), either the router itself is a group member, or there are no other routers on the network. In this case the router has complete information about group membership on the network and beyond. (Because there are no other routers on the network, there is no "beyond.") The router inserts its own router ID as the vertex ID.

If other routers exist on the network along with group members, then more group members may be residing "on the other side of" these routers. In this case, the designated router marks the vertex as type 2, and it lists its own IP address on that network as the vertex ID.

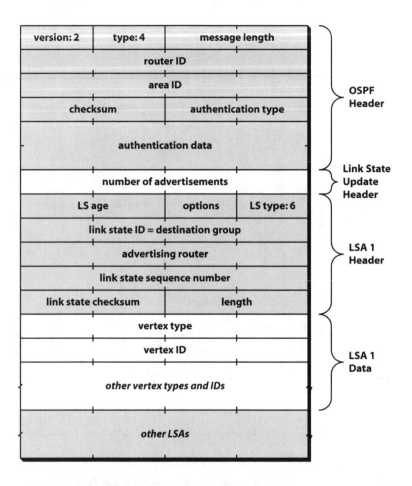

version: 2	type: 4	message length	OSPF Header
router ID			
area ID			
checksum		authentication type	
authentication data			
number of advertisements			Link State Update Header
LS age	options	LS type: 6	LSA 1 Header
link state ID = destination group			
advertising router			
link state sequence number			
link state checksum		length	
vertex type			LSA 1 Data
vertex ID			
other vertex types and IDs			
other LSAs			

NSSA Advertisements

As page 116 describes, areas designated as not so stubby areas differ from true stub areas in only one way—they permit the flooding of a special link state advertisement that carries the same information as an external advertisement.

The type 7 LSA, shown in figure 4.42, is that special advertisement. Because it carries the same information as an external LSA, it has the same format. Only the LS type field has a different value.

▲ **Figure 4.41**

This example shows a link state update message with group membership LSAs.

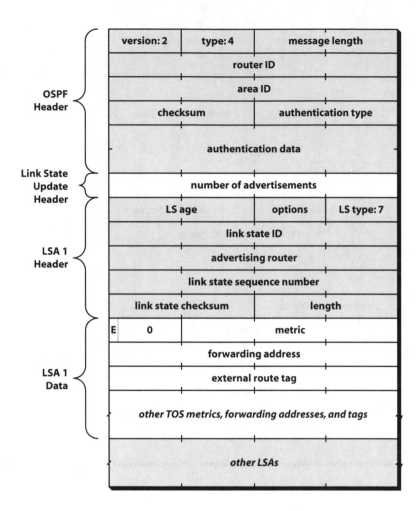

Figure 4.42 ▲

This example shows a link state update message advertising a not so stubby area.

Opaque Advertisements

The final three types of link state advertisements are opaque LSAs; they are type 9, 10, and 11 advertisements. The only difference between the three is the extent to which OSPF floods them. Type 9 advertisements are confined to a local network; type 10 advertisements remain in a single area, and type 11 advertisements flood through an entire autonomous system.

The OSPF protocol itself attaches no meaning to the data of an opaque LSA, and, as figure 4.43 indicates, it considers the

LSA data nothing more than a collection of bytes. Opaque LSAs provide a way to give OSPF new capabilities in the future. Even though today's routers won't be able to interpret them, they will still ensure that the data is flooded appropriately to routers that can understand them.

Reliable Flooding

Together, the different types of link state advertisements define the complete topology of a network. In order to distribute that information to all of the network's routers, OSPF floods link state update packets throughout the network. The OSPF protocol takes the flooding procedure one step further,

▼ **Figure 4.43**

This example shows a link state update message with an opaque LSA. The data carried in the advertisement is not specified.

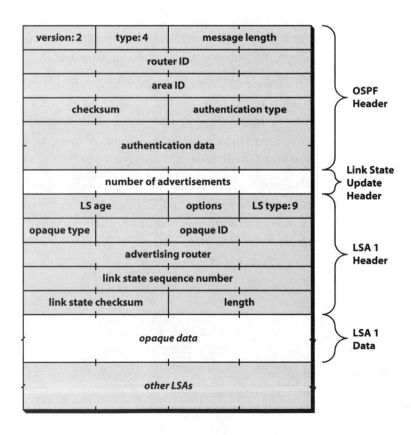

though. It requires routers to explicitly acknowledge when they receive an advertisement. Figure 4.44 shows the simple exchange on a point-to-point link.

The link state acknowledgment packet itself is shown in figure 4.45. As the figure shows, it contains a list of link state headers. Because the header is sufficient to identify an advertisement, there is no need to include the complete LSA. A single acknowledgment packet can acknowledge many link state updates.

Updating Neighbors

So far, this chapter has presented OSPF as if networks operated in a completely orderly manner. First routers learn their neighbors; they share that information, and then they compute routes. This approach almost gives the impression that there is a master switch for the network. Everything remains idle until someone turns on that master switch.

Of course, real networks never function this neatly. In particular, routers are usually introduced to networks that are already functioning. A new router cannot simply tell the rest of the network to start over. Instead, it must rapidly catch up and learn the network's topology.

To catch up with the rest of the network, a newly introduced router relies on its neighbors. As soon as two routers greet each other (with hello packets), they exchange information about their link state databases. They do so with database description packets.

Figure 4.44

Routers acknowledge link state updates by returning a link state acknowledgement.

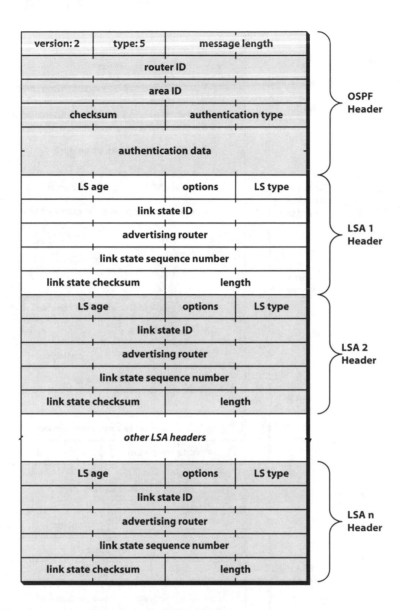

version: 2	type: 5	message length	
router ID			
area ID			
checksum		authentication type	
authentication data			
LS age		options	LS type
link state ID			
advertising router			
link state sequence number			
link state checksum		length	
LS age		options	LS type
link state ID			
advertising router			
link state sequence number			
link state checksum		length	
other LSA headers			
LS age		options	LS type
link state ID			
advertising router			
link state sequence number			
link state checksum		length	

OSPF Header

LSA 1 Header

LSA 2 Header

LSA n Header

Figure 4.46 shows a database description packet. The first two bytes after the common OSPF header carry the maximum transmission unit (MTU) size for the interface. This value is the largest IP datagram that the link or network can transmit in one piece.

▲ **Figure 4.45**

A link state acknowledgment message contains a list of LSA headers. These headers identify the specific LSAs acknowledged.

Figure 4.46 ▶

A database description message lists all the LSAs that the sender knows, even LSAs that originated with other routers. The message only contains the LSA headers, not the full LSAs. A receiving router can check the list for LSAs that it's missing and request their full contents explicitly.

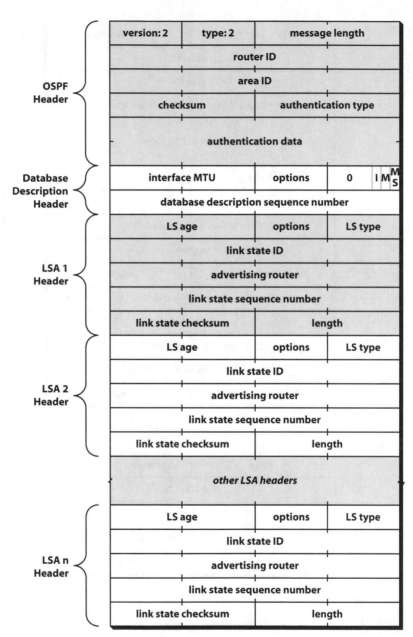

The next byte contains the standard OSPF options, and the fourth byte carries three additional flags. (The rest of the byte is zero.) The first two of these flags, labeled I and M, allow neighbors to exchange multiple database description packets. The first packet in the exchange will have the I (for *initial*) bit set, and all but the final packet will set the M (for *more*) bit. For each exchange, one of the two routers plays the role of master, while the other acts as a slave. The MS bit identifies which is which.

The next 32 bits carry a database description sequence number. This number has an arbitrary value for the initial packet in the exchange, but it increments by one with each successive description packet. The packet concludes with a list of link state headers. These headers describe the contents of the sender's link state database. Note that only headers are included; the link state data itself is not part of the description packet.

Once a router receives a complete set of database description packets from its neighbor, it examines its own link state database. (If the router has just powered up, its database will probably be empty.) Most likely, the router will find that its neighbor has at least some information that it lacks. The neighbor may have entirely new LSAs, or it may have more up-to-date versions of existing LSAs. In either case the router requests the updated information from its neighbor. It does so with a link state request packet, illustrated in figure 4.47.

The link state request contains a list of LSAs that the sender wishes to receive. These LSAs are identified solely by their type, link state ID, and advertising router. When the neighbor receives a request, it finds the advertisements in its link state database and forwards them in link state update packets.

After exchanging database description packets, link state requests, and finally link state updates, two routers will have successfully synchronized their link state databases. At that

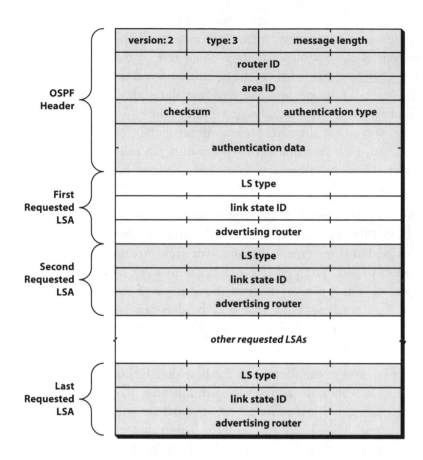

Figure 4.47 ▲

The link state request message asks for a full copy of the indicated LSAs.

point, both routers are up to date, and they can both participate in the network's routing.

Summary

Routers rely on routing protocols like OSPF to learn the map of a network, and from this map they see how to reach the network's destinations. The OSPF protocol is one of the family of link state routing protocols. Link state protocols proceed in three steps. First, each router learns the identities of its neighbors. Then it floods that information throughout the network. Finally, after collecting neighbor information from every other router, each router applies Dijkstra's algorithm to compute routes.

The OSPF protocol organizes networks into hierarchies. The highest level is an autonomous system. The AS boundary defines the limits of OSPF's influence. Within an AS, OSPF may further divide the network into areas. Each router knows the full details of the network within its areas, but it summarizes information only outside of the area.

The OSPF protocol has the flexibility to operate over a wide variety of links. In addition to point-to-point links, it supports broadcast networks like Ethernet, nonbroadcast multi-access networks like fully meshed frame relay and ATM, point-to-multipoint networks including frame relay and ATM configurations without a full mesh, and demand networks such as narrowband ISDN. In many cases, OSPF routers elect a designated router to reduce traffic demands on those networks.

The OSPF protocol also has experimental support for multi-cast routing. For link state protocols, multicast routing is a simple extension of normal routing. It can be computationally expensive, though. As the use of multicast increases, network engineers should gain greater understanding of OSPF's limitations.

CHAPTER 5

Distance Vector Routing and RIP

The OSPF protocol, the subject of chapter 4, provides fast and efficient routing. Its power carries a price, however, and that price is complexity. For smaller networks that do not require all of OSPF's power, there is an alternative routing protocol, the Routing Information Protocol (RIP).

Distance Vector Routing

The Routing Information Protocol relies on a *distance vector* algorithm to compute routes, and for that reason, it is a *distance vector routing protocol*. Distance vector routing differs significantly from the link state routing of OSPF. With link state algorithms, routers share only the identity of their neighbors, but they flood this information through the entire network. Distance vector algorithms adopt an opposite approach. Routers periodically share their knowledge of the entire network, but only with their neighbors.

At first, it might be hard to believe that such an approach actually works. After all, if routers share information only with their immediate neighbors, how can they learn about

The History of RIP

RIP actually began outside of the TCP/IP protocol suite. It was the original routing protocol of the Xerox Network Services (XNS) protocol suite. The University of California at Berkeley adapted RIP for TCP/IP, and Novell, Inc. adapted it for NetWare. Both Novell and TCP/IP's designers recognized the limitations of RIP, and both developed more powerful, link state replacements. For TCP/IP, that replacement is OSPF, while later versions of NetWare incorporated the Novell Link Services Protocol.

distant destinations? Here is the trick: When a router learns something from one neighbor, it adds that to its store of knowledge, and then it passes that knowledge on to other neighbors. Slowly but surely, the information makes it way across the network from one router to another.

To see distance vector routing in action, figure 5.1 turns once more to a (slightly distorted) part of the U.S. interstate highway system. Notice that this figure, unlike the link state example (figure 4.1) does not list distances between each city. Despite its name, actual distances are generally irrelevant in distance vector routing.

Before any routing information is exchanged, each city will know some information about each of its neighbors. Because neighbors must, by definition, share a link, they share an IP address prefix. When Seattle, for example, is configured with the IP address prefix of interstate I-84, it will implicitly know one of the IP address prefixes of Salt Lake City. While link state routing uses neighbor greeting to learn the precise identity of each adjacent router, distance vector protocols are content knowing only the address prefix of their connected networks and links.

With this information as a starting point, Seattle broadcasts its routing knowledge to all links. That knowledge consists of the IP address prefix (in this example, the highway number) and the cost to reach that destination. Most distance vector protocols, including RIP, measure cost by counting hops. To Seattle, any city on I-84 or I-5 is a single hop away, so the cost it advertises is "one." All cities broadcast this information simultaneously.

 Figure 5.1 ▶

A highway system can illustrate the principles behind distance vector routing.

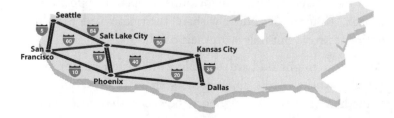

As figure 5.2 shows, each city includes every destination it knows in its broadcasts. (For clarity, the figure shows the actions of only three cities.) As the figure implies, a city broadcasts the same information on all of its links.

Now consider what happens when Seattle receives the broadcasts from its neighbors. Assume that it hears from San Francisco first. As Seattle examines each route in the broadcast it says, in effect, "I can reach San Francisco in 1 hop, so anywhere San Francisco can reach in n hops, I can reach in $n+1$ hops by forwarding through San Francisco."

For example, from this first update Seattle learns that San Francisco can reach I-80 in one hop. Seattle, therefore, considers I-80 to be two hops away and reachable via San Francisco. It performs the same calculations for the other routes in San Francisco's broadcast: I-10 and I-5. Of course, the result of the I-5 calculation is not important. Seattle already knows how to reach I-5 in one hop. The fact that it is two hops away via San Francisco is of no value.

Seattle treats the broadcast from Salt Lake City the same way. Through that update, it can add routes to I-90 and I-15. Each is two hops away via Salt Lake City.

Sometime later, it will again be time for Seattle to broadcast its routing knowledge on all links. (Distance vector routing calls for periodic broadcasts.) At this stage, Seattle has more information, and its update includes the newly learned

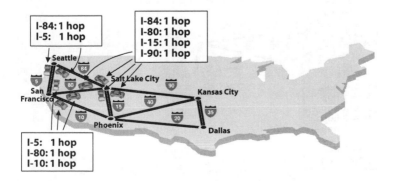

◀ **Figure 5.2**

This example shows how three cities begin distance vector routing by listing the links to which they connect. For clarity, the figure doesn't show the actions of Phoenix, Kansas City, or Dallas.

routes. Figure 5.3 shows the second round of routing updates for the same three cities. Note once more that each city sends exactly the same information in all of its updates.

After this second round, Seattle will once again be able to add information to its routing table. This time, the new routes are to I-35, I-20, and I-40. Seattle learns of I-35, for example, in the update it receives from Salt Lake City. (Salt Lake City learned how to reach I-35 from Kansas City in the first round.) Because Salt Lake City advertises a cost of two hops to reach I-35, Seattle adds one and calculates I-35 to be three hops away.

For the simple network of this example, three rounds are enough to disseminate complete routing information to all of the routers. After the third round, every router will have constructed a routing table that lists each destination on the network. For example, Seattle's complete routing table will look like table 5.1.

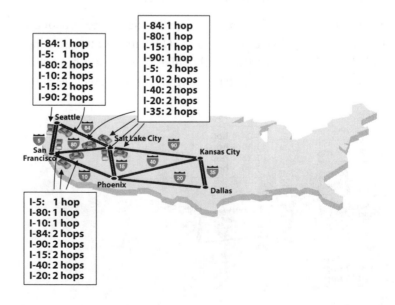

Figure 5.3 ▶

When each city learns of its neighbors' links, it adds those links to its update message. Since the new links are one city away from the sender, they are listed as two hops away.

Table 5.1 Complete Routing Table for Seattle

Destination	Cost	Next Hop
I-5	1 hop	N/A
I-84	1 hop	N/A
I-10	2 hops	San Francisco
I-15	2 hops	Salt Lake City
I-80	2 hops	San Francisco
I-90	2 hops	Salt Lake City
I-20	3 hops	San Francisco
I-35	3 hops	Salt Lake City
I-40	3 hops	San Francisco

Note that the table contains one additional piece of information for each destination—the next hop in the path to that destination. Routers determine this information by remembering where they learned of the route. For example, Seattle learns that I-15 is two hops away when it receives an update from Salt Lake City. Salt Lake City, therefore, is the next hop for that destination.

So far, this example has considered a stable, static network. Once cities learn how to route to each other, they can, based on this example, stop exchanging RIP updates. After all, they have learned the complete topology of the network. Of course, this approach will not do for real networks. The real world is rarely stable and never static. So how does RIP deal with changes in the network's topology? What happens if, for example, Salt Lake City experiences a power failure and routes through it are no longer available, as in figure 5.4?

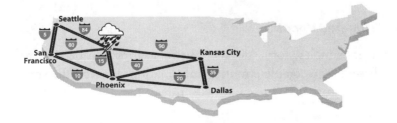

◀ Figure 5.4

If one of the cities is no longer available for routing traffic, a distance vector protocol must detect the failure and calculate new paths.

Unlike OSPF, RIP does not have routers exchange hello packets to assure each other of their health. The routing updates themselves serve that purpose. When Seattle first gets an update from Salt Lake City, it does not accept the update's routing information permanently. Rather, Seattle accepts the information provisionally. Seattle believes the information for only a short period of time, and Salt Lake City must periodically reassure Seattle that the information remains valid. This periodic reassurance explains the need for RIP-based routers to periodically rebroadcast their routing updates.

To return to the example of figure 5.4, once Salt Lake City loses power, it stops sending out its routing updates. After some period of time (typically three minutes) the routers that had previously heard from Salt Lake City will time out that information. They will then recalculate routes based on the information that they do have. Seattle, for example, will end up with a new routing table like that of table 5.2.

Table 5.2 Seattle's Routing Table after Salt Lake City Power Failure

Destination	Cost	Next Hop
I-5	1 hop	N/A
I-84	1 hop	N/A
I-10	2 hops	San Francisco
I-80	2 hops	San Francisco
I-15	3 hops	San Francisco
I-20	3 hops	San Francisco
I-40	3 hops	San Francisco
I-35	4 hops	San Francisco
I-90	4 hops	San Francisco

Triggered Updates

In its simplest form, distance vector routing can be slow to disseminate complete routing information. Even in the simple network of figure 5.1, it takes three full rounds of updates for routers to learn the network's routes. What does that mean for the network's routing? As one example, with the typical RIP update interval of 30 seconds, it could take Seattle as long as 90 seconds to learn that a bridge failure had closed I-35.

For computer networks, 90 seconds can be a very long time. As an extreme example, a single ATM link can transfer nearly 30 billion bytes of data in that time. Sending that much data along the wrong path is a substantial waste of network resources. Fortunately, distance vector protocols can use *triggered updates* to hasten the distribution of updated routing knowledge. The principle behind a triggered update is quite simple: As soon as a router learns of a change in the network topology, it immediately sends new routing updates. The router does not wait for its normal periodic update interval.

Figure 5.5 shows how Kansas City and Dallas respond to a failure of I-35. Each sends triggered updates to all their healthy links as soon as they detect the failure. The figure highlights three key features of triggered updates. First, routers indicate that a destination is unreachable by advertising it as an infinite number of hops away. Second, the triggered update includes all the routing information that has changed. Kansas City, for example, includes I-20 as well as I-35 in its list of unreachable destinations. It does so because, presumably, Kansas City was previously counting on reaching I-20 by forwarding along the failed I-35 link to Dallas. For the same reason, Dallas lists changed routes to I-40 and

Triggered Update Shortcomings

Triggered updates can drastically improve the responsiveness of a distance vector protocol, but they are not effective in every situation. Consider the earlier example in this chapter, a power failure that shuts down Salt Lake City. In that case, the router itself has failed, and it clearly cannot generate a triggered update to tell everyone that fact. Instead, Salt Lake City's neighbors must patiently time out the routes they learned from Salt Lake City. After 180 seconds, when that timeout occurs, they can then issue triggered updates themselves, informing the rest of the network quickly. They cannot, however, avoid that initial 180-second delay.

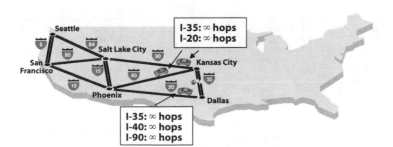

◀ **Figure 5.5**

Triggered updates can immediately indicate failure. They do so by listing the appropriate destination links as being infinitely far from the sender.

1-90 in addition to 1-35. It had been counting on Kansas City as the next hop for those destinations. As a third point, note that the triggered updates contain only the information that has changed. Kansas City does not include information for 1-40 and 1-90 in its triggered update. That routing information remains part of the normal, periodic update from Kansas City.

Counting to Infinity

In some ways, distance vector protocols are naïve protocols. Routers that implement them must place total trust in their neighbors. Of course, all protocols depend on mutual cooperation, and even link state protocols like OSPF function poorly when presented with a misbehaving peer. The Routing Information Protocol, however, has a particular vulnerability that shows up even when neighbors are not malicious. That vulnerability results in a problem known as *counting to infinity*.

Figure 5.6 shows a sample network that can illustrate counting to infinity. This example concentrates on the interaction between the center and right routers, and the figure illustrates the RIP updates they might exchange. Each advertises their own complete routing tables, including all three networks of the figure.

Now suppose the left router fails, as in figure 5.7. With that failure, the Token Ring network is not reachable. No one realizes this problem right away, though, and the remaining

Figure 5.6 ▶

This figure shows distance vector updates for a simple, stable network.

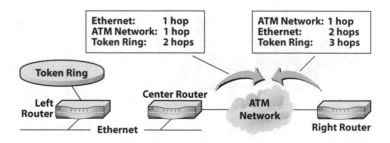

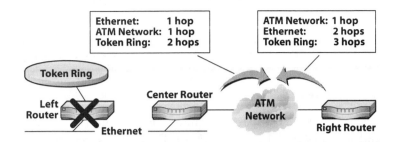

When one router fails, the remaining routers continue sending updates.

routers continue exchanging updates. The two routers do not behave identically, though. The right router regularly receives updates from its peer, and it has no suspicion that anything is amiss. But the center router no longer hears from the failed router. It steadily counts down the time remaining for the route to the Token Ring network.

After 180 seconds, that route expires. The center router realizes that the Token Ring is no longer reachable via the left router. The right router's information, on the other hand, is not even close to expiration. After all, it has been receiving regular updates from the center router. Shortly after the center router deletes all routes through the failed router, it receives a new update from the right router. As figure 5.8 shows, this update includes an advertisement for the Token Ring network.

This route is no longer valid. The right router does not know that, though. It has not timed out the route yet. Furthermore, the center router cannot know that the route is invalid either. The right router, after all, could have a "back door"

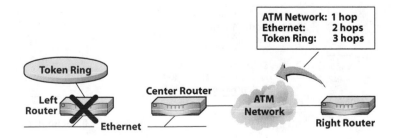

◀ **Figure 5.8**

Eventually, the center router recognizes that the left router has failed. It continues to receive updates from the right router, however. Significantly, those updates still include the Token Ring LAN as a destination.

path to the Token Ring network. With no other option, the center router believes that its peer does have a three-hop route to the Token Ring. And, if the right router is three hops away from the Token Ring, the center router must be four hops away.

The center router installs this "new" route to the Token Ring and includes it in its own updates. Figure 5.9 shows the resulting advertisement. Attention now turns to the right router. Previously, it thought the Token Ring was three hops away. But that belief was based on the network being only two hops away from the center router. Now the center router claims that the network is four hops away.

"Very well," one imagines the right router thinking, "my cost to reach the Token Ring has just grown from 3 (2+1) to 5 (4+1)." By now, the next step is obvious. The right router announces a new route to the Token Ring network with a cost of 5. The center router hears this, adjusts its own route accordingly, and announces a new route with a cost of 6.

Unfortunately, RIP has no easy way of stopping this process. The two routers continue exchanging updates, incrementing the Token Ring's cost with each exchange. Eventually, the cost reaches some artificially defined limit. That maximum value represents infinity, and, when the cost reaches that level, both routers finally agree that the Token Ring must be unreachable.

Distance vector protocols face a difficult decision when choosing the value to represent infinity. As the example

Figure 5.9 ▶

When the center router receives the right router's update, it believes a path exists to the Token Ring through the right router. It has no way of knowing that the right router was counting on it as part of that path. It increments the hop count and re-advertises the destination in its own updates.

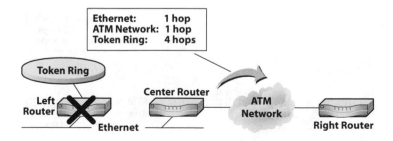

shows, it should not be too large. Otherwise, counting to infinity could take a long time and consume a lot of network resources. On the other hand, "infinity" should not be too small. Its value represents an upper limit on the true size of the network.

The Routing Information Protocol uses a distance of 16 as infinity. With this value, no destination can be more than 15 hops away from any other. For larger networks, this limit may represent a severe constraint on the topology. On the other hand, 16 may seem excessive by some measures. Without triggered updates, it can still take eight minutes for two routers to count to infinity. Fortunately, most RIP implementations employ triggered updates. They hasten the count to infinity considerably.

Split Horizon

It is not possible for RIP to eliminate counting to infinity in all topologies, but most RIP implementations employ a technique known as *split horizon* to avoid the most common situations that require counting to infinity. With split horizon, routers are more selective in the routes they advertise. The rule they employ is rather simple. If a router learns of a route from updates received on a particular link, it does not advertise that route on updates that it transmits to the same link. Consider figure 5.10. The topology remains the same, but both routers now use split horizon.

Notice the RIP updates sent by the center router. They no longer include the router's complete routing table. For example, the update it sends on the Ethernet omits any mention of the Ethernet or Token Ring networks. The center router learns about these destinations from the Ethernet, so it does not need to advertise them to that network. For the same reason, the router's updates on the ATM network do not mention that network, only the Ethernet and Token Ring.

Figure 5.10 ▶

To prevent counting to infinity, routers can omit destinations learned from their neighbors when they send updates back to those neighbors.

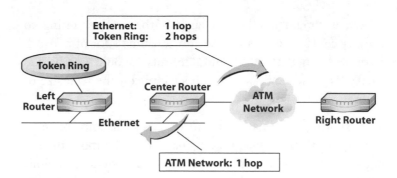

Split horizon has an even more drastic effect on the right router. Because the only routers it knows are learned from the ATM network, they will all be omitted on updates sent to that network. The right router has no need to send RIP updates at all.

Given the updates of figure 5.10, it is clear how split horizon avoids counting to infinity. When the left router fails, it will still take some time for the routes to the Token Ring to expire in the center router. Once that happens, however, the center router no longer hears of an apparent alternate path from the right router. Immediately after the route's expiration, the center router knows that the Token Ring is no longer reachable.

Some RIP routers employ an even more drastic form of split horizon called *poison reverse*. With poison reverse, routers do not omit destinations they learn from an interface. They include those destinations but advertise an infinite cost to reach them. Figure 5.11 shows poison reverse in action. Comparing it with figure 5.10 highlights the difference between simple split horizon and split horizon with poison reverse.

Poison reverse obviously increases the size of routing updates. In return, it provides a positive indication that a particular destination is not reachable through a router. This positive indication is less ambiguous, and sometimes safer, than simply relying on the absence of any information about

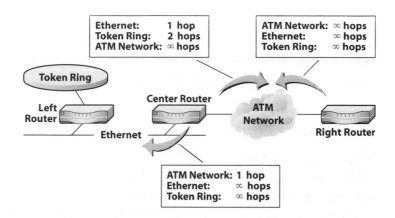

◀ **Figure 5.11**

A more aggressive defense against counting to infinity leaves neighbors' destinations in returned updates, but lists the distance to those destinations as infinite.

a route. It allows no room for misinterpretations or invalid assumptions.

From these discussions, it may appear that split horizon eliminates the counting to infinity problem altogether. Unfortunately, that is not the case. Some situations still require counting to recognize an unreachable destination. Figure 5.12 is a case in point. It shows an example network in which split horizon is ineffective. In that network, suppose the bottom router's connection to the Ethernet fails. At that point, the Ethernet is no longer reachable from anywhere else on the network.

Split horizon prevents the bottom router from being misled by any advertisements from the left or right routers. It does not, however, protect those routers from misleading each

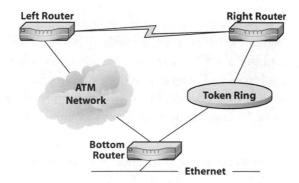

◀ **Figure 5.12**

Split horizon is not effective when paths can loop through multiple subnetworks, as in this simple figure. If the bottom router fails, the two top routers will still count to infinity among themselves before recognizing that the Ethernet LAN isn't reachable.

other. They will each include a route to the Ethernet in updates on the point-to-point connection. Once the path through the bottom router goes away, they will begin the steady march to infinity in exchanges across this link.

RIP Message Format

With the necessary background on distance vector routing, RIP's message formats become almost trivial. All RIP messages are carried in their own UDP datagrams, and RIP uses the UDP port of 520 to distinguish its traffic from other applications. (There is also a version of RIP for IPv6, which uses a separate UDP port; RIP for IPv6 is treated as a separate protocol from RIP for IPv4.)

All RIP messages share a common format, illustrated in figure 5.13. The first byte, labeled *command*, indicates whether the message is a request (when it contains a value of 1) or a response (value of 2). So far, all the update messages we've discussed have been unsolicited. They are sent as responses. The request command lets a router explicitly ask a neighbor for a route.

To request routing information for a specific destination, a router places that destination in a RIP request. The metric in the request is irrelevant. Any router that responds to a request fills in the metric in its response message. Split horizon processing is not applied to responses sent in reply to RIP requests.

A router can also use the request command to ask for a neighbor's entire routing table. To do that, it sends the neighbor a RIP request with a single entry. That entry has an IP address and subnet mask set to zero and a metric of 16. Routers that respond to this request return their entire routing table, possibly in several response messages.

The next byte in the RIP header indicates the version of the RIP protocol in use. The latest version of RIP is version 2. In

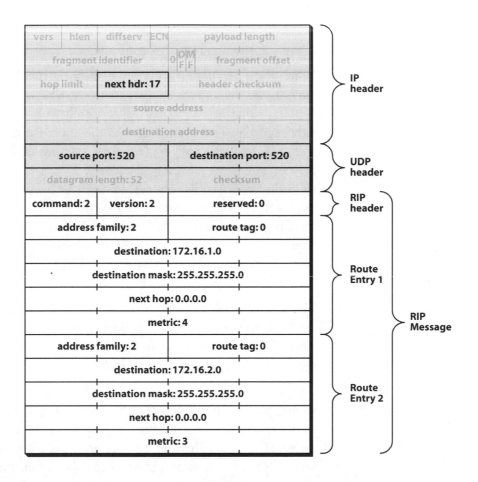

vers	hlen	diffserv ECN	payload length	
fragment identifier		0 DF MF	fragment offset	
hop limit		next hdr: 17	header checksum	
source address				
destination address				

source port: 520	destination port: 520
datagram length: 52	checksum

command: 2	version: 2	reserved: 0

address family: 2	route tag: 0
destination: 172.16.1.0	
destination mask: 255.255.255.0	
next hop: 0.0.0.0	
metric: 4	

address family: 2	route tag: 0
destination: 172.16.2.0	
destination mask: 255.255.255.0	
next hop: 0.0.0.0	
metric: 3	

IP header

UDP header

RIP header

Route Entry 1

Route Entry 2

RIP Message

▲ **Figure 5.13**

RIP messages are carried in UDP datagrams using source and destination ports 520. They contain a 4-byte RIP header and a list of route entries.

general, current RIP implementations use this version for all messages; however, RIP version 2 is backward compatible with RIP version 1. So if a router happens not to be using any of the features introduced in version 2, it may set the version number to 1 in order to interoperate with older neighbors. Two reserved bytes follow the version number. These bytes always contain zero.

After the 4-byte header, RIP messages contain a list of up to 25 route entries. Figure 5.13 shows two such entries. Each of these entries consists of 20 bytes. The first two bytes indicate that address family of the entry. Currently, RIP supports only IP addressing, and the value for this field is 2. A special value of this field, 65535, indicates that the entry contains authentication information rather than a route entry.

When the entry does carry a route, the next two bytes are a *route tag* for the entry. The RIP protocol itself does not interpret the value of the route tag; it merely ensures that the right tag value always remains with the entry. Route tags are used by systems that support other routing protocols such as OSPF or BGP along with RIP. Such systems can use the route tag to indicate whether a route was learned from a neighbor using RIP or whether it was imported from a different protocol. The distinction may be important because other routing protocols use different metrics than RIP, and comparing distances to arrive at the shortest path to a destination may require additional work.

The next two fields identify the route entry. Four bytes carry the IP address prefix, and four additional bytes contain the subnet mask. The message in figure 5.13's example advertises routes to 172.16.1.0/24 and 172.16.2.0/24.

The *next hop* field in the entry identifies the router that is serving as the next forwarding hop for destinations on the entry's network. Generally, the next hop router is the same as the router sending the RIP response, in which case this field may be set to zero. The RIP standard allows one router to advertise on behalf of another, a configuration that may be useful if not all routers on a network support RIP.

The final four-byte field is the metric for the route. Even though RIP messages allow four bytes for this field, RIP considers any value above 15 to be infinity.

RIP Authentication

If the first entry in the list of route entries has the address family $FFFF_{16}$, the entry contains authentication data for the message. The RIP standard itself defines authentication type 2, which indicates a simple password. Figure 5.14 shows a sample RIP message with such a password.

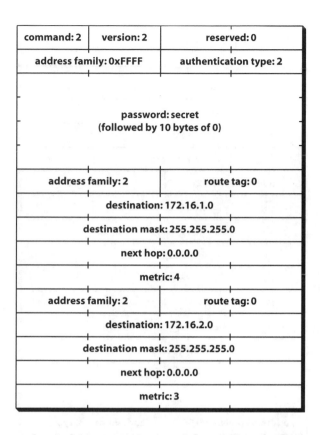

command: 2	version: 2	reserved: 0	
address family: 0xFFFF		authentication type: 2	
password: secret (followed by 10 bytes of 0)			
address family: 2		route tag: 0	
destination: 172.16.1.0			
destination mask: 255.255.255.0			
next hop: 0.0.0.0			
metric: 4			
address family: 2		route tag: 0	
destination: 172.16.2.0			
destination mask: 255.255.255.0			
next hop: 0.0.0.0			
metric: 3			

◀ **Figure 5.14**

As a very simple authentication scheme, RIP messages may include a secret password. This authentication method is not very secure, however, since the password is exposed to any potential adversary as the message travels across subnetworks.

Note that password authentication is not very secure. Because RIP messages are not normally encrypted, an attacker could easily eavesdrop on the network and discover the password. Password authentication is more useful to prevent accidental misconfigurations than malicious attacks.

An alternative authentication scheme relies on secure message digests using the MD5 algorithm. The MD5 authentication option relies on both the authentication entry and a special trailer. Figure 5.15 shows a sample message.

The first entry uses the special address family of $FFFF_{16}$ to indicate authentication, and it has an authentication type of 3. The next two bytes carry the length of the RIP message without the special authentication trailer. The entry then

Figure 5.15 ▶

Message digests provide a more secure method for RIP authentication. The special route entry contains information about the digest; the digest itself appears after the end of the message.

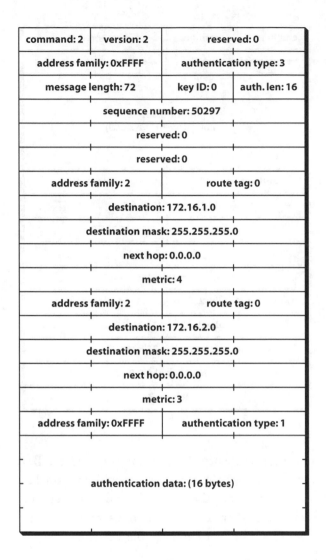

command: 2	version: 2	reserved: 0	
address family: 0xFFFF		authentication type: 3	
message length: 72		key ID: 0	auth. len: 16
sequence number: 50297			
reserved: 0			
reserved: 0			
address family: 2		route tag: 0	
destination: 172.16.1.0			
destination mask: 255.255.255.0			
next hop: 0.0.0.0			
metric: 4			
address family: 2		route tag: 0	
destination: 172.16.2.0			
destination mask: 255.255.255.0			
next hop: 0.0.0.0			
metric: 3			
address family: 0xFFFF		authentication type: 1	
authentication data: (16 bytes)			

contains a 1-byte key identifier and one byte that contains the length of the authentication trailer. For MD5 authentication, the trailer is always 24 bytes long. A 4-byte sequence number and eight reserved bytes that are always zero complete the initial authentication entry.

As figure 5.15 shows, the RIP message concludes with an MD5 authentication trailer. The trailer's first two bytes hold the value FFFF$_{16}$, and the next two bytes are set to 1. The final 16 bytes carry the result of the MD5 calculation.

To calculate the MD5 digest, a router replaces the trailer of figure 5.16 with a virtual trailer, which the figure also shows. The virtual trailer contains a 16-byte secret value, enough bytes of zero to force the entire message to a multiple of 16 bytes and eight bytes that hold the entire message length. Once a router calculates the digest, it replaces the virtual trailer with the actual trailer. This process means that the secret value itself is never transmitted on a network, so eavesdroppers cannot discover the secret value.

When a router receives a RIP message with MD5 authentication, it performs the same MD5 calculation. It replaces the

▼ **Figure 5.16**

To compute a message digest, the router adds three things to the end of the message: a shared secret, padding, and a count of the number of bits authenticated. These fields are replaced by the digest itself when the message is transmitted.

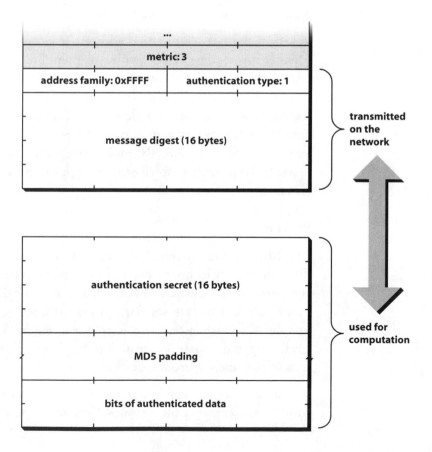

actual trailer with a virtual trailer, recalculates the digest and compares the result with the actual trailer. If the results are the same, the message is accepted as genuine.

Addressing RIP Messages

When a router sends a RIP update, it must be careful to use the appropriate source IP address. In particular, the router must use its own IP address on the network to which the update is sent. This distinction is important because routers typically interface to multiple networks. They are likely, therefore, to have multiple IP addresses. When a router receives a RIP update, however, it relies on the source address to define the next hop for routes included in the update. To ensure consistency, this next hop must be an address on the network from which the update arrived.

When picking a destination address, RIP must consider whether it is sending across a point-to-point link or a broadcast network. For point-to-point links, the destination address should be the IP address of the router at the far end of the link. For broadcast networks such as Ethernet LANs, RIP's destination address is a multicast address confined to the local network, 224.0.0.9. By multicasting RIP responses, a router sends its updates to all other routers on the network at once.

RIP Timers

The Routing Information Protocol relies on three different times to support its operation. The most obvious timer initiates periodic RIP updates. That timer has a nominal value of 30 seconds, but the RIP standard places extra restrictions on its value. In most cases, these restrictions require routers to randomize the update interval slightly. Randomization results in periodic RIP updates 25 to 35 seconds apart.

By randomizing its updates, a router avoids synchronizing with other routers on the network. Although researchers do not fully understand why routers synchronize with each other, the phenomenon definitely occurs.[1] Synchronization causes all routers to send their updates at the same time, stressing the network with a burst of traffic. Randomization reduces the probability of routers synchronizing, and it therefore spreads out their transmissions over time.

In addition to randomizing the periodic timer, RIP has an additional precaution to avoid synchronization. Triggered updates, regardless of when they are sent, do not reset the 30-second timer; otherwise, a major topology change could synchronize multiple routers. They would all restart their periodic timers simultaneously after sending the triggered updates. Instead, periodic updates take place as scheduled, even if their entire contents were just broadcast as a triggered update a few seconds earlier.

The second important timer on which RIP relies is the *expiration timer*. When a router hears a route to a particular destination, it initializes the expiration timer for that destination. The expiration timer is set for 180 seconds, but, in a stable network, it is always reinitialized about every 30 seconds when a new periodic update arrives. If the network is not stable, however, this timer may expire. Such an expiration indicates that the route is no longer valid.

The final RIP timer is the *garbage collection* timer. Should a route expire, routers do not immediately forget about that route. Instead, they mark the route as invalid (by setting its metric to infinity) and start the garbage collection timer. This timer runs for 120 seconds. During that time, the router continues to advertise the destination, though it does so with a metric cost of infinity. Advertising the route in this way forces neighbors to purge the route rapidly from their routing tables.

---

[1] Sally Floyd and Van Jacobson. "The Synchronization of Periodic Routing Messages." *Computer Communications Review* 23.4 (October 1993): 33-44.

RIP versus OSPF

A quick comparison of this chapter and the previous one should convince most readers that RIP is far simpler than OSPF.[2] Of course, even simplicity has a cost, and RIP has several significant limitations when compared to OSPF. It cannot support large networks, it is slower to respond to network changes, and it has no support for multicast routing.

Limited Network Diameter

The Routing Information Protocol defines infinity to be 16, and this definition places a strict limit on the size of any RIP-based network. Because RIP's metric must be an integer, all destinations must have a cost of at least 1. With all paths limited to less than an infinite number of hops, every system in a RIP-based network must be no more than 15 network hops away from all other systems. This measure is the network's *diameter*, and, with RIP, it is limited to 15.

There is another significant consequence of this limitation. It restricts the flexibility that administrators might otherwise have in assigning costs. Consider the simple example of figure 5.17. In that figure, the two primary routers are connected through ATM networks and by a narrow-band ISDN link. The path through the ATM networks requires an intermediate stop at a secondary router. Because of the much greater throughput available (155 Mbit/s vs. 128 Kbit/s) the ATM path is much more desirable than the ISDN link.

If an administrator assigns metric costs in the most straightforward way, he or she will give each network a cost of 1. With that assignment, however, RIP will choose the ISDN link as the lowest-cost path between the LANs. That path has only one hop, while the ATM networks require two hops.

---

[2] Indeed, such a comparison actually minimizes the differences between the two. Chapter 4 offers only a brief overview of the OSPF protocol. A careful study of all its RFCs is essential to a correct implementation. This chapter, on the other hand, presents a fairly complete picture of RIP.

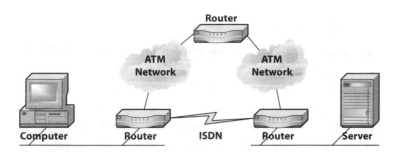

In this network, the path with the fewest hops isn't necessarily the best. The one-hop ISDN link may have much less bandwidth than the two-hop path through the ATM network.

To force a more appropriate decision, the administrator can artificially inflate the cost of the ISDN link. To make sure that the ATM networks become the preferred path, he or she can assign the ISDN link a cost of 3. With this assignment, the ATM networks provide a lower-cost path, but the ISDN link remains available as a backup.

This flexibility comes at a cost. If links have typical costs of 2 or 3, the maximum network diameter shrinks accordingly. Because of the counting to infinity problem, RIP is always stuck with a maximum cost of 15. In contrast, OSPF metrics are 16-bit quantities, and it has no artificial limit to allow for counting to infinity.

Responsiveness to Network Changes

Another disadvantage of RIP is its responsiveness. Triggered updates help, but they can still require the exchange of more than a dozen packets to count to infinity. There are also scenarios that force RIP to wait 180 seconds before it recognizes routes that have become invalid.

The OSPF protocol, on the other hand, suffers no such delays. With suitable tuning, it can recognize failed neighbors in a few seconds. Regardless of how OSPF learns of a network change, it can reconstruct the correct network topology as soon as it floods the appropriate advertisement. Instead of the 180 seconds (and more) that RIP sometimes requires, OSPF typically responds to changes within a second or two.

Distance Vector Multicast

Although link state protocols like OSPF are more naturally suited for distributing multicast routing information, it is possible to design a distance vector protocol that supports multicast routing. RFC 1075 documents just such an experimental protocol.

Multicast Routing

A final shortcoming of RIP is its lack of support for multicast routing. Because RIP has no way to disseminate group membership information, it offers no help in forwarding multicast packets. The OSPF protocol, on the other hand, includes explicit support for multicast routing in the form of special extensions. Indeed, link state protocols in general are well suited for distributing group membership. A network with multicast services can still use RIP, but only for unicast routing. Such a network would need an additional protocol or manual configuration to support multicast routing.

Summary

The Routing Information Protocol offers a simpler alternative to OSPF. Like OSPF, RIP is designed for routing within an autonomous system, but RIP differs from OSPF in its basic technology. Instead of link state routing, RIP relies on distance vector algorithms. Distance vector algorithms are less complex than link state approaches, but they suffer from significant limitations. In particular, RIP places limits on the size of its networks and on the speed with which they can respond to topology changes. Because of these limitations, RIP is better suited for small networks. Complex networks require the sophistication of OSPF.

CHAPTER 6

Path Vector Routing and BGP

Both RIP and OSPF are interior gateway protocols, routing protocols that operate within an autonomous system. The Internet, of course, includes a lot of autonomous systems, and it needs a way to route between them. Protocols that provide this routing are *exterior gateway protocols*. (Gateway is an old name for a router.) The exterior gateway protocol in use on the Internet today is version 4 of the Border Gateway Protocol (BGP).

As OSPF demonstrates, routing within an autonomous system can get complicated. Ultimately, though, it has a simple, unconstrained goal: figure out the best way to get from here to there. When paths cross AS borders, however, even the goals get complicated. An example that first appeared in chapter 2 introduces some of the issues. Figure 6.1 repeats the network from that example.

Big Company's network has connections to both Giant Company and one of Giant's suppliers. It is not surprising that these connections exist, as Big needs to exchange information with both other firms. Big is adamant about one

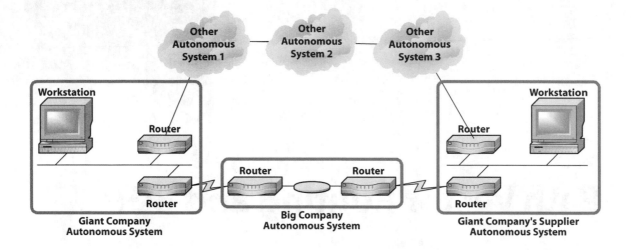

Figure 6.1 ▲

In a network like this example, Big Company may not want to carry traffic between Giant Company and its supplier. Policy tools give Big Company this type of control.

thing, though; it does not want to provide a service to Giant. That means that traffic between Giant and its supplier should not travel through Big's network. Such traffic must take the long way around, through the other autonomous systems at the top of the figure.

No longer is the routing goal simply to figure out the best way to get from here to there. Instead, the network now needs the best way to get from here to there without passing through a restricted area. Restricted areas define policies, and policies make routing between ASs especially complex.

In chapter 2, the source system solves the policy problem by adding a source route option to all its datagrams. In theory, this approach always works. In practice, it places much too great a burden on the host systems. Furthermore, it requires Big to trust both Giant and its supplier to use appropriate source routes. In all but the simplest configurations, policy must be transparent to the hosts involved in the communication. Through its support of policy-based routing, BGP provides just such a service.

Implementing Policy

Policies constrain communications. If every system were allowed to communicate with every other system without restrictions, then networks would not need policies. Policies can take many complex and sophisticated forms, but they all ultimately amount to a limitation on communication between systems.

Networks can implement policies in at least three different ways. Each approach corresponds to a different way to place limitations on communications. The simplest approach is based on bandwidth. If, for example, Big Company wants to make sure that Giant Company uses no more than 56 kbit/s of bandwidth in its network, then Big Company can limit the connections between the two networks to 56 kbit/s. Figure 6.2 illustrates this configuration. Clearly, with only 56 kbit/s of bandwidth available, Giant must conform to Big's policy. In the extreme case, Big can simply decline to connect with Giant, limiting the bandwidth to 0 kbit/s.

Another place to implement policies is in the forwarding process. Every IP datagram that crosses Big's network travels

▼ **Figure 6.2**

A crude way to implement policy it to simply restrict the bandwidth available for a particular path. This approach doesn't restrict the type of traffic, however, and it indiscriminately affects all traffic crossing the restricted link.

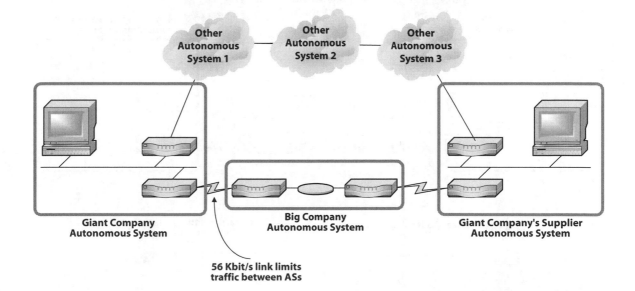

through its routers, and the ip layer in each router must make a forwarding decision. Routers can implement policies by constraining their forwarding decisions. Most commercial routers, in fact, support this form of policy through *packet filters*.

Packet filters, symbolized by the traffic lights of figure 6.3, allow administrators to define exactly which datagrams routers will and will not forward. Unfortunately, these filters place a substantial burden on the routers. They must check every single datagram against the defined constraints. Administering packet filters is also quite a challenge. It usually requires in-depth knowledge of messages and application protocols.

The Border Gateway Protocol relies on a third way of implementing policy, *policy-based routing*. Policy-based routing places constraints on how routers distribute routing information. The idea is simple: If Giant's routers do not know that

Figure 6.3 ▼

Another way to implement policy is through special packet filters in the routers. Packet filters often require extensive manual configuration, however, and can be difficult to administer.

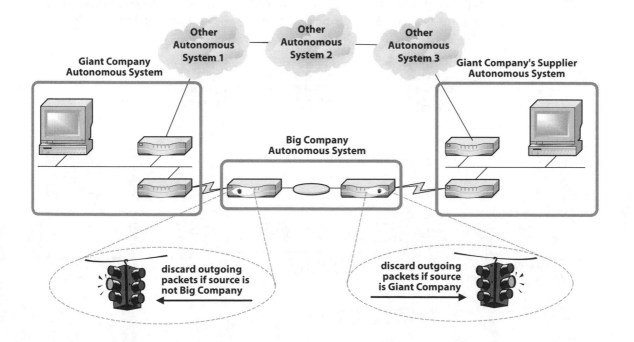

the supplier lies on the other side of Big's network, they do not forward traffic through it. In figure 6.4, Big's routers consider that information "secret," refusing to advertise it to Giant's network.

This approach does not require special calculations for every IP datagram. Instead, routers simply implement their normal forwarding decision (although with less than complete information). Giant's routers find an alternate path to reach the supplier, and they forward traffic along that path.

Influencing Routing Information

Even though BGP exists mainly to support policy-based routing, it is not concerned with the details of routing policies. The protocol has no understanding of the format, structure, administration, or any other aspect of policies. It merely acknowledges their existence, and it allows them to influence routing information. Figure 6.5 begins a discussion of this approach.

▼ **Figure 6.4**

With policy-based routing, Big Company's routers simply omit any paths to Giant's supplier when advertising to Giant's routers. Giant's routers never learn of these hidden paths and calculate a different router for such traffic.

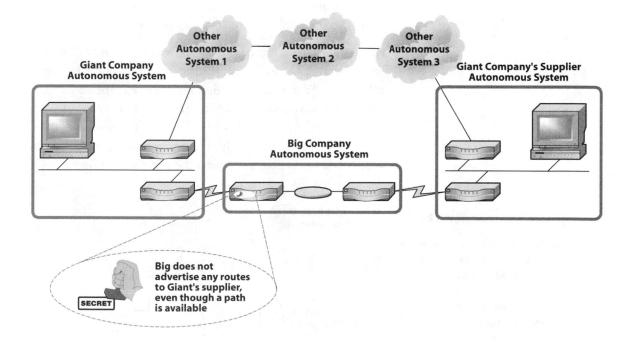

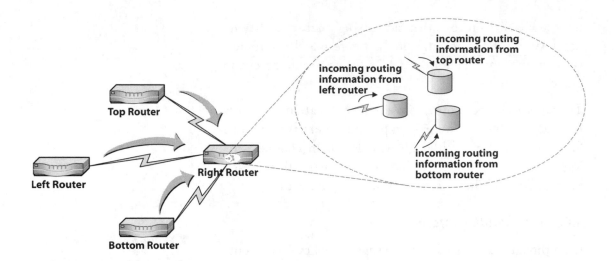

Figure 6.5 ▲

The right router stores routing information from each of its neighbors in its incoming database.

In the figure, the right router is connected to several other routers in different autonomous systems. These routers exchange routing information with each other using BGP. This routing information describes the topology of the network, as the sender understands it. Conceptually, the right router accepts routing information from each of its neighbors, and BGP is the protocol that conveys that information.

The right router then has to do something with the routing information it has gathered. It ultimately must decide how it will forward datagrams. As figure 6.6 shows, the router applies policies to decide what information it keeps and what information it ignores. This process creates a database of local routing information. The incoming routing information describes how its neighbors view the network, while the local

Figure 6.6 ▶

Policy rules determine how information from the incoming databases is added to the router's local routing database. This local database is what the router uses for its own forwarding decisions.

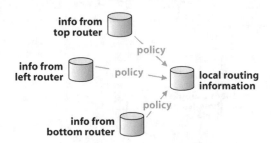

routing information defines how the router itself views the network.

This view is also what the router advertises as external routes in its OSPF link state advertisements or RIP updates. Other routers within the autonomous system will reach a consistent view of the greater network beyond their AS.

Routing policies can also affect the information that a router shares with its neighbors. For these policy decisions, the router starts with its own local routing information, and then it decides what information BGP should send to its neighbors. Logically, it constructs outgoing routing information for each neighbor. Again, this decision, depicted in figure 6.7, is based on policy.

This step is where Big solves the problem of preventing Giant's routers from using its own network. Big implements a policy in its routers that prohibits them from including routes to Giant's supplier in the information they send to Giant's routers.

Path Vector Routing

So far, routing between autonomous systems sounds a lot like routing within an autonomous system. The inter-AS approach has to support policy-based routing, but policies themselves are not part of the protocol. So why is another

◀ **Figure 6.7**

Policy rules also determine which information in the local routing database the right router extracts and places into outgoing databases for transmission to other routers. Just as each neighbor had its own incoming database, each neighbor may have its own outgoing database, in case the local router wants to advertise different information to different neighbors.

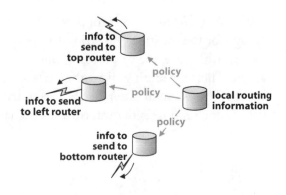

protocol required? What is wrong with using OSPF or even RIP for exterior routing?

The answer to these questions lies in the goals of the protocol. Both OSPF and RIP assume that all routers have the same goal. That goal is to figure out how to get from here to there. Exterior routers also loosely share a goal: figure out how to get from here to there, subject to certain restrictions. The problem arises because the restrictions vary from router to router. Some organizations may have no concerns forwarding traffic through Big Company's network, while others (such as Giant Company) have different ideas. Giant's routers have a different restriction than other routers, and so Giant's routers and other routers do not share the same goal. Without a common goal, routers using OSPF or RIP cannot calculate paths consistently, and routing loops are almost certain to arise.

The root of this problem is the protocol's reliance on metrics. Both OSPF and RIP attach a metric, or cost, to possible paths. Link state advertisements in OSPF include a metric for each link, and RIP assigns a metric to each route in its update packets. The protocols count on every router attaching the same meaning to each metric, allowing consistent, and therefore loop-free, calculation of routes. When routing policies are in place, routers value some metrics differently than others, invalidating the assumptions on which OSPF and RIP rely.

Distance Vector Routing without Distance

The Border Gateway Protocol solves this problem by eliminating (for the most part) metrics. Its approach is essentially that of a distance vector protocol, but without explicit distances. The BGP routing algorithm is known as *path vector routing*. The essential difference between distance vector and path vector routing is the information exchanged in routing updates.

Distance vector protocols advertise a cost to reach each destination; path vector protocols explicitly list entire paths to each destination. Consider the example network of figure 6.8. (In that network, autonomous systems are unrealistically small. Real ASS contain many networks connected by many routers.)

If the center router used a pure distance vector protocol like RIP, it would advertise a routing table listing all reachable networks, along with their distance metrics. Figure 6.9 shows the router generating such advertisements. The neighboring routers receive the advertisements and calculate their own routes to those destinations by adding one (the cost of the

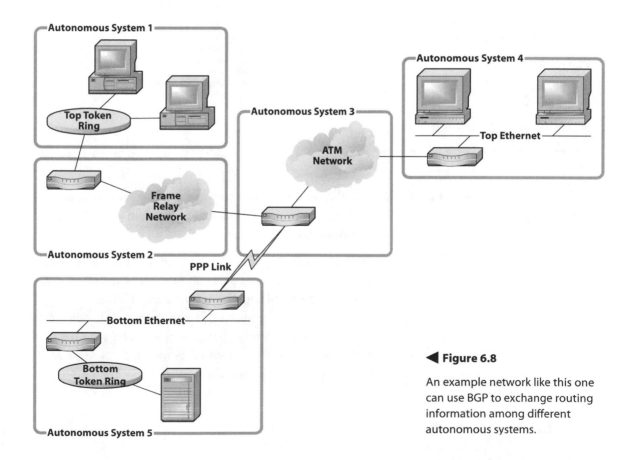

◀ **Figure 6.8**

An example network like this one can use BGP to exchange routing information among different autonomous systems.

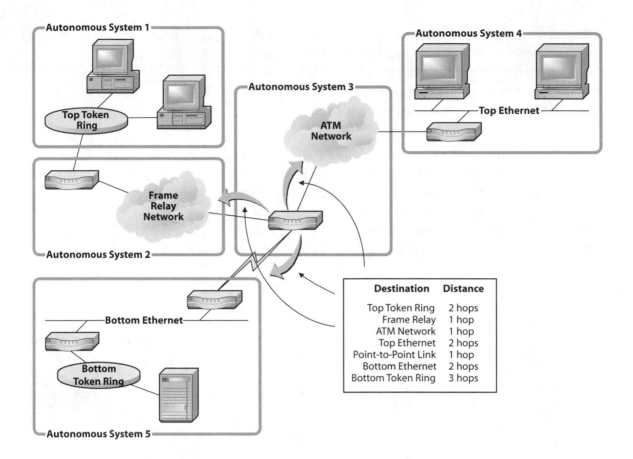

Destination	Distance
Top Token Ring	2 hops
Frame Relay	1 hop
ATM Network	1 hop
Top Ethernet	2 hops
Point-to-Point Link	1 hop
Bottom Ethernet	2 hops
Bottom Token Ring	3 hops

Figure 6.9 ▲

If BGP were a true distance vector protocol, each router would simply advertise the number of hops to each autonomous system.

link to the central router) to the advertised cost and accepting the new route if it is less expensive than any other route to that destination.

In the path vector approach, the center router advertises a routing table listing reachable networks, along with the full path the router would use to reach them. Figure 6.10 highlights the difference between this approach and distance vector advertisements. When a neighboring router receives such an advertisement, it can compute its own paths to the destinations. These calculations define the incoming routing information from the central router. The neighboring router can then base its local route information on any appropriate

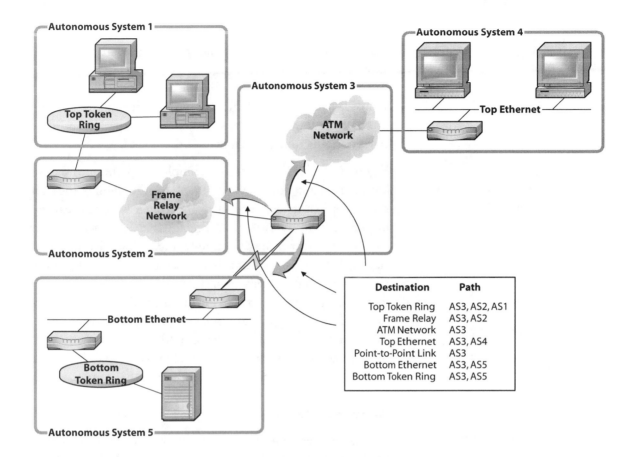

Destination	Path
Top Token Ring	AS3, AS2, AS1
Frame Relay	AS3, AS2
ATM Network	AS3
Top Ethernet	AS3, AS4
Point-to-Point Link	AS3
Bottom Ethernet	AS3, AS5
Bottom Token Ring	AS3, AS5

policies. For example, the top right router, after hearing from the center router, knows a path to the Token Ring LAN. That path runs through ASs 3, 2, and 1. If the router's policy forbids it from using AS 2, then it will note that the Token Ring is unreachable.

Counting to Infinity

Path vectors also provide a convenient solution to the counting to infinity problem. Recall that distance vector protocols sometimes must count to infinity to break a routing loop. Such loops can arise because, when one router receives an advertisement from another, it knows only the cost of the

▲ **Figure 6.10**

With path vector routing, BGP advertises the full path to each destination, not just the number of hops. This additional information is critical for policy-based routing, since policy may apply to an entire path, not just the next hop.

advertised destinations; it does not know the path to those destinations. In particular, the receiving router does not know if the advertising router is actually counting on the receiving router to reach the destination. With a path vector approach, on the other hand, receiving routers know the entire path. If they themselves are part of the path, then they can ignore the route, avoiding a loop.

Figure 6.11 gives a concrete example of path information breaking a potential routing loop. In the figure, the left router has lost its connection to the Token Ring and can no longer reach that destination directly. It does, however, hear an advertisement from the center router. That advertisement claims that the Token Ring is reachable. The path, however, includes the left router's own autonomous system. The left router recognizes that it would do no good to send packets for the Token Ring to the center router. After all, that router would simply turn them right around and send them back through autonomous system 2. The left router can detect the potential routing loop and avoid accepting that route.

Route Aggregation

In a network as large as the Internet, the number of potential destinations is quite large. The number, in fact, is so large

Figure 6.11 ▶

Because BGP advertises full path information, it is easy for routers to avoid routing loops. When the left router receives the message from the center router, it sees its own autonomous system in the path to the top Token Ring LAN. The left router, therefore, knows that the path through the center router is no longer available.

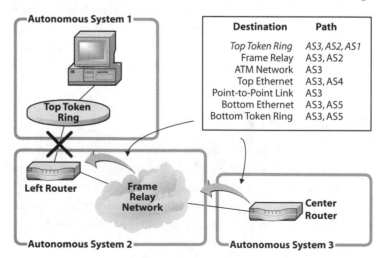

that it is not practical for routers to actually track every separate destination in their routing tables. To avoid overwhelming routers with too many destinations, BGP supports *route aggregation*. Route aggregation lets a BGP router combine multiple destinations and create a single advertisement for all of them. Routers that hear this advertisement treat the combined destinations as a single destination, so aggregation reduces the number of individual destinations that other routers must remember. It also shrinks the network overhead that route update packets require.

Route aggregation relies on the fact that destinations are just IP address prefixes. Sometimes multiple prefixes together specify all of a larger prefix. (In this sense, "larger" means to include more systems; the prefix itself actually contains fewer specified bits.) For example, suppose a router knows a path to the two different destinations of table 6.1. If the router has a path to both of these 17-bit prefixes, then it must also have a path to the 16-bit prefix 172.16.0.0/16. Any destination that matches the larger prefix (172.16.0.0/16) must, by definition, match one or the other of the smaller prefixes. The seventeenth bit of the destination address must either be a 1 (in which case it matches 172.16.128.0/17) or a 0 (which matches 172.16.0.0/17).

Table 6.1 Routes Subject to Aggregation

Prefix Bits	Prefix Value	Binary Representation
17	172.16.0.0/17	10101100 00010000 0xxxxxxx xxxxxxxx
17	172.16.128.0/17	10101100 00010000 1xxxxxxx xxxxxxxx

Figure 6.12 shows how route aggregation can work in a real network. The left router knows paths to the two destinations in table 6.1, When it creates an advertisement for the left network, though, it does not have to list each destination separately. Instead, it uses the larger prefix 172.16.0.0/16.

The figure does highlight a dilemma facing BGP: When a router combines destinations, what path does it advertise for

Figure 6.12 ▶

The left router autonomous system 3 receives advertisements for two different destination subnets. When it sends its own advertisement, it can aggregate those two subnets into a single destination. The left router must adjust the path appropriately by listing both of the autonomous systems that reach the two subnets; it lists them both as a set rather than the normal sequence.

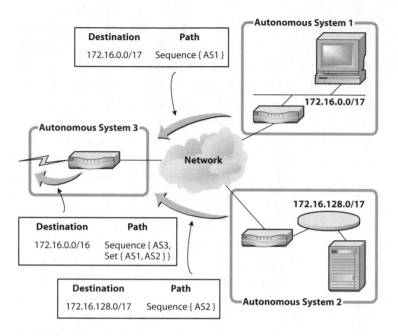

the aggregate? In the figure's example, the two destinations do not lie on the same path. The path to the top destination is AS 1, while the bottom network is in AS 2. Nonetheless, the left router must list a single path to the combined route in its update. The path it selects is the union of the paths to each separate destination; in other words, both AS 1 and AS 2 are listed in the path to 172.16.0.0/16. To indicate that this path is a union, the left router marks it as a *set*. In contrast, regular paths that have not been aggregated are termed *sequences*.

Normal BGP Operation

Unlike the other routing protocols we've discussed, BGP uses a reliable transport service; BGP routers communicate with each other over TCP connections. As a consequence, BGP has no mechanism that lets routers automatically discover each other. Instead, the identities of a router's BGP peers are administratively configured. That approach is consistent, however, with BGP's focus on policy. The set of peers for any given router is another aspect of routing policy, and it is entirely appropriate that BGP defer that decision to a human administrator.

Once two BGP routers establish a TCP connection, they introduce themselves and then exchange their complete routing tables. An OPEN message carries the introductions, while UPDATE messages transfer routing tables. As the network topology changes, the routers send each other incremental updates with additional UPDATE messages.

The BGP specification also defines NOTIFICATION messages that routers can send each other to indicate errors, and it defines a KEEPALIVE message for routers to transmit periodically, when there is no other traffic on the connection.

The KEEPALIVE message is important because it lets routers assure each other that they're still active. Absent any traffic, TCP does not provide this service, and it won't discover a failed connection unless one of the peers attempts to transmit data. The TCP connection is critical to the peering of BGP routers. If a router discovers that the connection has failed, it must immediately disregard all information it has learned from that peer.

A fifth type of BGP message is the ROUTE-REFRESH message. Routers use this message to request a new copy of their peer's full routing table.

The MD5 Signature Option for TCP

Because the TCP connection is so critical to BGP, BGP implementations have even introduced a special TCP option to afford it extra protection. That option is the MD5 signature option, and, even though it was created specifically for BGP implementations, other protocols have begun to use it as well.

Unlike other TCP options, MD5 signatures are not negotiated by the peers during connection establishment. Instead, they

Implementing MD5

The MD5 algorithm performs a set of convoluted calculations on its input and derives a 128-bit digest. The algorithm itself is moderately complicated, and it is certainly filled with various random and other magic numbers. Fortunately, RFC 1321 includes a complete implementation of MD5 in the C language.

MD5 Vulnerability

After the MD5 Signature option had been introduced by key BGP implementations, cryptographic researchers discovered a theoretical vulnerability in the algorithm's security. Because the practical implications of the vulnerability are rather minor, however, and because MD5 had already been widely deployed on the Internet, there has not been a major effort to replace MD5 with a more secure algorithm.

must be administratively configured. Routers either use them or not, and the configuration in both peers must match.

The option itself relies on a secret value that both routers share. When a router sends a TCP segment, it uses this value, along with the TCP header, message data, and other key values, as input to the Message Digest 5 algorithm.

Once the peer router has calculated a message digest, it can fill in the TCP option. As table 3.5 shows, the option type is 19, and its total length is 18 bytes. The 16 bytes of data are the message digest result.

If a router has been configured to use the MD5 signature option and it receives a TCP segment that doesn't include the option, the router simply discards that segment. If the option is present, the recipient verifies its value by duplicating the MD5 calculation. If the result agrees, the router accepts the segment for processing. Otherwise, it discards the segment with no further action.

The MD5 signature option protects against a malicious party injecting false information into a network of BGP routers. The malicious party won't know the secret value that legitimate routers share, so it won't be able to calculate correct message digest values for its messages. As a result, any segments that the malicious party does send will be ignored by the legitimate routers. This protection is critical to the successful operation of the Internet.

BGP within an Autonomous System

Even though BGP was originally designed for routing between autonomous systems, it has several properties that are useful just within a single autonomous system. The most important of those properties is BGP's ability to manage large routing databases. Consider the network of figure 6.13. The autonomous system in that figure has several connections to the external Internet, and a different BGP router coordinates

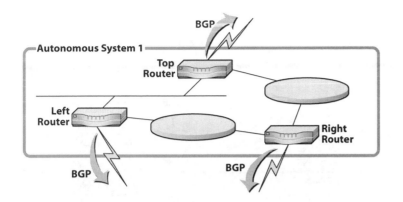

◀ **Figure 6.13**

BGP was designed for routing external to an autonomous system; however, when multiple routers within an AS use BGP, they must coordinate the information they advertise to present a consistent view of the AS to the rest of the network.

each of those connections. Those BGP routers must coordinate their actions to provide a consistent view of the AS's routing to the external Internet.

Because all three routers are within a single AS, they could use OSPF or RIP to exchange routes with each other. Indeed, such operation is possible, but it may require OSPF or RIP to carry a tremendous number of external routes—enough to describe the entire Internet. That can definitely present scaling protocols for those protocols.

Interior BGP

One way around this problem is for the routers to use BGP to communicate among the three routers, as in figure 6.14. This type of operation, where BGP is used among routers within a single autonomous system, is known as *Interior BGP* (sometimes abbreviated as IBGP). With IBGP, the routers can communicate directly with each other, without burdening OSPF or RIP with a lot of extra traffic.

For the most part, Interior BGP operates just like normal BGP. There is, however, one important exception: avoiding routing loops. As we saw earlier in this chapter, BGP avoids routing loops by listing the full AS path to each destination in its updates. If a router receives an update that lists its own AS in that path, it knows that the update has looped back and can

Figure 6.14 ▶

Interior BGP is one way multiple
routers can coordinate their BGP
exchanges outside the
autonomous system.

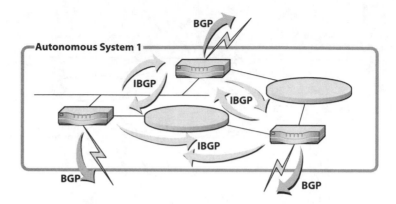

be ignored. This approach won't catch routing loops within
an AS, though, because all the routers have the same AS value
in the path.

Figure 6.15 shows the problem more explicitly. Suppose the
top router advertises its paths in an update to the right
router. Because those paths all pass through the top router,
they will all include that router's AS in their path vectors. If
the right router were using traditional BGP, it would ignore
these paths when it receives the update, because it would

Figure 6.15 ▶

When the top router sends an
IBGP update to the right router, it
adds its own autonomous system
to the path. Because the right
router sees its own AS in the path
already, under normal BGP rules, it
would reject this information as
suggestive of a routing loop.

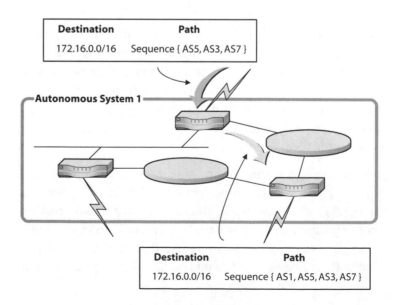

find its own AS in the path lists. But with interior BGP, ignoring the routes is exactly the wrong thing to do. The whole point of using IBGP is to let the routers update each other.

When routers use BGP within an autonomous system, they have to modify the normal BGP behavior. Instead of rejecting paths that include their own AS path, they accept them. A BGP router, however, cannot re-advertise these same paths in its own updates, even to routers other than their source. Doing so introduces the possibility of routing loops. We can see such a loop start to form in figure 6.16. There, the right router inappropriately re-advertises the top router's paths to the left router. Now the left router thinks the top destinations on the Internet can be reached through either the top or right routers. If the left router, acting just as badly, re-advertises the top router's paths to the right router, the right router will believe those top destinations are reachable via the left router. When the top router fails, both the left and right routers believe the other has a valid path, and traffic circulates endlessly between the two routers.

To avoid possible routing loops, IBGP routers have to adjust their behavior one more time: They cannot re-advertise

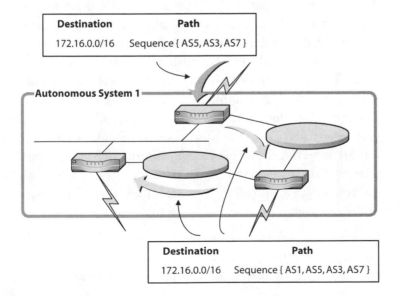

Destination	Path
172.16.0.0/16	Sequence { AS5, AS3, AS7 }

Autonomous System 1

Destination	Path
172.16.0.0/16	Sequence { AS1, AS5, AS3, AS7 }

◀ **Figure 6.16**

In this example, the right router violates an important interior BGP rule by re-advertising a route it has learned from an interior peer. Since the left router can't—by IBGP rules—reject information with its own AS in the path, the potential for a routing loop exists.

paths learned from other routers in their own autonomous system. That behavior introduces an important restriction on the possible configurations of IBGP routers. All IBGP routers must establish sessions with all other IBGP routers in the same autonomous system, a configuration known as a *full mesh*. If, for example, the left router in figure 6.14 had no BGP session with the top router, it would never learn of the top router's paths. Even though the right router knows those paths, IBGP prohibits it from disseminating them.

In autonomous systems with just a few IBGP routers, requiring a full mesh configuration may be reasonable. As the number of routers grows, however, the resources required to support the full mesh grow even faster. At some point the resource requirements may become unacceptable. To make interior operation more scalable, BGP has introduced two special extensions, *route reflectors* and *confederations*.

Route Reflectors

A route reflector is a BGP router that—by design—breaks the normal rules for BGP operation. In particular, it re-advertises routing information within the same autonomous system. The concept is apparent from figure 6.17. All three routers belong to a single autonomous system, and they use interior BGP to distribute routing information within that AS. Routers A and B, however, do not establish a BGP session with each other. This configuration violates the full mesh architecture for interior BGP, and normally it would present a serious problem: How does router A learn of router B's routes (and vice versa)? The solution, in this case, is router C. Router C is a route reflector; it accepts routing information from A and reflects that information to B. In the same way, it reflects B's information to A, and all three routers learn the full topology of the autonomous system.

Of course, there's more to route reflection than this simple exchange. Interior BGP normally prohibits route reflection, and there's a good reason for that prohibition: routing loops.

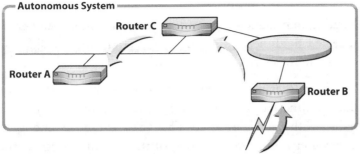

◄ Figure 6.17

If routers A and B don't have a direct session with each other, router C, acting as a route reflector, can relay information between the two.

Because route reflection violates BGP's normal operating rules, something special is required to prevent routing loops.

To avoid loops, route reflection introduces the concept of *clusters*. A cluster is a route reflector and all the other BGP routers that depend on the reflector. In the example of figure 6.17, routers A, B, and C form a single cluster. Figure 6.18 shows a more comprehensive network. In that figure routers A, B, C, and D form a cluster. Both C and D are reflectors within the cluster. Having multiple reflectors is generally a good idea because it provides redundancy. If router C fails, router D can continue reflecting routes between A and B. The other routers in the figure, E, F, and G, are not part of the cluster. As the figure shows, they must maintain a full mesh configuration among themselves and with the route clusters.

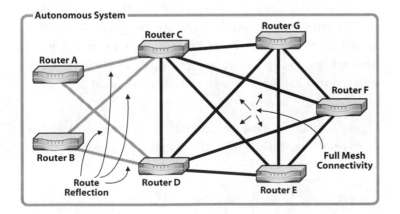

◄ Figure 6.18

Routers that don't peer with every other router—like A and B in this example—must peer with at least one router reflector that is part of the full mesh. Otherwise, their information won't real all routers in the autonomous system.

The rules that govern a route reflector are straightforward. Routing information that it receives from cluster members is reflected to all peers. Routing information from outside the cluster, however, is reflected only to cluster members.

To ensure that misconfiguration or other errors don't introduce routing loops, route reflectors tag all information they reflect with an *originator ID*. This value is unique among all BGP routers. (Generally it's one of their IP addresses.) If the router receives a router that's already tagged with its own originator ID, it knows that the information has looped back, and it can discard it without reflecting it further.

Reflected routing information also carries a *cluster list*. This attribute identifies all the route reflection clusters through which the information has passed. If a route reflector sees its own cluster in routing information it receives, it knows that the information has already passed through its cluster and need not be reflected further. Cluster lists break routing loops that could develop when a cluster has more than one route reflector within it, a situation that might not be caught with just the originator ID.

Confederations

Autonomous system confederations offer a different approach for avoiding the full mesh requirement of interior BGP. An AS confederation takes an existing autonomous system and subdivides it into many smaller groups. Each smaller group acts as a full autonomous system on its own, so, within each group, the full mesh requirement still holds. Between groups, however, BGP can operate much as it does between real autonomous systems. Most notably, a full mesh topology is not necessary.

Figure 6.19 shows how confederations may be deployed on an example network. The real autonomous system is subdivided into three smaller groups. Each group maintains a full mesh among its members, but a single BGP session is all that is required between groups.

The most confusing aspect of AS confederations may well be its terminology. The groups of systems within the real autonomous system are known as *member ASs*, while the real autonomous system itself is known as a *confederation*. This terminology can be confusing because it changes the meaning of autonomous system, depending on whether one is inside or outside of the confederation. Outside the confederation, the autonomous system *is* the confederation, and BGP's AS number refers to the confederation. Within the confederation, however, the autonomous system is the member AS. Here BGP's AS number refers to the member AS group, and a new attribute, the *confederation identifier*, denotes the full confederation.

▼ **Figure 6.19**

When an autonomous system divides into islands of full mesh connectivity, the individual islands, known as member ASs, operate like a full BGP autonomous system. The full autonomous system becomes a confederations of these member ASs.

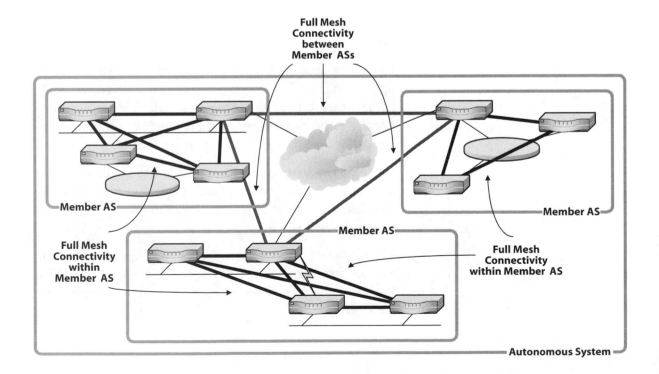

As you might expect, this change of perspective makes life a little tricky for routers in the confederation that also peer with other real autonomous systems. Those routers have to modify routing information that leaves the confederation so that the internal structure of the confederation remains hidden to exterior peers. Some routers within the confederation—namely those that peer with routers outside their own member AS—also have to exercise a little extra care. For the most part, those routers treat the peering session between other routers just like an exterior BGP session. There are a few attributes of the routing information, however, that receive slightly different treatment. Those attributes are normally removed from UPDATE messages sent outside an autonomous system, mainly because another AS has no use for the information. In the case of confederations, however, it is useful to propagate the information to all routers within the confederation, so it isn't stripped when transferred to another member AS.

BGP Messages

Every BGP message begins with a 19-byte header, shown in figure 6.20. The first 16 bytes, known as the *marker*, generally have all their bits set to 1. Originally, this field was intended to carry authentication information, but that task is now performed by the MD5 signature option for TCP.

The next two bytes contain the total length of the BGP message, including the common header. The minimum value for this field is 19, and the BGP specification restricts the maximum value to be no more than 4096.

The header's final byte indicates the message type. As table 6.2 indicates, there are five different BGP message types. The format of the rest of the message depends on the specific message type.

Table 6.2 BGP Message Types

Value	Message Type
1	OPEN message to establish a peering session
2	UPDATE message to exchange routing information
3	NOTIFICATION message to report errors
4	KEEPALIVE message to maintain the TCP connection
5	ROUTE-REFRESH message to request full routing information

OPEN Message

The OPEN message is how BGP routers introduce themselves. It is the first message peers exchange over a TCP connection. Figure 6.21 shows a complete OPEN message. The first byte

▼ **Figure 6.20**

BGP messages travel within TCP segments. A special marker identifies the start of each BGP message.

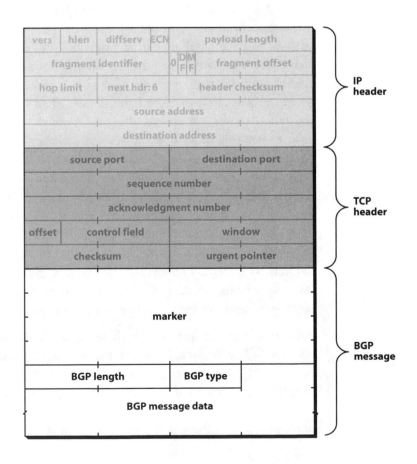

Figure 6.21 ▶

A BGP open message introduces a
router to its peer. Open messages
carry just a few parameters.

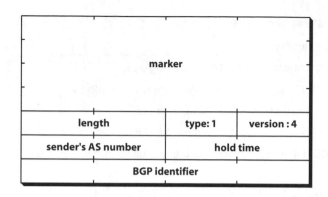

after the common header contains the BGP *version* number;
the most recent value is 4. The next two bytes carry the
sender's autonomous system number. They are followed by a
2-byte *hold time*, in seconds. With this value the sender indicates the maximum amount of time its peer should wait
without hearing anything further from the sender. If nothing
arrives from the sender within this time period, the recipient
should consider the sender to have failed, and the recipient
should immediately disregard any routes it had learned from
the failed router. Of course, the sender must take steps to
ensure that this timer does not expire as long as it remains
healthy. If it has no other traffic to send, it can transmit
KEEPALIVE messages. The BGP specification allows a router to
set the hold time to zero in its OPEN message and forgo
sending KEEPALIVE messages. This practice is discouraged,
however, and a router receiving such an OPEN message may
reject the BGP session with that peer. The final field of an
OPEN message is a four-byte *BGP identifier*. By convention,
this is one of the sender's IP addresses. A router must use the
same BGP identifier for all of its BGP sessions.

An OPEN message may also include several options. These
options follow the fixed part of the message. Each option
begins with a parameter type byte, followed by a parameter
length byte, followed, if appropriate, by any data for the option. As table 6.3 shows, BGP currently supports only two options, and one of those is not used. The capabilities option is

an important one, though, as it allows routers to advertise their support for new capabilities. To allow for the graceful introduction of new capabilities within BGP, routers use the new capabilities only if they receive, in the peer's OPEN message, a positive indication that the peer can support that new capability.

Table 6.3 BGP Options

Type	Option
1	Authentication information (not currently used)
2	Capabilities supported by the sender

The capabilities option itself is nothing but a list of capabilities. Each has a capability code (one byte in size), a capability length (also one byte long), and, optionally, a capability value that further defines the sender's level of support for the capability. Table 6.4 lists the capability codes defined at the time of this writing; several of the associated capabilities have not yet been fully defined and are not, therefore, discussed further in this text.

Table 6.4 BGP Optional Capabilities

Code	Length	Capability
1	4 bytes	Multiprotocol support
2	0 bytes	Route refresh
3	varies	Cooperative route filtering
64	varies	Graceful restart

One of the more interesting optional capabilities is multiprotocol support. Through it, routers can use BGP to distribute routing information for protocols other than version 4 of IP. The most notable of such protocols is the next version of the Internet Protocol, IPv6. To identify other protocols, BGP uses address family identifier (AFI) values, along with a special subsequent address family identifier (SAFI) that distinguishes unicast from multicast addresses. Table 6.5 lists

Assigning Capability Codes

The BGP specifications divide the possible values for capability codes into three groups. Code values from 1 to 63 are selected using the normal IETF standards process, which requires consensus approval of the Internet's technical community. Code values from 64 to 127 are assigned on a first-come-first-served basis by the Internet Assigned Numbers Authority. Finally, code values from 128 to 255 are reserved for private use and will not be standardized.

several common AFIs, while table 6.6 indicates the SAFI values that BGP recognizes.

Table 6.5 Address Family Identifiers

AFI	Network Address Family
1	IP version 4 addresses
2	IP version 6 addresses
3	ISO network addresses (NSAPs)
11	Novell IPX addresses
12	AppleTalk addresses
13	DECnet phase IV addresses
14	Banyan VINES addresses

Table 6.6 Subsequent Address Family Identifier Values

SAFI	Meaning
1	Addressing for unicast forwarding
2	Addressing for multicast forwarding
3	Addressing for both unicast and multicast forwarding
4	Address including MPLS label information

UPDATE Message

The UPDATE message is how BGP actually transfers routing information. As figure 6.22 shows, each UPDATE message may contain two separate blocks of information. The first block identifies routes that are no longer available. The first two bytes of this block carry the length (in bytes) of the *withdrawn routes* field. That field contains a list of routes that are no longer available through the sending router.

Each route in the list begins with a single byte that contains the length, in bits, of an IP address prefix. The prefix, in as few bytes as necessary, follows. Figure 6.23 shows how a router would withdraw a route to 172.16.0.0/16. Note that the length byte has a value of 16, but only two bytes make up the value.

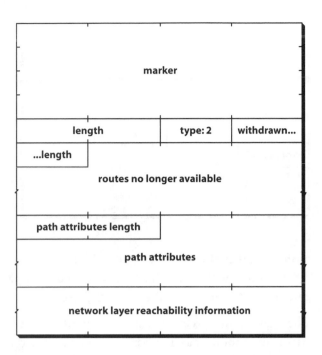

◀ Figure 6.22

A BGP update message first lists routes that are no longer available. It then contains a series of attributes (including, for example, an AS path), and it concludes by describing the destination to which these attributes apply. To advertise paths to multiple destinations, a router must use multiple update messages.

The second block of information in each UPDATE message describes routes that are valid, with one exception. Preceding the routes themselves is a list of attributes that describe the routes. The next section details all the attributes that BGP defines, but they include important characteristics such as the AS path for the routes. The exception to this general rule is a special attribute used to withdraw routes for network

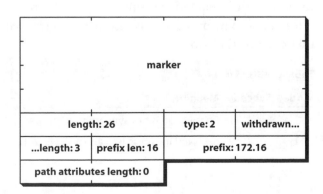

◀ Figure 6.23

This example shows how a BGP router withdraws a router to 172.16.0.0/16. Note that the destination being withdrawn is carried in as few bytes as possible, two in this case.

Figure 6.24 ▶

The BGP notification message reports errors.

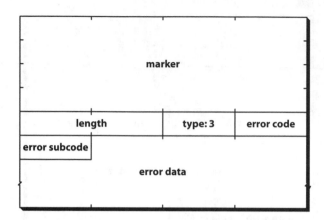

protocols other than version 4 of IP. This attribute, naturally, describes routes that are no longer valid, but it appears in the path attributes section of the UPDATE message.

The valid routes section concludes with a list of routes. Again, each route is an IP address prefix identified by a prefix length (in bits) and the minimum number of bytes required to hold its value. Because the messages attributes apply to all routes in this list, routes can be combined in the same UP-DATE message only if they share the same attributes.

NOTIFICATION Message

Routers use the NOTIFICATION message to report errors to their peers. As figure 6.24 shows, the message contains both an *error code* and an *error subcode*. The code describes the error at a high level, and the subcode provides more detailed information. The message may also include error data to further describe the error.

Table 6.7 BGP Errors

Code	Subcode	Meaning
1	1	Connection is not synchronized properly.
1	2	Received message had an invalid length.
1	3	Received message had an unrecognized type.

Table 6.7 continued

Code	Subcode	Meaning
2	1	OPEN message had an unsupported version number.
2	2	OPEN message had a bad AS.
2	3	OPEN message had a bad BGP identifier.
2	4	OPEN message had an unsupported option.
2	5	OPEN message authentication failed.
2	6	OPEN message had an unacceptable hold time.
2	7	OPEN message included unsupported capability.
3	1	UPDATE message had a malformed attribute list.
3	2	UPDATE message had an unrecognized attribute.
3	3	UPDATE message had a missing attribute.
3	4	UPDATE message attribute flags in error.
3	5	UPDATE message attribute length in error.
3	6	UPDATE message had an invalid ORIGIN attribute.
3	8	UPDATE message had an invalid NEXT HOP attribute.
3	9	UPDATE message optional attribute error.
3	10	UPDATE message had an invalid network field.
3	11	UPDATE message had a malformed PATH attribute.
4		The hold timer has expired.
5		An unexpected event occurred.
6		Connection will be closed.

KEEPALIVE Message

The KEEPALIVE message is BGP's simplest message. Because its only purpose is to provide traffic for the TCP connection, it carries no BGP information itself. As figure 6.25 shows, the message consists of nothing more than the common BGP header.

ROUTE-REFRESH Message

The ROUTE-REFRESH message requests that a peer send its entire routing table. Figure 6.26 shows an example ROUTE-

Figure 6.25 ▶

A BGP keepalive message carriers no information, but it does exercise the TCP connection between the peer routers, keeping that connection active and alive.

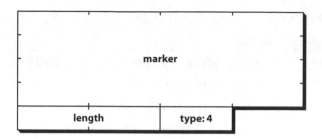

REFRESH message. The only contents of the message are an address family identifier, a reserved byte of zero, and a subsequent address family identifier. The AFI and SAFI, using the same rules as for multiprotocol BGP, identify the specific network protocol for which the sender is requesting a routing table. As in the example figure, the AFI, SAFI values of 1, 1 request IP version 4 routing tables.

Path Attributes

In addition to the routes themselves, path attributes are an important part of every update message. They describe the properties of the routes, including such key properties as the Autonomous System path for the route.

All BGP path attributes generally follow a common format. As figure 6.27 shows, however, the general format has two different manifestations. Both forms begin with a two-byte *attribute type*. An attribute length follows; this length is either one byte or two bytes, depending on the value of a bit in

Figure 6.26 ▶

A BGP route refresh message asks for the entire routing table for a particular network address family.

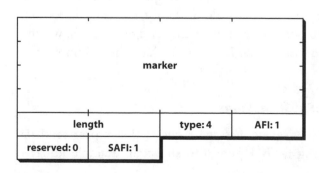

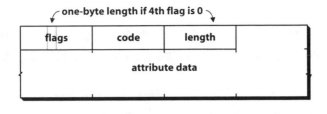

◀ **Figure 6.27**

BGP path attributes have a variable length. The length field identifies the attribute's length, but that field can itself vary in size. A special flag indicates whether the length field is one byte or two bytes in size.

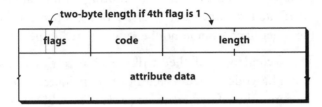

the attribute type. The third part of each attribute is the actual attribute data.

The first eight bits of the attribute type field carry flags that indicate general characteristics for the attribute. Table 6.8 lists the attributes that have so far been defined. (Note that the table numbers the most significant bit of this byte as bit 7, which differs from the convention adopted by the BGP specification.)

Table 6.8 BGP Attribute Type Flags (MSB to LSB)

Bit(s)	Meaning
7	If 1, understanding the attribute is optional.
6	If 1, the optional attribute is transitive and should be redistributed even if it is not understood.
5	If 1, the attribute contains only partial information.
4	If 1, the attribute length field is two bytes in size.
3-0	Reserved; must be transmitted as zero and ignored on reception.

The first two flag bits are important for BGP operation. The first bit designates an attribute as either optional or mandatory. Its setting determines how a router responds when it receives a path attribute that it does not understand. If the attribute is marked as mandatory, the receiving router must report an error. If the attribute is optional, the receiving router can ignore the attribute and continue processing the message.

The second bit further refines the treatment of optional attributes. If the bit is set, the attribute is transitive, and it should be included if the routing information is redistributed to other BGP peers. Nontransitive attributes, on the other hand, should not be redistributed to peer routers.

The second byte of the attribute type carries the *attribute code*. This code actually identifies the attribute. Table 6.9 lists the currently defined attribute codes. The table also indicates which attributes must be understood by all implementations and, if so, whether the attributes must be included in all UPDATE messages. (An attribute whose "Mandatory" column is blank need not be understood by all implementations.) The final column indicates if the optional attributes are transitive or not.

Table 6.9 BGP Attributes

Code	Attribute	Mandatory	Transitive
1	ORIGIN	●	
2	AS_PATH	●	
3	NEXT_HOP	●	
4	MULTI_EXIT_DISC	○	
5	LOCAL_PREF	IBGP	
6	ATOMIC_AGGREGATE	○	
7	AGGREGATOR	○	
8	COMMUNITY		●
9	ORIGINATOR_ID		○
10	CLUSTER_LIST		○
14	MP_REACH_NLRI		○
15	MP_UNREACH_NLRI		○
16	EXTENDED_COMMUNITIES		●

ORIGIN Attribute

The ORIGIN attribute indicates how the network of BGP routers first learned of the routes. This attribute is set by the first BGP router to introduce the routes to its peers. The attribute value consists of a single byte that takes one of three values. A value of 0 indicates that the route originally came from an interior routing protocol such as RIP or OSPF. A value of 1 identifies routes learned through an exterior gateway protocol. Other sources for the routes require a value of 2; this generally means that an administrator statically configured the routes.

AS_PATH Attribute

The AS_PATH attribute lists the autonomous systems that form the path to the routes' destinations. It contains a series of path segments. Each path segment begins with a 1 for SETs and a 2 for SEQUENCEs. The segment then contains a one-byte length field, and it concludes with one or more autonomous system numbers, each 16 bits in size.

NEXT_HOP Attribute

The NEXT_HOP attribute carries the IP address of the router that should be used as the next hop to reach the routes' destinations. Often, this address is that of the router sending the BGP message, but the specification permits a BGP router to advertise a route on behalf of another router.

MULTI_EXIT_DISC Attribute

The MULTI_EXIT_DISC attribute, commonly abbreviated MED, lets an autonomous system express a preference for different routes to the same destination. Figure 6.28 shows an example configuration that can make use of this attribute. In the figure, the two autonomous systems connect to each other on two different links, and they each have BGP routers supporting both links. When autonomous system A needs to

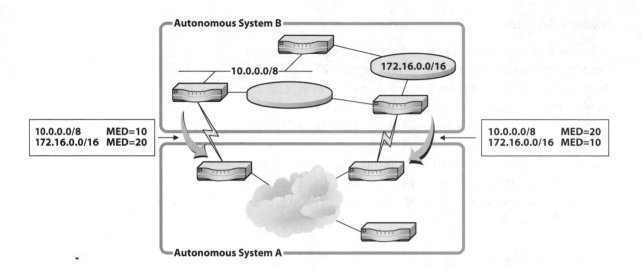

10.0.0.0/8   MED=10
172.16.0.0/16 MED=20

10.0.0.0/8   MED=20
172.16.0.0/16 MED=10

Figure 6.28 ▲

In this example network, there are two different links that connect the autonomous systems. When AS B advertises the subnetworks within it, it can attach a multi-exit discriminator attribute to those destinations. Autonomous system A should prefer the link with the lowest associated MED value when forwarding traffic to a destination. The left link should receive traffic for the Ethernet subnetwork, while the right link is the preferred path to the Token Ring subnetwork.

choose a route through AS B, it has two choices: the left link or the right link.

Autonomous system B can help out AS A by marking destinations with a MED attribute. For example, on the BGP session across link 1, it may mark destinations close to link 1 with a MED value of 10. On the BGP session across link 2, those same destinations may have a MED value of 20. When AS A needs to forward traffic, it will recognize that either link 1 or link 2 can reach those destinations. To choose between the two links, it picks the one with the lower MED value—link 1.

LOCAL_PREF Attribute

While the MULTI_EXIT_DISC attribute helps other ASs pick between multiple paths, the LOCAL_PREF attribute performs a similar function *within* an autonomous system. Administrators can assign local preference values to information learned from various external peers, and BGP routers will include that value in updates distributed within the autonomous system. When a router needs to choose from among several forwarding paths, it picks the path with the highest local preference value.

ATOMIC_AGGREGATE Attribute

The ATOMIC_AGGREGATE attribute has no data value and, therefore, always contains an attribute length of 0. This attribute indicates that the routes were created by aggregating more specific routes together.

AGGREGATOR Attribute

The AGGREGATOR attribute is an optional attribute that identifies the router that originally aggregated the routes. The attribute's length is six bytes; its value is the aggregating router's autonomous system number and IP address.

COMMUNITY Attribute

The COMMUNITY attribute associates routing information with a particular community of users. Such communities generally share some property, and tagging the routes as belonging to the community makes it easier to routers to identify that property and enforce appropriate policies.

The attribute's data consists of a list of four-byte community values. Any autonomous system is free to create its own community values and decide on their meaning. To avoid conflicts, the first two bytes of a community value are the autonomous system number of the AS that created the value. The BGP specification also defines a few community values that begin with $FFFF_{16}$ (which is not a valid AS number). Table 6.10 lists those values.

Table 6.10 Well-Known BGP Community Values

Value	Name	Meaning
$FFFFFF01_{16}$	NO_EXPORT	Routes should not be advertised outside of the confederation (or outside of the autonomous system if confederations are not being used). *continues...*

Table 6.10 Well-Known BGP Community Values (continued)

Value	Name	Meaning
FFFFFF02$_{16}$	NO_ADVERTISE	Routes should not be advertised at all.
FFFFFF03$_{16}$	NO_EXPORT_SUBCONFED	Routes should not be advertised outside of the local member AS within a confederation.

ORIGINATOR_ID Attribute

The ORIGINATOR_ID is one of two attributes that help route reflectors avoid routing loops. Whenever a BGP router reflects a route, it adds this attribute, which carries a value of the router's BGP identifier. If the reflector later receives a route with its own ORIGINATOR_ID value already present, it knows to break the potential loop as it has already seen the route.

CLUSTER_LIST Attribute

The second attribute used with route reflection is the CLUSTER_LIST attribute. This attribute consists of a list of clusters through which a route has been reflected, and every route reflector adds its own cluster ID to the list. If a router receives a route that already contains its own cluster ID in the cluster list, it can ignore the route.

MP_REACH_NLRI Attribute

The MP_REACH_NLRI attribute describes routes for network protocols other than IP version 4. The attribute identifies the network protocol with an address family identifier and a subsequent AFI. It then contains the network address of the next hop router for the destinations, as well as the link level (e.g., Ethernet) addresses for that next hop. The attribute concludes with the destinations expressed as prefixes.

MP_UNREACH_NLRI Attribute

The MP_UNREACH_NLRI attribute withdraws non-IPv4 routes, marking them as no longer available. It includes the route's AFI, SAFI, and network address prefixes.

Summary

Routing between autonomous systems has much the same goal as routing within an AS: figure out how to reach a destination. There are, however, key differences. First among those is the effect of policy. Routing is constrained by policies adopted by each autonomous system, and inter-AS routing protocols must respect those policies. In addition, on a network as large as the Internet, inter-AS routing must pay careful attention to scalability. The Internet includes hundreds of thousands of separate destination routes.

The Internet's inter-AS routing protocol, BGP, addresses these concerns by using path-vector routing. A variant of distance-vector routing, path-vector routing advertises the full path to a destination in addition to the next hop. By exposing the full path, BGP lets its routers make informed policy decisions. Path-vector routing also eliminates the flooding traffic of link-state protocols, and, by using reliable TCP connections, BGP avoids the periodic broadcasts of RIP. These steps significantly enhance the protocol's scalability, allowing it to cope with the full Internet.

CHAPTER 7

MPLS—Multi-Protocol Label Switching

Until this chapter, we have focused on traditional IP routing. All systems in the path between two communicating hosts are routers, and those routers rely on routing protocols to learn the network topology and IP headers to make forwarding decisions. Traditional IP routing, however, does have a few limitations that, in some networks, can be significant.

One of the problems with traditional IP routing is that it forces a "winner-take-all" forwarding decision. Generally, all datagrams with the same IP destination address follow the same path through the network, even if other paths are available. That behavior can result in a situation shown in figure 7.1. In that figure, the top path carries so much traffic that it becomes congested, even though the bottom path, which also reaches the destination, remains idle.

Another problem with traditional IP routing is that it relies on rather coarse attributes for picking the best paths. Routing protocols like RIP, OSPF, and BGP generally select paths by minimizing the number of hops to the destination. Administrators have a limited ability to influence route selection by,

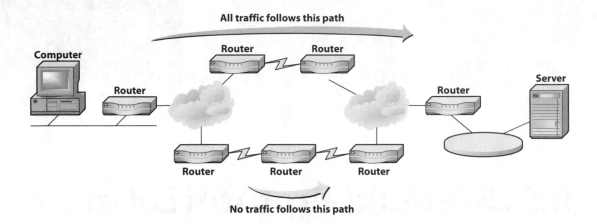

Figure 7.1 ▲

Traditional IP routing forces all traffic bound for the same destination along the same path. This behavior can leave some parts of a network idle, while others are at capacity.

for example, artificially inflating RIP's metric cost. This capability is difficult to employ in a concerted way, however, and it doesn't allow subtle adjustments based on multiple factors.

Traditional IP routing and forwarding can also be complex. As we've seen in the previous three chapters, routing protocols are not simple, and they can require significant computational and memory resources. The forwarding process can also be rather complex, as it generally requires parsing and processing the entire IP header, as well as looking up an appropriate path in the routing tables.

MPLS Operation

A new addition to the IP architecture—IP switching—addresses these concerns. In fact, the technology can support architectures built on protocols other than IP as well. Its official name is Multi-Protocol Label Switching, or MPLS.

Labels

The central concept behind MPLS is the *label*. Packets are assigned a label when they enter an MPLS network, and the network uses that label, rather than an IP address, to deliver packets to their destination. Figure 7.2 shows an example.

The PC in that figure is simultaneously communicating with two different servers, and it can reach both servers across an MPLS network. As the figure indicates, routers in an MPLS network are known as label switched routers, or LSRs.

When the PC sends a datagram for the top server, the ingress router recognizes the destination and assigns that packet a black label. Packets bound for the bottom server, on the other hand, receive a gray label. Once the packets have their appropriate labels, LSRs within the network no longer have to care about IP routing or forwarding. They simply direct the packet based on its label. The second router in the path, for example, has a very simple switching decision. If the label is black, send the packet to router C, and if it's gray, send it to router D.

Figure 7.2 shows different labels as shades of gray, but, generally, that's not what appears in real packets. (In optical networking, however, MPLS labels may literally be DWDM colors.) On most networks, labels are numbers. And, because a label determines how to forward a packet, it is a little like an IP destination address. A big difference between the two, however, is their scope. A legitimate IP address is unique in all the world. Its assignment must be coordinated among all

▼ **Figure 7.2**

When a router assigns an MPLS label to a datagram, that label defines the datagram's full path through the MPLS network.

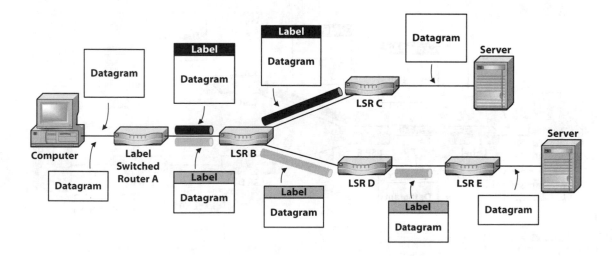

possible systems, and it is possible to unambiguously interpret an IP address anywhere on the network. Those properties make IP routing and forwarding complicated. An MPLS
label, on the other hand, has only local significance. A given
label value is significant only on a particular link between
two LSRs. Two other LSRs elsewhere in the network can reuse
the same label value without conflict. Label assignments do
not have to be coordinated across an entire network, and a
given LSR has to understand only label values that it directly
uses.

Because labels have only local significance, their actual values
can change as a packet traverses an MPLS network. Take a
look at figure 7.3. This time we've added actual label values to
the colors. As you can see, a label changes its value as it
moves from LSR to LSR, and the same value can appear in
different places. The label value 44, for example, is used between LSRs A and B and between LSRs D and E. Even though
the actual label value may change as a packet travels across a
network, however, the packet's path through the network is
completely determined by the initial label the ingress LSR
assigns it. This complete path is known as the *label switched
path* (LSP). Each router along the path maintains a mapping

Figure 7.3 ▼

Actual label values may change at
each hop, but the path that the
labels represent does not change.
Label values are just a local
identifier for that path; they only
have significance on a single link.

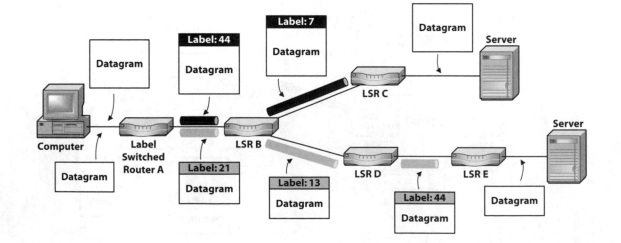

table. That table takes an incoming interface and label value and maps it to an outgoing interface and label value. When a packet arrives, the LSR finds its incoming interface and label value in the table, changes the label to its new value (from the table), and sends it on the outgoing interface. This process is much simpler than traditional IP forwarding, and it is easily more relegated to special-purpose (and extremely fast) hardware.

Selecting Labels

When the ingress router assigns an initial label to a packet, that label determines the packet's full path through the MPLS network. The task of making that initial assignment is critical to the network's operation. Ingress routers select a label by determining the packet's *forwarding equivalence class*, or FEC. The FEC controls the packet's path through the network and the forwarding treatment it will receive along that path.

One of the features that MPLS offers network administrators is greater control over the forwarding behavior of their networks. The FEC is the heart of that control. Unlike traditional IP forwarding, which is generally based strictly on the IP destination address and possibly the diffserv codepoint, forwarding equivalence classes can take into account many different factors. Ingress routers can consider the packet's application protocol, its source host, the link on which it arrived, quality of service constraints, service level agreements, current network conditions, virtual private network requirements, and an almost unlimited list of other factors. This flexibility, combined with the accelerated forwarding performance, is what makes MPLS so attractive.

Distributing Labels

Even though an MPLS label doesn't have global significance, its value does matter to the two systems that use it. As figure 7.4 shows, MPLS refers to those two systems as the upstream router and the downstream router. Any particular label

Figure 7.4 ▶

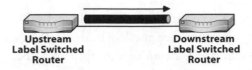

At every hop along an MPLS path one router is the upstream router and its peer is the downstream router. The downstream router for one hop becomes the upstream router for the next hop.

switched path consists of a series of upstream-downstream hops. The downstream router for one hop becomes the upstream router for the next hop.

For any given hop, the downstream and upstream routers must agree on the meaning for all MPLS labels. The process by which they reach that agreement is label distribution. Full-featured label distribution protocols are the subject of the next two chapters, but there are some important general principles.

The most important principle is that the downstream router ultimately picks the label values. This procedure is critical when MPLS operates over multi-access links such as Ethernet. It's the only way to ensure that a label value for an incoming link is unique. Consider figure 7.5. If the downstream router (on the right) let the upstream routers pick label values, both upstream routers might pick the same value. That would complicate the operation of the downstream router; the path corresponding to any particular label would depend not just on the incoming interface, but also on the previous hop. Having the downstream router pick label values avoids this problem. When making its choices, the downstream router merely makes sure that, as far as it is concerned, all label values are unique for an interface.

Figure 7.5 ▶

Because a single router may serve as the downstream router for many paths at once, that downstream router picks label values to ensure their uniqueness. If the upstream routers picked, they might both pick the same value.

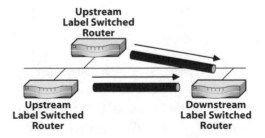

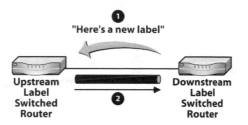

◀ Figure 7.6

If a downstream router wishes, it can simply announce a new label to its upstream peer. This approach is downstream unsolicited label distribution.

Even though downstream routers pick label values, the trigger that generates a new label can come from either router. When the downstream router decides, on its own, to create a new label switched path, it simply informs the upstream router of its decision. This process, shown in figure 7.6, is known as *downstream unsolicited* label distribution.

Figure 7.7 shows a different process. In that figure, the upstream router makes the decision to create a new MPLS label. The upstream router cannot pick the label value, however. Instead, it sends a request to the downstream router, asking that router to pick a label. This mode is *downstream on demand* label distribution.

Label Stacks

Although we've discussed a straightforward implementation of MPLS so far, the specification does suffer a bit from "if one is good, two labels are better." Based on that philosophy, the MPLS standards define the concept of a label stack. Label stacks allow the creation of nested label switched paths, in

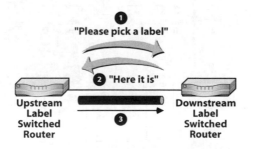

◀ Figure 7.7

The upstream router can't announce a new label; it must explicitly ask for one. This approach is downstream on demand label distribution.

Figure 7.8 ▶

This autonomous system provides transit services and connects to three other autonomous systems. Because router D has to know how to forward transit traffic appropriately, it must maintain full routing information for all the external autonomous systems.

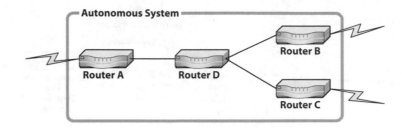

which one large LSP uses several smaller LSPs on the way to its destination.

To understand the usefulness of label stacks, consider the example of figure 7.8. That figure shows an autonomous system that provides transit services to the three other ASs that connect to it. In this figure, no MPLS services are used. Consequently, routers within the autonomous system must understand the full Internet routing, even if they don't participate in BGP sessions. Router D, for example, has to know which BGP router should be the next hop for every transit packet. Effectively, this requires router D to maintain a routing table for the full Internet. This requirement can represent a considerable burden for router D.

Figure 7.9 uses MPLS to ease the burden on router D (and on any other interior routers in the AS). Here, the three BGP routers have established label switched paths among themselves. When a transit packet arrives at A, it determines

Figure 7.9 ▶

If the autonomous system supports MPLS, router D can avoid maintaining full routing tables. Instead, the border router simply assigns an appropriate label to the traffic as it enters the transit AS. Since the border routers do have to know the full external routing, they'll know which path to use.

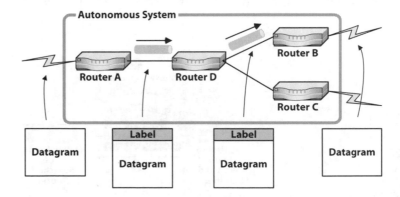

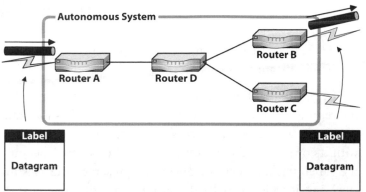

◀ **Figure 7.10**

Autonomous systems providing transit services may wish to provide transit for MPLS paths. In such cases, the AS must treat those paths appropriately within its network.

which path to use and adds the appropriate label information. Router D, which is also a label switched router, merely looks at the MPLS label and forwards the packet on to router B. With MPLS, the interior routers need not track the full Internet routing table.

So far, we haven't uncovered a need for label stacks, but now consider figure 7.10. In that figure, transit packets are themselves using a label switched path. The AS's BGP routers are merely LSRs on the transit traffic's paths. One implementation of this scenario is to extend the label switched paths into the autonomous system, as in figure 7.11. Using appropriate label distribution techniques, router D becomes a hop in all label switched paths. The problem with this approach,

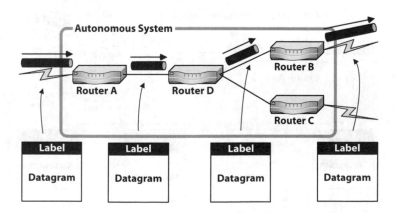

◀ **Figure 7.11**

If an autonomous system simply extends external paths into its network, interior routers again face a problem. They have to maintain information for all external paths passing through the network.

though, is that it requires router D to track all possible LSPs through the network. If the autonomous system handles a lot of transit LSPs, then the burden on router D once again becomes significant.

Figure 7.12 shows how label stacks solve this problem. In the figure, the BGP routers continue to maintain their short label switched paths to each other. When a transit packet arrives with its own label, the ingress router pushes a new label onto the label stack. The push operation preserves the existing label, but it adds a new label that takes priority. The new label serves to deliver the packet to the egress router for the AS. There, the new label is popped off the stack, restoring the original MPLS label. From the egress router the packet resumes its travel using the original label switched path.

Support for label stacks does add one more complication to MPLS processing in label switched routers. Without stacks, LSRs merely needed to map <incoming interface, label> to <outgoing interface, label>. With stacks, LSRs now have to take into account stack processing. When a packet arrives, the LSR may have to push a new label onto the stack or pop an old label off of the stack, in addition to its normal switching behavior.

Label stacks highlight a potential optimization that's available to all MPLS routers—*penultimate hop popping*. Figure 7.13

Figure 7.12 ▶

With label stacks, interior routers don't have to know about all the external MPLS paths. Instead, the ingress router assigns the datagram to an interior path which carries the datagram through the autonomous system. The egress router removes the interior path information, allowing the datagram to continue along its external path.

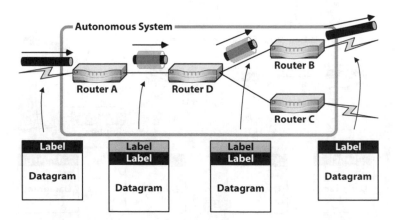

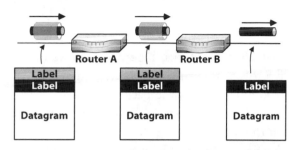

◀ **Figure 7.13**

When label stacks are in use, the egress router may have to perform two MPLS lookups on a single datagram. Here, router B has to first lookup the interior (gray) label to determine that it should pop the label stack. That action uncovers the external (black) label, which router B also has to look up to determine where to send the datagram.

offers a good example. In the figure, the packet arrives at router B with a stack depth of two labels. The topmost label represents the short path through the autonomous system, and the second label represents the longer path across the transit AS. When the packet arrives at router B, it has to perform two distinct MPLS operations. First, it has to examine the topmost label. Its mapping table for that label will tell it to pop the label stack. Doing that exposes the second label, and the router has to consult its mapping table once again to determine the next hop for the packet. For high-speed switching devices, doubling the number of MPLS operations can slow down performance.

As an optimization, router D could pop the label stack before sending the packet on to router B. Figure 7.14 illustrates this operation. In this scenario, both router B and D need only perform one MPLS mapping operation. Router D determines from its mapping table that it should (1) send the packet to router B, and (2) pop the stack. When router B receives the packet, the label stack is already adjusted for the transit path, so router B needs to use only its mapping table to find the next hop.

▼ **Figure 7.14**

Penultimate hop popping removes the topmost label from a label stack one hop earlier than necessary. Here, router A looks up the interior (gray) label and determines that the next hop is router B. It also determines that router B is the last router in the path. Knowing this information, router A takes a shortcut and removes the topmost label from the stack before forwarding the datagram. Note that router A doesn't have to perform a second lookup on the datagram; it already knows router B is the next hop.

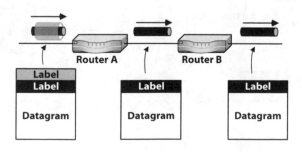

Penultimate hop popping is a relatively obvious optimization for label stacks, but it can also benefit MPLS implementations that don't use stacks. Figure 7.15 shows the same network as figure 7.2; this time, however, router B pops the label stack before it forwards the packet to router C. When there's only one label on the stack, popping it simply removes all label information, restoring the packet to its non-MPLS format. As the figure shows, this means that router C receives a normal IP datagram, which it subjects to normal IP forwarding. Assuming that the label switched path ends at router C (rather than the top server), the router would have to perform normal IP forwarding anyway to send the packet to the server. By popping the stack, however, router B saves router C from having to do an MPLS mapping.

MPLS Message Formats

Figure 7.15 ▼

Penultimate hop popping is also effective when there are no label stacks in use. Here, LSR B pops the MPLS stack on hop earlier than normal. This action saves LSR C from having to perform an MPLS lookup, though it still must look up the datagram's destination address to forward it appropriately.

The MPLS specifications actually provide many different ways to carry labels in packets. Some network technologies—notably frame relay and asynchronous transfer mode—have natural mechanisms for carrying labels built into their protocols. For those networks, MPLS simply uses the existing protocol fields. Other network technologies, however, don't have natural label mechanisms included within them. The generic MPLS format accommodates those technologies.

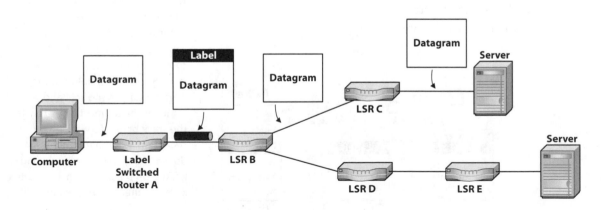

Generic MPLS

The generic MPLS format is deliberately simple. The label stack is simply prepended to the IP datagram. Figure 7.16 shows an example. As the figure shows, each entry in the stack is 32 bits in size. Each entry consists of a 20-bit label, three bits whose use is reserved for future extensions, one bit that flags the bottom of the stack, and eight bits for a hop limit.

The stack bottom bit is set only on the last (bottom) entry of the label stack. When an LSR pops an entry off the stack, this bit tells the LSR whether the remaining packet has any additional labels or whether it is a standard IP datagram.

The hop limit field (also known as the *time to live*, or TTL, field) replaces the IP datagram's hop limit count. Because label switched routers don't normally process the IP header of the datagrams they forward, they don't have an opportunity to adjust the hop limit appropriately. Including this field in the MPLS header lets LSRs achieve the same results.

When an ingress router first attaches a label to a datagram, it should take the hop limit value from that datagram and insert that value in the label stack. As the packet traverses its label switched path, each LSR decrements the hop limit by one. Should the hop limit reach zero, the label switched

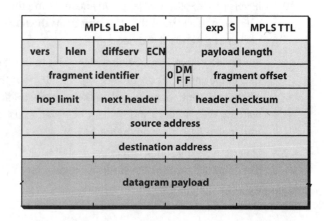

◀ **Figure 7.16**

MPLS adds a simple four-byte header to IP datagrams.

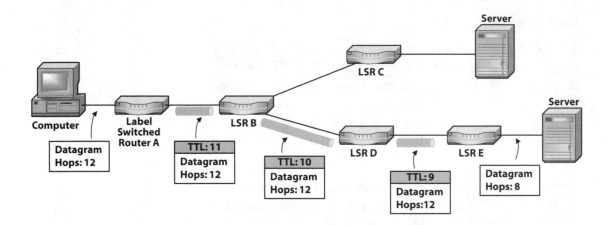

Figure 7.17 ▲

The MPLS header includes its own time-to-live field, which serves as an IP hop limit within the MPLS network. Once the datagram leaves the MPLS path, the egress router adjusts its IP hop limit to account for the MPLS hops.

router should pop the entire label stack and return an ICMP time exceeded message to the datagram's source. Once a datagram reaches the egress LSR, that router must replace the datagram's IP hop limit with the hop limit value it would use on the LSP. Figure 7.17 shows the interaction between IP and MPLS hop limits as a packet travels across a network.

The label value itself can take on almost any value. The MPLS specification, however, reserves a few key values. Table 7.1 lists those reserved values.

Table 7.1 Reserved MPLS Label Values

Value	Meaning
0	IP version 4 explicit null label. On encountering this label, an LSP immediately pops the stack and treats the remaining packet as a standard IP datagram.
1	Router alert label. This label provides a hint to the LSR that the packet may need special processing. The LSR pops this label off the stack and routes based on the next label. Before forwarding the packet to another LSR, however, it pushes the router alert label back on the stack.
2	IP version 6 explicit null label. On encountering this label, an LSP immediately pops the stack and treats the remaining packet as a standard IPv6 datagram.

Table 7.1 continued

Value	Meaning
3	Implicit null label. This label never appears in an actual datagram, but label distribution protocols may use this value to indicate that it should pop the stack rather than adding a new label.
4-15	These values are reserved for future extensions.

By adding a label stack, generic MPLS increases the size of the datagram. That creates a problem if the new packet grows so large that it no longer fits across a link. This can cause particular headaches to applications that try to precisely judge the size of their data to make sure that packets fit across all links on the network, but it is an unavoidable consequence of adding a label stack.

One solution has the ingress LSR of every path know the smallest maximum packet size supported by the path. If it receives a datagram bigger than this maximum (and the datagram's don't fragment bit in the IP header is clear), the router can fragment the datagram before labeling it.

If an LSR inside an MPLS network finds that a labeled packet won't fit across a link, it reverts to a normal IP router. First, it removes all the labels from the datagram. If the resulting IP datagram permits fragmentation, the router fragments it appropriately and adds a copy of the original label stack to each fragment. If the datagram does not allow fragmentation, the router returns an ICMP error message to the datagram's source.

MPLS and Frame Relay

If, as in figure 7.18, an MPLS network includes frame relay switches, then MPLS can take advantage of inherent characteristics of the network technology. In particular, label switched routers can use the frame relay *Data Link Connection Identifier* (DLCI) as the topmost label of the label stack. The rest of the stack (including the topmost entry) is still

Figure 7.18 ▶

In a frame relay network, the data link connection identifier (DLCI) serves as the MPLS label. No MPLS headers are needed.

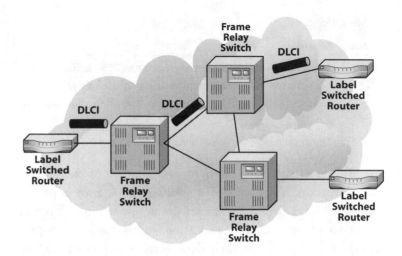

carried in the packet as with generic MPLS; the generic encoding carries the time to live and bottom of stack indicator.

In a frame relay network, the DLCI acts much the same as an MPLS label. It identifies a path through the network, and it has local significance between frame relay switches. Unlike generic MPLS labels, DLCI values are either 10 bits or 23 bits in size, but, because they have only local significance anyway, that presents no problem. More troublesome is the fact that frame relay does not support the hop limit concept. To compensate, ingress LSRs should decrement the hop limit before placing the packet onto the label switched path. If possible, they should decrement the hop limit by a number equal to the number of frame relay switches in the path. Unfortunately, this information may not be available to the ingress LSR. In such cases, the switch can decrement the hop limit only by one, and the entire label switched path will be treated as a single hop by the datagram.

MPLS and Asynchronous Transfer Mode

Asynchronous transfer mode (ATM) networks can also provide natural support for MPLS. For ATM, the combination of *virtual path identifier* (VPI) and *virtual circuit identifier* (VCI) distinguishes connections between adjacent switches. If the switches are both label switched routers, then the VPI/VCI value can serve as an MPLS label value. As with MPLS generic labels, the VPI/VCI combination has only local significance.

Even when two switches are not adjacent in an ATM network, they can still serve as adjacent label switched routers. Figure 7.19 shows this case. In the figure LSR A and LSR B are separated by an entire ATM network, none of whose interior switches understand MPLS. Nonetheless, A and B can establish an MPLS adjacency through a virtual path between them. For such a link, only ATM's VCI is available to MPLS, and it is that field alone that carries the MPLS label.

Just as is the case with frame relay, ATM switches are not able to track the hop limit field. Consequently, the ingress LSR should decrement the hop limit by a number equal to the number of ATM switches in the path. If the ingress router doesn't know that value, it can decrement the hop limit by one, treating the entire ATM network as a single IP hop.

MPLS and ICMP

Because MPLS distorts the standard IP architecture, it influences not only IP routing and forwarding, but also associated

▼ **Figure 7.19**

In ATM networks, the virtual path and virtual circuit identifiers serve as MPLS labels.

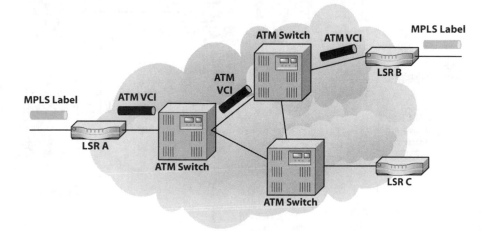

network protocols such as ICMP. There are two different types of interactions between MPLS and ICMP. First, ICMP must continue to operate appropriately in an MPLS environment, and, second, ICMP can enhance the operation of MPLS networks by providing diagnostics specific to MPLS.

As we've seen, there are several cases in which a label switched router in the middle of a path needs to return an ICMP error message to a datagram's source. The datagram's hop limit may run out, or the packet may encounter a link over which it cannot fit. In most of these cases, the LSR can simply pop the original datagram's label stack and perform normal ICMP processing. In some cases, however, that approach won't work. Consider the example of figure 7.20. In that figure, MPLS provides a virtual private network between two locations. The MPLS network operates across the public Internet, yet the two subnetworks use private IP addresses.

Figure 7.20 ▼

In this example, LSR D faces a dilemma. It needs to report an ICMP error to the datagram's sender, but that sender is using an IP address that LSR D does not know how to reach.

When a label switched router within the network needs to return an ICMP error message, it may be distressed to find that the source IP address in the offending datagram is a private address. Because the LSR is in the middle of the public Internet, it will have no way to route to that IP address.

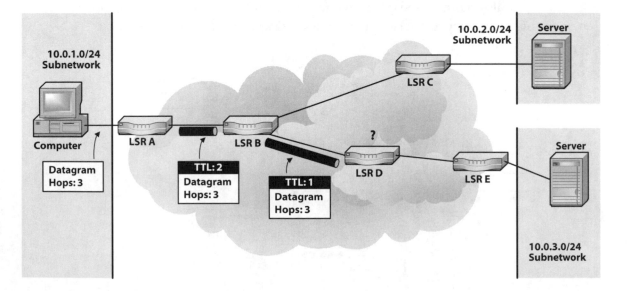

Figure 7.21 shows the solution to the LSR's dilemma. The router creates the ICMP error message and then adds the original datagram's label stack. In most cases the router will modify the stack's hop limit to ensure that the ICMP message won't expire. The router then takes the resulting packet and switches it normally. As the figure illustrates, this approach has the curious effect of initially sending the packet away from its destination. That behavior, however, makes sure that the packet reaches a point that can successfully interpret its addresses. The egress LSR must be able to understand the original datagram's IP addresses. Once the ICMP message reaches the egress LSR, it reverses direction and travels to its ultimate destination.

The main purpose of ICMP is to report errors and provide diagnostic information. In an MPLS network, it might often be useful to include MPLS-specific details along with any ICMP diagnostic information. One useful service, for example, would be to return MPLS label stacks to the `traceroute` application. The sample output below shows how an enhanced `traceroute` could display MPLS information from

▼ **Figure 7.21**

To resolve its dilemma, LSR D forwards the ICMP error message onward though the same path that the datagram was taking. This direction may seem backwards, but once the error message reaches the egress router, that router must know how to reach the original datagram's source. LSR E can send the error to its destination.

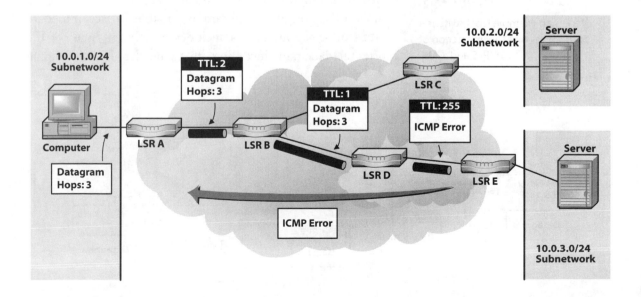

the network in figure 7.22. Notice that only hops 2, 3, and 4, return label information in their ICMP response.

```
> traceroute -n -q 1 166.45.2.7

traceroute to 166.45.2.74, 30 hops max

    1   166.45.5.1   101 ms
    2   166.45.4.1   120 ms   mplsLabel1=2001
    3   166.45.3.1   130 ms   mplsLabel1=2002
    4   166.45.6.1   131 ms   mplsLabel1=2003
    5   166.45.2.7   120 ms
>
```

To provide these kinds of services, label switched routers can modify several ICMP message types, including destination unreachable and time exceeded. Unfortunately, the ICMP specification does not include an easy way to add options to its messages, so LSRs have to resort to a bit of trickery to add MPLS information to these messages.

As we saw in figure 2.27 on page 55, ICMP error messages conclude with a copy of the datagram that caused the error. The ICMP standard specifies that only the first 8 payload bytes of the original datagram are carried in error messages, although other Internet standards suggest appending as much of the original datagram as possible. To accommodate MPLS information, an LSR includes exactly 128 bytes of the original datagram, including its IP header. If the original

Figure 7.22 ▼

Here is an example label switched path that shows the interaction of MPLS and ICMP.

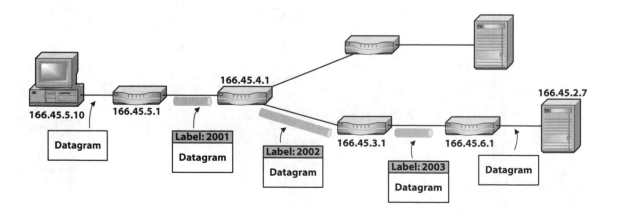

datagram is less than 128 bytes in size, then the LSR should add enough bytes, each with a value of zero, to lengthen the message. Then, at the 129th byte after the start of the original datagram, the LSR appends its MPLS diagnostic information. Figure 7.23 shows a resulting time exceeded message.

The MPLS-specific information uses the format shown in figure 7.23. Each MPLS object begins with a common header. The first four bits of this header carry a version number. (The current version is 2.) The last two bytes are a standard IP one's complement checksum of the object, and the bits in between are reserved for future extensions. The object then continues with a two-byte length field, one byte for the object class and another byte for the object type. The object data follows. To add an MPLS label stack, LSRs use a class and type of 1. The object data is then simply the label stack itself, as in the figure.

The only other class and type so far defined are a class of 2 and a type of 1. That object is the extended payload object, and it is used to carry the rest of the original datagram, beginning with byte number 129.

▼ Figure 7.23

Here is a sample ICMP message with MPLS information. The sender indicates the presence of MPLS information by including exactly 128 bytes from the original datagram in error.

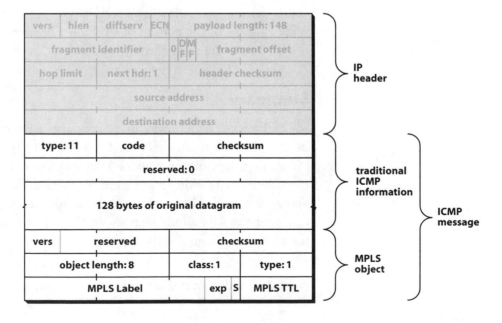

This trick format does present a challenge to a system that receives an ICMP error message: How is that system supposed to know whether the message contains any MPLS extensions? Unfortunately, there are no foolproof ways to make that determination. If the original datagram part of the message is greater than 128 bytes in length, and if the information at the 129th byte looks like an MPLS extension (in other words, it has an appropriate version, checksum, length, class, and type), then the recipient can probably assume that an MPLS extension really is there.

MPLS and BGP

If two BGP peers are also label switched routers, they can use BGP itself to exchange label information. To do that, they associate an MPLS label with each destination they advertise. To carry that information, the routers uses the multi-protocol extensions to BGP. Label stacks are carried in the same attribute as the destination addressing information, except that the subsequent address identifier is set to 4. A SAFI value of 4 indicates that label information precedes the actual destination address. The recipient must parse the label stack looking for the bottom of stack bit to determine where the label stack ends and the network address begins.

Summary

Multi-Protocol Label Switching introduces a major wrinkle in the standard IP architecture. In addition to routing and forwarding, intermediate nodes take on the additional responsibility of IP switching. In return, these nodes may recognize a considerable performance improvement, and they can offer network administrators much greater control over the routing of the network's traffic.

For network technologies such as frame relay and ATM, MPLS is a trivial addition; it simply attaches additional meaning to fields that are already present in those technologies' protocol headers. To accommodate other network technologies, MPLS prepends a shim header before the normal IP datagram. This header carries the MPLS label information.

As of this writing, MPLS is still a very new technology, and network engineers are still developing the experience they need to use it effectively and appropriately. The technology holds great promise, however, in improving the performance and flexibility of IP-based networks.

CHAPTER 8

LDP—Label Distribution Protocol

Multi-Protocol Label Switching can provide important benefits to IP networks, but only if label switched routers can successfully share label values. Sharing labels is the job of the Label Distribution Protocol, or LDP. Even though LDP was developed specifically for MPLS, however, it is not the only way that LSRs can share their label information. As chapter 7 discusses, routers can use BGP to exchange labels, and similar extensions are under development for other routing protocols such as OSPF. Despite those efforts, LDP is expected to be one of the two primary label exchange protocols. The other, RSVP, is the subject of the next chapter.

LDP Operation

In its operation, the Label Distribution Protocol resembles a combination of OSPF and BGP. Like OSPF, LDP provides a way for neighbors to meet each other automatically. And like BGP, LDP neighbors use TCP connections to establish a reliable communication channel. Unique to LDP are its procedures for exchanging label information.

Meeting Neighbors

Before two label switched routers can exchange label information, they have to meet each other. Neighbor greeting is the first phase in LDP's operation. The basic discovery procedure is much the same as OSPF's: Each LSR multicasts a hello message on all its interfaces. Figure 8.1 shows this step for a router connected both to a local area network and a point-to-point link.

One advantage that LDP has over OSPF is that LDP can rely on an operating IP network. LDP can, like any application protocol, use standard UDP to send these multicast messages. Multicast hello messages have as their destination the all routers multicast address and the well-known UDP port of 646.

Because LDP can safely use regular IP forwarding to transfer its hello messages, LDP "neighbors" don't have to be adjacent to each other on the network. In some cases, it's useful for label switched routers on the opposite sides of entire networks to exchange information with each other. Consider the example of the previous chapter, where an internal label switched path acts as a tunnel across a backbone network for an external LSP. Figure 8.2 repeats the example of figure 7.12. In this case LSR A and LSR B need to exchange information for the external path, even though the entire backbone network separates them. For these two routers to meet each other, they must exchange a targeted hello message. A targeted hello message looks the same as the normal hello message, except that its destination IP address is a specific IP address rather than the all routers multicast address. How each router learns the IP address of its "neighbor" is not, in this case, a concern of the label distribution protocol.

Figure 8.1 ▶

Label switched routers first use LDP to meet their peers. They do so by exchanging hello messages.

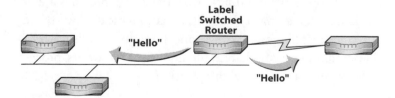

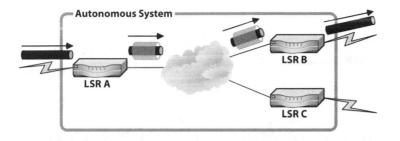

◀ **Figure 8.2**

As this example illustrates, LDP peers—such as LSR A and LSR B—don't have to be adjacent to each other. They may be separated by many subnetworks. Because hello messages travel in UDP datagrams, however, the peers can still establish communications.

Each hello message, indeed every LDP message, has an LDP identifier. This parameter uniquely identifies the label space appropriate to the message. Because downstream routers define label values, part of the LDP identifier is a unique, 32-bit router ID. Generally this router ID is one of the IP addresses assigned to the router because that's guaranteed to be unique. The LDP identifier also includes two bytes to distinguish different label spaces within the same router. A router may choose to maintain only one label space, in which case these two extra bytes are always zero. Alternatively, a router may manage multiple label spaces simultaneously. The latter case may be useful, for example, if the router wants to manage separate label spaces for each of its interfaces.

In addition to the LDP identifier, hello messages can optionally carry an IP address. This value tells recipients how to contact the router in the next LDP phase, session establishment. If there is no IP address parameter present, recipients use the source IP address from the hello message.

Establishing Sessions

Once two label switched routers exchange hello messages, they are ready to establish an LDP session. The LSR with the numerically greatest IP address initiates a TCP connection; the other router passively listens. If desirable, LDP can require the use of TCP's MD5 signature option. This feature works just as it does for BGP. The two routers share a secret value and create a message digest of each TCP segment combined with this secret value. The receiving router can check the message digest value and, if it doesn't match what it would have computed, reject the segment. This option provides some protection against malicious (or accidental) injection of false label information into an LSR network.

The same router that initiates the TCP connection continues the session establishment by sending the first LDP initialization message. This message proposes several parameters for the session, including LDP version, distribution method, timer values, and, if appropriate, ATM or frame relay parameters. The peer LSR responds with its own initialization or error notification message that accepts or rejects those parameters. If it doesn't like the response, the first router can propose new parameters with a new initialization message. This router, known as the *active LSR*, must be careful, however, to avoid an endless propose/reject cycle. The first time it proposes new parameters, the active router waits 15 seconds. The next time the delay doubles to 30 seconds. With each rejection the active router doubles its delay until the delay reaches a value of 2 minutes.

Exchanging Labels

As chapter 7 mentions, either the upstream or the downstream router can initiate the creation of a label switched path. If, as in figure 8.3, the downstream router initiates the path, it informs the upstream router in an advertisement discipline known as *downstream unsolicited*. If, on the other hand, the upstream router initiates creation of the LSP, the upstream router requests a new label in an advertisement

Figure 8.3 ▶

When LDP operates in downstream unsolicited mode, the downstream LSR initiates a label exchange independent of any actions by the upstream LSR.

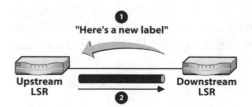

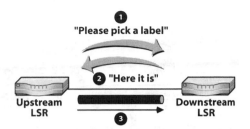

◀ Figure 8.4

With downstream on demand operation, the upstream LSR uses LDP to explicitly request a label from its downstream peer.

discipline known as *downstream on demand*, shown in figure 8.4. In either case, though, it is the downstream router that assigns the label to the path.

In addition to these advertisement disciplines, LDP supports two different label distribution control modes: *independent* and *ordered*. Under independent control, each LSR advertises label mappings at will. In an unsolicited discipline, independent LSRs will generally advertise new labels whenever the IP routing information changes. Figure 8.5 shows this case. When the OSPF advertisement arrives, the router learns of a new route and advertises a corresponding new LSP. If the advertisement discipline is on demand, an independent LSR responds to new requests immediately, without any action with other LSRs further downstream, as in figure 8.6.

Ordered control, on the other hand, requires coordination of all the LSRs in a path. In this mode an LSR advertises a label mapping only if the next hop mapping already exists. For independent routers, this mode requires that all path advertisements originate at the egress router. As in figure 8.7, only the rightmost LSR can initiate the path. Its label advertisement messages travel upstream to the ingress router. If the

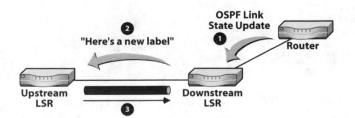

◀ Figure 8.5

Independent control allows each hop to establish labels independent of any other hops along the ultimate path. Here, the downstream LSR creates a new label on its own when a new router is available.

Figure 8.6 ▶

Independent control for downstream on demand puts each downstream LSR completely in charge of the hop. Here, LSR B assigns a label before consulting with LSR C.

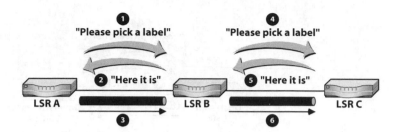

advertisement discipline is on demand, then a request from the ingress router triggers additional requests, one after the other, downstream to the egress router. As figure 8.8 shows, only after the egress router answers the request can a response travel upstream to the initial requester.

Label Retention

Label switched routers using LDP can choose from two different strategies for keeping label information. One strategy, known as *conservative label retention*, retains label mappings only if they correspond to the next hop in the IP forwarding path. In figure 8.9, for example, LSR B initially has a path to the destination through LSR C. When the network topology changes and LSR C is no longer the next hop in the IP forwarding path, LSR B discards the label switched path through LSR C as well. When LSRs combine conservative label retention with a downstream-on-demand advertising discipline, they request mappings only from next hops in the IP forwarding path. In the case of figure 8.9, LSR B requests a label only from LSR D, the new next hop for the destination.

Figure 8.7 ▼

Ordered control requires coordination of the entire path before any labels are assigned. With unsolicited distribution, only the egress router can initiate a new label distribution.

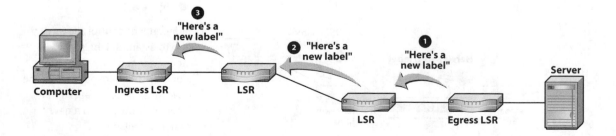

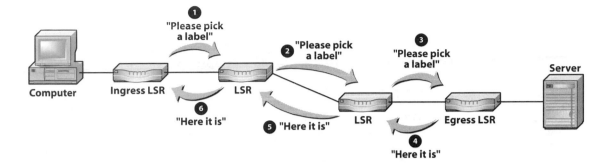

As an alternative to this approach, routers may use *liberal label retention*. With liberal retention, a router remembers label mappings even if they don't correspond to IP forwarding paths. In the case of downstream-on-demand advertising, a router may request a mapping from all of its neighbors, not just the next IP hop. Figure 8.10 shows the situation in this case; LSR B asks each of its neighbors for a label to the destination server. If, as in the figure, the next hop path changes, LSR B may already have a new LSP ready, so it can react to the routing change almost immediately.

▲ **Figure 8.8**

Ordered control for on demand distribution has each LSR wait on its downstream peer before responding to a request.

▼ **Figure 8.9**

Conservative label retention means LSR B can only ask for a backup LSP after the primary fails.

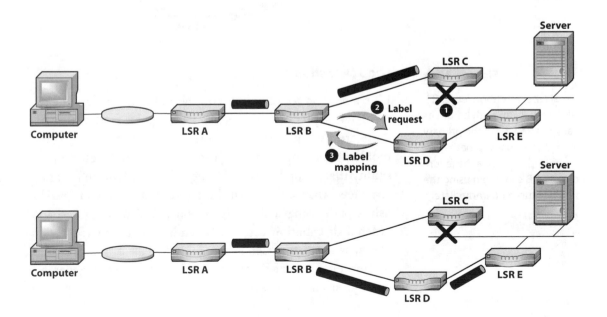

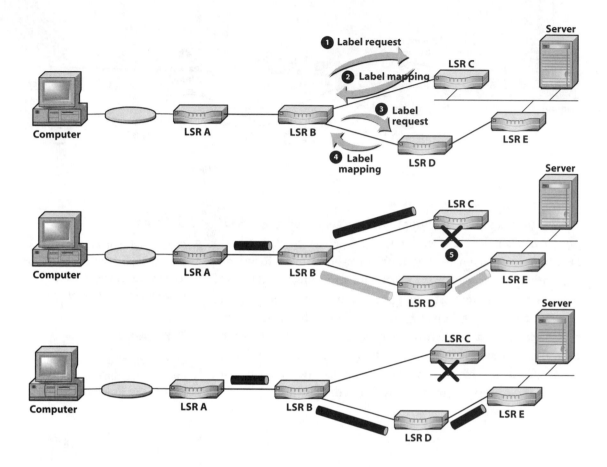

Figure 8.10 ▲

Loop Detection

Liberal label retention lets LSR B ask for a backup path before its actually needed. Until the primary path fails, this backup path goes unused, but once the failure occurs, LSR B can begin using the backup path immediately.

Like any good routing protocol, the Label Distribution Protocol takes precautions against looping. In fact, with LDP, there are two different loop possibilities. In addition to the problem of a loop in the path itself, LDP introduces the possibility that mapping requests might loop indefinitely. Figure 8.11 shows that scenario. In the figure, LSR A wants to establish a path using a downstream-on-demand discipline and ordered distribution control. It sends a mapping request to LSR B, who, in turn sends a request to LSR C. Because of a routing error or misconfiguration, however, LSR C generates its request and sends it to LSR A. As the figure highlights, a

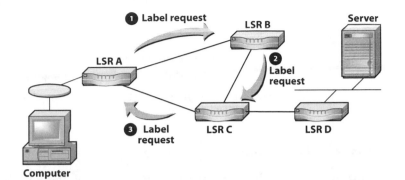

loop has developed and, without any measures to detect and eliminate it, will cause the requests to cycle indefinitely.

As a microcosm of the entire development of MPLS, the Label Distribution Protocol defines two different ways to detect loops, both borrowed from traditional IP protocols. One approach mirrors the traditional IP hop count. An LSR that initiates either a label request or a label mapping includes a hop count field in its message. As that message spawns subsequent messages, the hop count increments by one. If the hop count ever reaches a maximum value, the LSR that detects the problem sends an LDP notification message. In figure 8.12 the administrator has configured a maximum hop count of 5, so the loop ends the second time the message reaches LSR C.

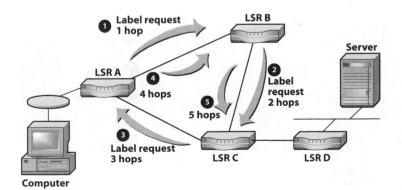

Figure 8.12

One way to prevent endless looping is to define a hop limit for requests. When the hop count reaches this limit, the request causes an error notification. In this example the hop limit is 5, so LSR C detects an error the second time it sees the request.

Figure 8.13 shows the alternative approach for loop detection—path vectors. This technique works the same as it does with BGP. Each router inserts its own LSR ID in the path vector field of the message. When the message loops back to LSR A, that router sees that its own LSR ID is already in the path vector, so it breaks the loop.

Constraint-Based Routing

Those of you who have been waiting for some of the advanced capabilities advertised for MPLS may feel a little disappointed so far. Indeed, the Label Distribution Protocol, as it has been described, really supports only one use of MPLS—faster IP forwarding. The label switched paths it sets up follow the same paths as for traditional IP forwarding. Improved performance is not insignificant, but it's only one of the reasons for using MPLS.

One of the major advantages of MPLS forwarding is precisely that it doesn't have to follow the same paths as IP forwarding. Administrators can construct MPLS paths to balance traffic across different links, to provide specific service qualities, and to steer traffic more finely than IP routing defines. Label distribution protocols like LDP are still a long way from automatically supporting the full set of traffic engineering capabilities of MPLS, but some LDP extensions for *constraint-based routing* offer a start. These extensions, collectively

The Status of CR-LDP

As of this writing, the CR-LDP extensions had not yet been accepted by the IETF as a draft standard. Although it is almost certain that CR-LDP extensions will eventually become a standard part of LDP, it is not certain that they will take the exact format described in this text.

Figure 8.13 ▶

Another way to prevent endless looping is to track the path a request takes through the network. If an LSR finds itself already included in that path—as LSR A does here—it detects the loop and responds with an error message.

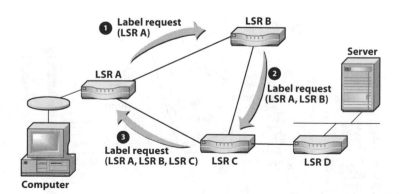

known as CR-LDP, allow an ingress LSR to select an entire path for a traffic flow, not just the next hop. The extensions also give the ingress router a way to reserve network resources for the traffic.

One issue that CR-LDP does not resolve is how the ingress LSR knows which path is best for a given traffic flow. There are proposals to add special extensions to routing protocols such as OSPF to carry current network conditions (such as current bandwidth utilization, maximum available bandwidth, and relative priority). There are also proposals to add this type of information to LDP itself, primarily in the response to mapping requests. As of this writing, however, these proposals remain works in progress. When a complete constraint-based routing architecture is fully defined, it is likely to operate something like table 8.1.

Table 8.1 Constraint-Based Routing

Step	Action
1	Ingress routers collect information on the state of the network (bandwidth utilization, available bandwidth, priorities, etc.).
2	New traffic flow commences with defined resource requirements.
3	Ingress router calculates path for traffic flow.
4	Ingress router requests label switched path for flow and reserves necessary resources.
5	Flow commences using label switched path.

The first three steps are outside the scope of label distribution, and the final step is standard MPLS forwarding. Constraint-based routing LDP, therefore, focuses on step 4. As the table makes clear, there are two distinct components to that step: specifying complete paths and reserving resources.

To specify a full label switched path, the ingress router includes an explicit route as part of its label request. Individual steps along this explicit path are known as *abstract nodes*. The CR-LDP specification calls them "abstract" because they don't necessarily have to represent individual, physical routers. An abstract node can be a group of routers, in which case any member of the group is acceptable for the path. Groups may be identified by an IP address prefix or by an autonomous system number.

Each hop along a label switched path is designated as either *strict* or *loose*. A strict hop gives the LSRs setting up the path no leeway at all; the strict hop must be the next hop in the path. A loose hop, on the other hand, is more flexible. If the LSRs setting up the path cannot reach a loose hop directly, they can set up the path through other intermediate routers, so long as the path eventually traverses the indicated hop.

If an ingress router specifies a path using loose hops, or if any abstract nodes in the path are groups of routers, then it might be possible for the actual path to change during its lifetime. If that behavior is undesirable, the ingress router can request *route pinning*. Route pinning tells the LSRs to keep the exact path fixed for its duration.

To reserve network resources, the ingress router includes a description of the traffic flow in its label request. That description includes the minimum required data rate and burst size, the peak data rate and burst size, and an excess burst size. Along with the parameters themselves, the ingress router can identify whether the resource requirements are negotiable, and it can indicate the relative priority of the flow for resources above and beyond its minimum requirements.

When downstream LSRs return their label mapping messages, they can also include the traffic flow description. In this case, this description indicates that the downstream LSR has reserved the indicated resources. If the ingress router marked any resource requirement as negotiable, the label mapping traffic flow may be less than that of the request. The ingress router, when it receives the final label mapping, can decide if the reserved resources are adequate for the traffic flow.

Along with resource reservation, CR-LDP provides for resource preemption. Preemption allows a new label request to preempt resources already in use by another label switched path, provided the new request has higher priority than the existing path. Each label mapping request may include both a setup priority and a holding priority. The setup priority is the priority for the path as it is being established. The holding priority is the path's priority once it has been established. A new path request can preempt an existing path only if the new path's setup priority is greater than the existing path's holding priority. (Note that CR-LDP uses a value of 0 to indicate the highest priority and 7 for the lowest priority.)

LDP Message Formats

The Label Distribution Protocol uses both UDP and TCP to carry its messages. In both cases, though, the message format is the same. As figure 8.14 indicates, individual messages are grouped together into a *protocol data unit*, or PDU. The PDU begins with an LDP header.

The LDP header carries a protocol version number (currently 1), a length, and an LDP identifier. The LDP identifier is six bytes long, and it consists of the sender's 32-bit router ID plus a 16-bit label space identifier. If the sending router doesn't use multiple label spaces, it sets these last two bytes to zero.

General LDP Messages

Each LDP message has the format of figure 8.15. The first bit—known as the *unknown message* (U) bit—tells a recipient what to do if it doesn't understand the message. If the U bit is clear, the recipient responds with an error message. Otherwise, it simply ignores the unknown message.

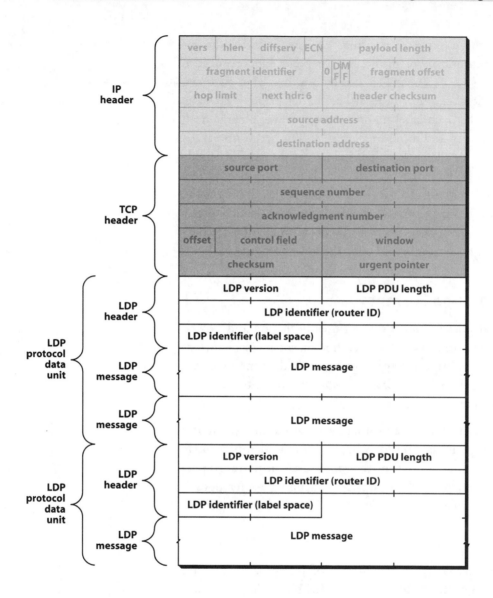

The IP header includes:

vers	hlen	diffserv	ECN	payload length
fragment identifier		0 D M F F	fragment offset
hop limit	next hdr: 6	header checksum
source address		
destination address		

- **IP header**

- **TCP header**

source port	destination port
sequence number	
acknowledgment number	
offset	control field	window
checksum	urgent pointer

- **LDP header**
LDP version	LDP PDU length
LDP identifier (router ID)	
LDP identifier (label space)	

- **LDP message**
  | LDP message | |

- **LDP message**
  | LDP message | |

- **LDP protocol data unit**

- **LDP header**
LDP version	LDP PDU length
LDP identifier (router ID)	
LDP identifier (label space)	

- **LDP message**
  | LDP message | |

- **LDP protocol data unit**

Figure 8.14 ▲

An LDP protocol data unit consists of an LDP header and at least one LDP message. A single TCP segment can carry multiple PDUs.

The *message type* identifies the specific type of message. As table 8.2 indicates, LDP defines 11 different message types, plus room for vendor and experimental extensions. After a two-byte length field, the next four bytes carry a unique message ID. This value is important if a router needs to report an error in received message. The resulting error

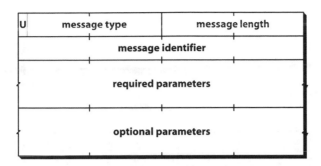

U	message type	message length
	message identifier	
	required parameters	
	optional parameters	

◀ **Figure 8.15**

Each LDP message begins with a message type and length, followed by a unique (to the sender) message identifier. Any required parameters are next, and the message concludes with optional parameters.

message includes the message ID of the original message, and it can help to diagnose the specific problem. The rest of each message consists of required and optional parameters specific to the message type. Vendor-specific messages have an additional field before the parameters, as figure 8.16 indicates. That field is a *vendor ID*; it contains the IEEE-assigned organizational unit identifier for the vendor that has defined the message type.

Table 8.2 LDP Message Types

Decimal	Hexadecimal	Message
1	0001	Notification
256	0100	Hello
512	0200	Initialization
513	0201	KeepAlive
768	0300	Address
769	0301	Address Withdraw
1024	0400	Label Mapping
1025	0401	Label Request
1026	0402	Label Withdraw
1027	0403	Label Release
1028	0404	Label Abort Request
15872-16127	3E00-3EFF	Vendor extensions
16128-16383	3F00-3FFF	Experimental extensions

Figure 8.16 ▶

Vendor-specific messages have an additional field between the message identifier and any parameters. The vendor identifier is taken from a value assigned by the IEEE to any manufacturer of network equipment.

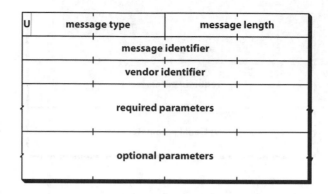

Both the mandatory and optional parameters in each LDP message have a format similar to the message itself. Figure 8.17 shows a generic parameter. The unknown bit has the same meaning as it does with messages. If a router receives a message containing a parameter it does not understand, it either reports an error (if the parameter's U bit is clear) or simply ignores that parameter. The next bit is the *forward unknown* (F) bit; it matters only if the U bit is set and a router receives an unknown parameter. If, in that case, the F bit is set, the router forwards the unknown parameter in subsequent messages, even though it doesn't understand the parameter's meaning. On the other hand, if the F bit is clear, the router drops the unknown parameter from forwarded messages.

After the U and F bits is the 14-bit parameter type. The LDP standard defines 19 of the parameters of table 8.3, as well as room for vendor and experimental extensions. The CR-LDP extensions define 10 additional parameters.

Figure 8.17 ▶

Individual LDP parameters have their own type and length fields, followed by the parameter value.

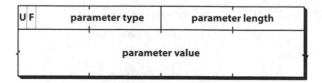

Table 8.3 LDP Parameter Types

Decimal	Hexadecimal	Parameter Type
256	0100	Forwarding Equivalence Class
257	0101	Address List
259	0103	Hop Count
260	0104	Path Vector
512	0200	Generic Label
513	0201	ATM Label
514	0202	Frame Relay Label
768	0300	Status
769	0301	Extended Status
770	0302	Returned PDU
771	0303	Returned Message
1024	0400	Hello Parameters
1025	0401	IPv4 Transport Address
1026	0402	Configuration Sequence Number
1027	0403	IPv6 Transport Address
1280	0500	Session Parameters
1281	0501	ATM Session Parameters
1282	0502	Frame Relay Session Parameters
1536	0600	Label Request Message ID
2048	0800	Explicit Route (CR-LDP)
2049	0801	IPv4 Prefix Explicit Route Hop (CR-LDP)
2050	0802	IPv6 Prefix Explicit Route Hop (CR-LDP)
2051	0803	AS Number Explicit Route Hop (CR-LDP)
2052	0804	LSP ID Explicit Route Hop (CR-LDP)
2064	0810	Traffic Parameters (CR-LDP)
2080	0820	Preemption (CR-LDP)
2081	0821	LSP ID (CR-LDP)
2082	0822	Resource Class (CR-LDP)
2083	0823	Route Pinning (CR-LDP)
15872-16127	3E00-3EFF	Vendor extensions
16128-16383	3F00-3FFF	Experimental extensions

Figure 8.18 ▶

Vendor-specific parameters also
have the vendor identifier field.

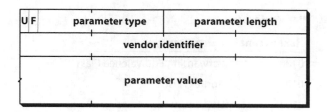

As is the case for vendor-specific message types, vendor-specific parameters include the unique vendor ID field immediately before the parameter value, as in figure 8.18. This vendor identifier allows each vendor to define its own special parameters, without worrying that other vendors might pick the same value for their special parameters.

Notification Message

Label switched routers use the LDP notification message to report errors to their peers. Errors may be fatal, in which case the LSRs terminate the LDP session immediately after exchanging the notification message. Other errors are merely advisory, in which case they don't require the session's immediate termination.

Figure 8.19 shows a sample notification message. The status parameter is required in all notification messages, while the other three parameters (extended status, returned PDU, and returned message) are optional.

The status parameter is the key element of a notification. It contains an indication of whether the error is fatal (the E bit), whether the notification should be forwarded (the F bit), and the type of error. If the notification message is in response to a specific message from the router's peer, the message ID and message type identify the original message; otherwise, those fields are zero. Table 8.4 lists the status code values defined by the LDP and CR-LDP specifications.

The optional parameters in a notification message include extended status, returned PDU, and returned message. The

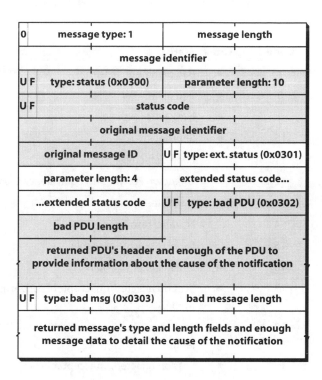

Figure 8.19

An LDP notification message reports errors. It carries a status code to indicate the type of error and an optional extended status to provide additional information. The message also carries information to identify the PDU that caused the error.

extended status parameter can provide additional details about the notification status, although the current version of the LDP specification doesn't define any extended status values. The returned PDU and returned message parameters can hold a copy of the PDU and the message that caused the error. Their information may help diagnose LDP problems.

Table 8.4 LDP Status Codes

Code	Fatal	Status
0		No error.
1	●	Bad LDP identifier.
2	●	Bad protocol version.
3	●	Bad PDU length.
4		Unknown message type.
5	●	Bad message length.
6		Unknown parameter.

continues…

Table 8.4 LDP Status Codes (continued)

Code	Fatal	Status
7	●	Bad parameter length.
8	●	Bad parameter value.
9	●	Hold timer expired.
10	●	Shutdown
11		Loop detected.
12		Unknown Forwarding Equivalence Class.
13		No route.
14		No label resources.
15		Label resources available.
16	●	Session rejected; no hello.
17	●	Session rejected; unacceptable advertisement mode.
18	●	Session rejected; unacceptable max. PDU length.
19	●	Session rejected; unacceptable label range.
20	●	Keep alive timer expired.
21		Label request aborted.
22		Missing message parameters.
23		Unsupported address family.
24	●	Session rejected; unacceptable keep alive time.
25	●	Internal error.
1140850689		Bad explicit route parameter (CR-LDP)
1140850690		Bad strict node (CR-LDP).
1140850691		Bad loose node (CR-LDP).
1140850692		Bad initial explicit route hop (CR-LDP).
1140850693		Resource unavailable(CR-LDP).
1140850694		Traffic parameters unavailable(CR-LDP).
1140850695		LSP preempted (CR-LDP).
1140850696		Modify request not supported (CR-LDP).
67108885		Setup abort (CR-LDP).

Hello Message

Label switched routers introduce themselves to each other with hello messages, a sample of which appears in figure 8.20. The common hello parameters are present in all hello messages. Optional parameters include the IPv4 transport address and configuration sequence number. Although it's not present in the figure, there is also an IPv6 transport address parameter.

The main hello parameter is the hold time. This parameter specifies the maximum number of seconds any recipient should wait without hearing another hello from the router. If the specified time expires without another hello message, recipients should consider the sending router to have failed. Normal values for hello hold times are 15 seconds for hello messages sent to the all routers multicast address and 45 seconds for hello messages sent to specific destinations. Routers can pick any value up to 65535, however, which is treated as infinite. If two routers propose different hold times in the hello messages they exchange, both routers use the minimum value. In figure 8.21, for example, LSR A and LSR B have a hello hold time of 15 seconds, while LSR C uses 5 seconds. Because s C has the smaller hold time, all routers on the LAN must use its value. Once a router has established a hello hold time, it sends periodic hello messages at a frequency that's

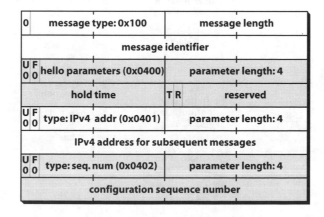

◀ **Figure 8.20**

An LDP hello message introduces an LSR to its peer. It carries essential information about the sender.

Figure 8.21 ▶

When LSRs on the same subnetwork propose different hold times in their hello messages, they all resort to the smallest proposed value, five seconds in this example.

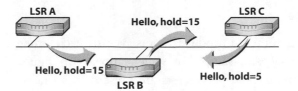

about a third of the hold time. That way, a recipient would have to miss three consecutive hello messages to inappropriately consider a peer to have failed.

The other flags in the common hello parameters indicate whether the message was targeted at a specific destination or sent to all routers, and whether a specific (targeted) reply is requested.

The configuration sequence number is an optional value that the sender increments whenever its configuration changes. This parameter may help break a session initialization deadlock quickly. To see its use, consider figure 8.22. In the figure, the LSRs have successfully exchanged hello messages but cannot agree on session parameters. The active router, LSR A,

Figure 8.22 ▶

The configuration sequence number lets an LSR tell its peer that it has a new configuration. That gives the peer a hint that it can immediately retry a negotiation that was rejected under the previous configuration. Without the hint, the peer might wait for a lengthy timeout before retrying.

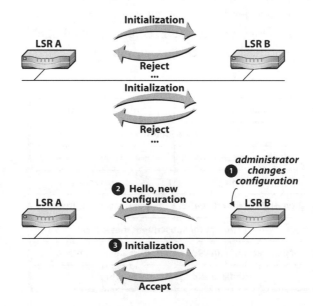

continues to propose a session, but LSR B rejects its request. Because this has been going on for a while, LSR A has backed off to its maximum value and is retrying the session initialization only every two minutes.

At the point of time in the figure, the network administrator has recognized the deadlock and reconfigured LSR B. Now LSR B is prepared to accept LSR A's proposed session. The problem, however, is that it may be as long as two minutes before LSR A retries its request. In this case, the configuration sequence number can hasten the session establishment. Because LSR B's configuration has changed, it increments the configuration sequence number in its hello messages. When LSR A sees the new sequence number, it can skip the full two-minute wait and try a new session initialization immediately.

Initialization Message

Initialization messages actually establish an LDP session between two LSRs. Once a TCP connection between the routers is established, the active router sends its initialization message. If the passive router accepts the parameters this initialization message proposes, it sends its own initialization message, as well as a keep alive message. The active router completes the negotiation by responding with its own keep alive message. Figure 8.22 illustrates the process. If either router doesn't like the session parameters proposed by its peer, it rejects the session with a notification message.

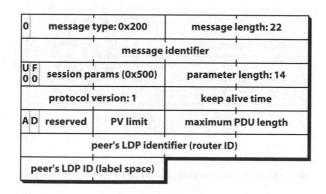

◀ **Figure 8.23**

An LDP initialization message begins a session negotiation by proposing parameters for the session.

Figure 8.23 shows a sample initialization message. The keep alive time indicates how many seconds must elapse without an LDP message from a router before its peer considers the session to have failed. The *advertisement discipline* (A) bit proposes either downstream unsolicited (if it has a value of zero) or downstream on demand (a value of one). If the two peers propose different values, then ATM or frame relay sessions use downstream on demand, while other sessions use downstream unsolicited. The D bit indicates whether or not the session uses path vectors for loop detection. If its value is 1, then the path vector limit field indicates the maximum permitted size of path vectors. Path vectors that exceed this size are treated as if a loop had been detected. The maximum PDU length field tells the recipient the largest size LDP PDU the sender can accept; the default value is 4096 bytes. The final required field is the receiver's LDP identifier. This field echoes the LDP identifier field from the peer's hello message. It allows a router that receives an initialization message to

Figure 8.24 ▶

When MPLS uses ATM virtual path or virtual circuit identifiers as labels, the LDP initialization message carries the VPI and VCI ranges that are available for assignment to labels.

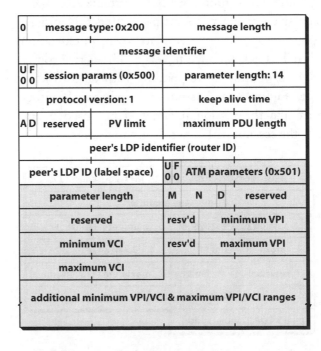

determine the specific hello message (and label space) to which it refers.

When the LSRs operate over ATM or frame relay networks, the initialization messages can carry additional information. Figure 8.24 shows an initialization message with ATM parameters, and figure 8.25 shows a message with frame relay parameters. In both cases the M field indicates whether the LSR can merge connections or paths, and the D field indicates whether the virtual circuits are bi-directional. The N field carries the number of label ranges, and the ranges themselves identify the virtual path identifiers, virtual circuit identifiers, and data link connection identifiers that are available as labels for mapping.

Keep Alive Message

The LDP keep alive message, shown in figure 8.26, has no parameters at all. Label switched routers use the keep alive

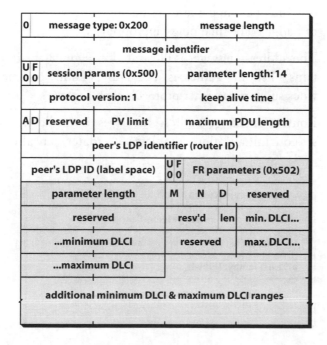

◀ **Figure 8.25**

When MPLS uses frame relay data link connection identifiers as labels, the LDP initialization message carries the DLCI ranges that are available for assignment to labels.

Figure 8.26 ▶

The LDP keepalive message has
no parameters at all. It simply lets
an LSR's peer know that it is still
alive and functioning, and that
nothing has changed.

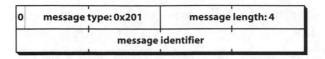

message to prevent the keep alive timer for a session from expiring. If a router has no other LDP message to send, it sends a keep alive message to reset its peers timer.

Address Message

When label switched routers manage label mappings, they often need to track the next hop address of downstream peers. If, as an example, an LSR operating in downstream unsolicited mode sees the next hop for a given forwarding equivalence class change, it needs to find a new label mapping for that FEC. Because the router will only know the new next hop address, it must be able to find a label corresponding to that next hop address. The LDP address message lets downstream routers advertise their interface addresses. With the information they carry, an upstream router can keep track of which next hop addresses belong with which labels, and it can adjust label mappings appropriately.

The address message, as illustrated in figure 8.27, simply contains a list of IP addresses. The address family parameter provides support for other protocols such as IPv6.

Routers exchange address messages immediately after the session initialization completes. A router can also send an

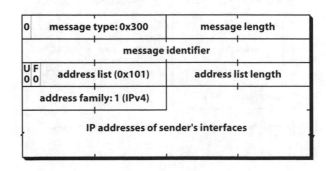

Figure 8.27 ▶

An LDP address message tells a
peer which IP addresses belong to
an LSR's interfaces.

address message whenever it activates a new address on the interface. If an address is removed from a router's interface, the address withdraw message signals the peer LSR.

Address Withdraw Message

As figure 8.28 illustrates, the address withdraw message has the same parameters as an address message. Its address list, however, indicates interface addresses that are no longer in service.

Label Mapping Message

The label mapping message is the heart of LDP; it is the message that a downstream router uses to tell the upstream router of a label mapping. The downstream router can send this message on its own initiative (in the case of downstream unsolicited discipline) or in response to the upstream router's request (for downstream on demand).

Figure 8.29 shows a label mapping message for basic LDP. It does not include any extensions for constraint-based routing. The forwarding equivalence class and the label parameters are required; the hop limit parameter is optional.

Label request messages allow two different types of forwarding equivalence class parameters. One type defines an IP address prefix. The label switched path applies to all destinations that match the address prefix. The example FEC parameter of figure 8.29 indicates a 24-bit prefix of 172.16.1.0.

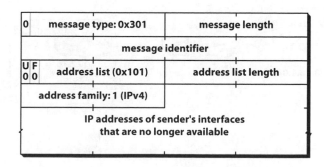

◀ **Figure 8.28**

An LDP address withdraw message tells a peer that some IP addresses no longer belong to an LSR's interfaces.

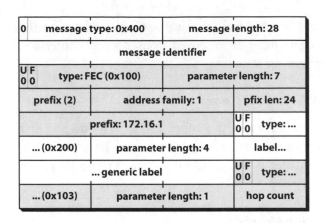

0	message type: 0x400		message length: 28	
	message identifier			
U F 0 0	type: FEC (0x100)		parameter length: 7	
prefix (2)	address family: 1		pfix len: 24	
prefix: 172.16.1			U F 0 0	type: ...
... (0x200)	parameter length: 4		label...	
... generic label			U F 0 0	type: ...
... (0x103)	parameter length: 1		hop count	

Datagrams with destination address of 172.16.1.1, 172.16.1.100, or 172.16.1.200, for example, could be mapped to this label switched path. A datagram destined to 172.16.2.1, however, would not match.

In addition to matching the destination IP address, a router may map a datagram to a path if the path's FEC prefix matches the address of the egress router for the path. Figure 8.30 shows the effect of this mapping. The ingress router has a path for 172.16.1.0/24. Even though the datagram's destination is 172.16.3.1, the ingress router knows that the destination is directly connected to an egress router that does match the path's prefix. The ingress router, therefore, maps the datagram to that path. The Label Distribution Protocol itself

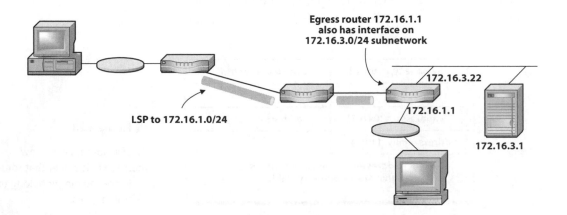

doesn't tell the ingress router the identify of the egress router, but the information may be available to the ingress router from another source.

In the example message of figure 8.29, the first byte of the parameter value (2) indicates that the FEC defines a prefix. The next two bytes identify the address family. The fourth byte carries the prefix length, in bits, and the rest of the parameter value holds the address prefix itself.

The alternate FEC type, a host address, is the example of figure 8.31. As the figure shows, the format is actually the same as for a prefix. The address length byte, however, indicates the size of the entire address, and its units are bytes rather than bits. Figure 8.31's example specifies a label switched path to the destination host 172.16.1.1. Note that host address FECs match the destination address of only a datagram. Unlike prefix FECs, they cannot match the egress router.

The second required parameter of a label mapping message is the label itself. Figures 8.29 and 8.31 both show a generic

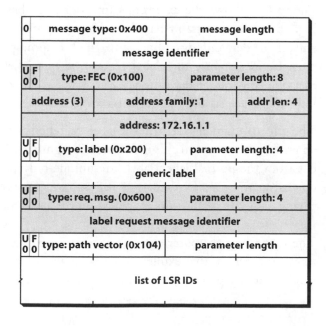

◀ **Figure 8.31**

LDP label mapping messages can also use a host address as a forwarding equivalence class, as in this example. This message is the result of downstream on demand operation, as it includes the message identifier from the label request message that triggered it. The message concludes by listing the path through which it has traveled, allowing receiving LSRs to detect looping.

Figure 8.32 ▶

When ATM VPI/VCIs or frame relay DLCIs act as MPLS labels, the Label Distribution Protocol uses a special parameter format to exchange their values.

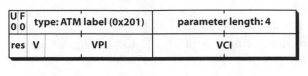

label, suitable for use over links like PPP and Ethernet that don't have special support for MPLS. There are also label parameters for ATM and frame relay networks. Figure 8.32 shows their formats. Instead of generic labels, they identify VPI/VCI combinations or DLCI values.

The label mapping optional parameters include hop count, path vector, and label request message ID. Figure 8.29's example includes a hop count, and figure 8.31 has a label request ID and a path vector parameter. The hop count parameter helps prevent routing loops. Unlike hop counts used in protocols such as IP, the hop count increments rather than decrements. The path vector is simply a list of LSR IDs.

Figure 8.33 shows the extensions for constraint-based routing. Because constraint-based routing requires a downstream-on-demand discipline, any label mapping message must be in response to a label request, so the label request message ID parameter will be present. The two new parameters are the LSP ID and the traffic parameters.

The LSP ID uniquely identifies a label switched path within an entire MPLS network. This function is significantly different from the normal label; labels are unique only to a single downstream router. Particularly with CR-LDP, however, identifying a specific path from anywhere on the network may be very useful. It allows the behavior of figure 8.34, for example. There the ingress router uses CR-LSP to specify an explicit route, and part of that explicit route is an already established label switched path. The ingress router uses the LSP ID to

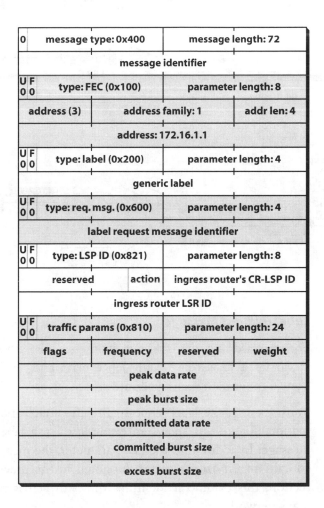

0	message type: 0x400	message length: 72		
	message identifier			
U F 0 0	type: FEC (0x100)	parameter length: 8		
address (3)		address family: 1		addr len: 4
address: 172.16.1.1				
U F 0 0	type: label (0x200)	parameter length: 4		
generic label				
U F 0 0	type: req. msg. (0x600)	parameter length: 4		
label request message identifier				
U F 0 0	type: LSP ID (0x821)	parameter length: 8		
reserved		action	ingress router's CR-LSP ID	
ingress router LSR ID				
U F 0 0	traffic params (0x810)	parameter length: 24		
flags	frequency	reserved	weight	
peak data rate				
peak burst size				
committed data rate				
committed burst size				
excess burst size				

◀ **Figure 8.33**

Constraint-based label distribution adds two extra parameters to the label mapping message. The LSP ID uniquely identifies the path anywhere in the network. Unlike the label value itself, the LSP ID does not change at each hop. The second extra parameter specifies the resources that have been reserved by the network for the LSP.

identify that path in its request. As figure 8.33 indicates, the LSP ID consists of the path's ingress router ID plus a value assigned to the path by that ingress router.

The final CR-LDP parameter in the label mapping message contains the traffic parameters. In a mapping message, this parameter indicates the resources that have been reserved for the traffic, including the peak data rate, peak burst size, committed data rate, committed burst size, and the excess burst size. Each of these fields is a floating-point number with units of bytes or bytes per second.

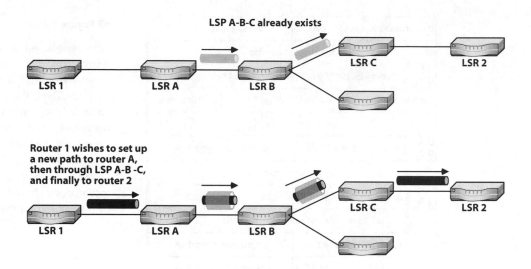

Figure 8.34 ▲

Because the LSP ID is valid anywhere in the network, an LSR such as LSR 1 can use the LSP ID to refer to a path somewhere else in the network. In this example LSR 1 wants to use an already-established LSP as part of a new path it is requesting.

Label Request Message

For standard LDP, the label request message is rather simple. It carries a forwarding equivalence class and, optionally, a hop count or path vector parameter.

With CR-LSP, the label request can carry much more information. Figure 8.35 shows an example CR-LSP label request message. In addition to the FEC parameter, the message must contain an LSP ID parameter. As noted in the previous subsection, this parameter identifies the path across the entire MPLS network.

The optional CR-LSP parameters include an explicit route, traffic characteristics, route pinning, resource class, and preemption. The explicit route describes the path the ingress router is requesting for the path. It consists of a series of explicit route hops. Each explicit route hop is one or more IPv4 address prefixes, IPv6 address prefixes, autonomous system numbers, or LDP IDs. Associated with each hop is the *loose*, or L, bit, which determines whether the hop must be the very next hop (L is zero) or if (L is one) other, unspecified, hops may intervene.

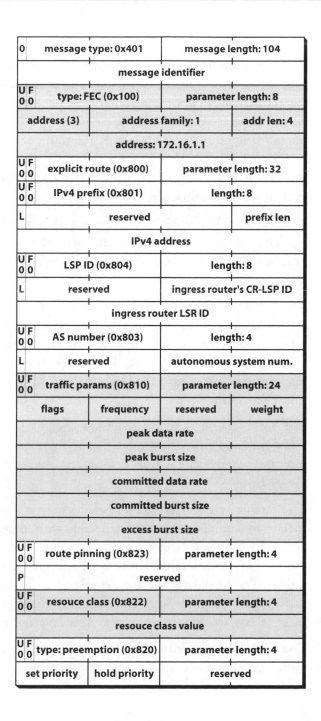

0	message type: 0x401	message length: 104		
	message identifier			
U F 0 0	type: FEC (0x100)	parameter length: 8		
address (3)		address family: 1		addr len: 4
	address: 172.16.1.1			
U F 0 0	explicit route (0x800)	parameter length: 32		
U F 0 0	IPv4 prefix (0x801)	length: 8		
L	reserved			prefix len
	IPv4 address			
U F 0 0	LSP ID (0x804)	length: 8		
L	reserved	ingress router's CR-LSP ID		
	ingress router LSR ID			
U F 0 0	AS number (0x803)	length: 4		
L	reserved	autonomous system num.		
U F 0 0	traffic params (0x810)	parameter length: 24		
flags	frequency	reserved		weight
	peak data rate			
	peak burst size			
	committed data rate			
	committed burst size			
	excess burst size			
U F 0 0	route pinning (0x823)	parameter length: 4		
P	reserved			
U F 0 0	resouce class (0x822)	parameter length: 4		
	resouce class value			
U F 0 0	type: preemption (0x820)	parameter length: 4		
set priority	hold priority	reserved		

◀ **Figure 8.35**

This example shows an LDP label request message, including parameters only available with constraint-based label distribution. The explicit route parameter specifies a complete path through the network, allowing an ingress router to define appropriate traffic-engineered paths. The group of traffic parameters identify resources the network should reserve for the path.

The traffic characteristics parameter has the same format as in the label mapping message. With a label mapping request, however, several of its fields take on additional meaning. The flags field contains six individual flag bits. They indicate whether the resource requirements are negotiable. The frequency field hints at the granularity the traffic requires for its committed data rate. A value of 2, indicating "very frequent," implies that the committed data rate must be guaranteed even at very small time scales.

The weight field is a value from 0 to 255. When bandwidth is available in the network above and beyond what has been guaranteed to individual paths, routers should try to give the excess to those paths with higher weights.

The remaining fields are individual resource requirements for the traffic. They have the same meaning as in the label mapping message, except that in a label mapping request, the values are those requested by the ingress router. The label mapping message reports the resources actually reserved back to the requesting router.

The route pinning parameter, although eight bytes in size, really contains only a single bit that is significant. That bit indicates whether the ingress LSR requests route pinning for the path.

The resource class parameter allows the ingress router to associate an administratively defined value with its requests. A network provider, for example, might choose to offer its customers different service levels, perhaps gold, silver, and bronze. The provider could then configure its ingress routers to add the appropriate "color" to each label mapping request. Interior LSRs would see this color and react accordingly.

The final optional parameter, preemption, is how an ingress router specifies the setup and hold priorities for the request.

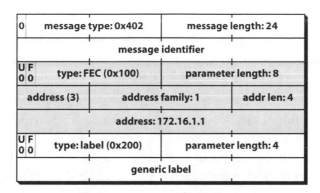

◄ **Figure 8.36**

An LDP label withdraw message lets a downstream router tell its peer that a label switched path is no longer available.

Label Withdraw Message

The label withdraw message indicates that a label mapping is no longer available. A downstream router sends this message when it is no longer supporting a specific label switched path. As figure 8.36 indicates, the message includes a forwarding equivalence class and, optionally, a label.

Label Release Message

As the label withdraw message acts as the opposite of a label mapping message, the label release message is the opposite of a label request. Upstream routers send label release messages to indicate that they no longer need a previously requested label mapping. Figure 8.37 shows an example. Like the label

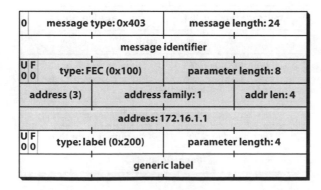

◄ **Figure 8.37**

An upstream LSR uses an LDP label release message to ask its downstream peer to withdraw a path.

withdraw, the label release always includes the forwarding equivalence class and may include the label value.

Label Abort Request Message

The last LDP message is the label abort request. Upstream routers use this message to cancel a label mapping request that has not yet completed. (If the request completes, the upstream router uses the label release message.) In addition to the forwarding equivalence class, label abort requests carry the message ID of the original label mapping request message. Figure 8.38 shows an example.

Summary

Multi-Protocol Label Switching offers significant improvements to the performance of IP-based networks, but MPLS alone is not a complete solution. Label switched routers need to exchange label information, just as traditional IP routers need IP routing protocols. The Label Distribution Protocol is designed specifically for exchanging label information. It defines a way for upstream routers to request a label mapping and for downstream routers to identify label mappings to their upstream peers.

Because LDP's function is similar to that of IP routing protocols, LDP can borrow many concepts from those protocols. It

Figure 8.38 ▶

The LDP label abort message cancels a label request currently in progress.

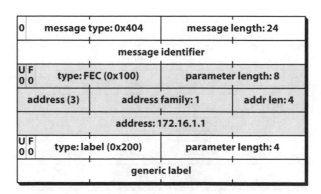

has a neighbor greeting phase like OSPF, and then, like BGP, it establishes reliable TCP connections to actually exchange label information.

Standard LDP provides support for only one of the important features of MPLS—its ability to speed up forwarding performance. For more advanced MPLS features such as traffic engineering, a separate set of LDP extensions define support for constraint-based routing. Those extensions, known as CR-LDP, let an ingress router explicitly specify an entire path, and they let the ingress router reserve network resources for traffic flowing on the path.

CHAPTER 9

RSVP-TE—Resource Reservation for Traffic Engineering

With its constraint-based routing extensions, the Label Distribution Protocol gains the ability to reserve network resources for traffic flows. Another protocol—one that has been deployed for several years—has that functionality as well. That protocol is the Resource Reservation Protocol, or RSVP. And, just as LDP has expanded its functions to include resource reservation, RSVP has expanded its functions to include label distribution.

The need for RSVP grew out of increasing use of IP networks to carry real-time traffic such as telephony and video conferencing. Real-time traffic usually has tight time constraints and must reach its destination within a certain time period. Without assistance from protocols such as RSVP, real-time applications are at the mercy of the Internet Protocol's delivery service, and IP is an unreliable protocol, as it makes only a best effort to deliver data.

Some real-time applications can accommodate unreliable delivery. They perform their own reordering and, if necessary, disregard or approximate any missing data. Other applications require more from the network. To ensure that networks serve their needs, these applications reserve network resources. Once reserved, these resources are dedicated to the application.

The Resource Reservation Protocol offers applications just such a reservation service. It defines how applications place reservations and how they can relinquish those resources once their need concludes.

Resource Reservation

Subnetwork Bandwidth Management

For network technologies such as Ethernet that don't naturally provide performance guarantees, RSVP has special extensions for subnetwork bandwidth management (SBM). Through these extensions, routers elect a designated subnetwork bandwidth manager. The designated manager coordinates the traffic flows of all routers across the subnetwork.

Even though IP offers only unreliable delivery, in many cases the underlying network technologies can provide performance guarantees. And even when those guarantees cannot be absolute, such as is the case with Ethernet LANs, they may be of high enough probability that applications can still function adequately.

If the networks themselves can provide suitable performance, success or failure of the application rests with IP. Consider the example of figure 9.1, in which a real-time video stream traverses a network. To keep the video acceptably smooth, the client must display 30 frames per second. That is the rate at which the server transmits the data. To prevent the client from falling behind, the network must deliver 30 frames per second to the destination. If each video frame contains about 1 million bits of data, then the application requires 31 Mbit/s of network bandwidth. (Fortunately, actual digital video traffic does not require nearly this much bandwidth.)

Now consider the task facing a router inside the network. That router must support the real-time video traffic flow, as well as other traffic on the network. Suppose, as figure 9.2 illustrates, a separate file transfer is temporarily peaking at 30 Mbit/s. If the intervening network is a low-speed ATM network with an access rate of 51 Mbit/s, then the router cannot

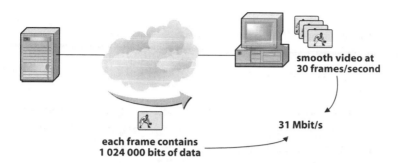

To deliver this video stream across an IP network, the network must provide at least 31 Mbit/s of bandwidth. (This number is an example only; actual IP-based video technology normally uses much less bandwidth.)

support both traffic flows at full speed. Their combined bandwidth requirement exceeds what the link can provide.

The router might try to share the limited resource (the ATM link) evenly between the two flows. The video flow might receive 26 Mbit/s of bandwidth and the file transfer 25 Mbit/s. Of course, that allocation would be fine for the file transfer, but unacceptable to the real-time video stream. It would be better if the router maintained the video transfer rate of 31 Mbit/s by limiting the file transfer to 20 Mbit/s. That allocation would satisfy both applications. The file transfer might take a bit longer, but it would still succeed. More important, the real-time video would continue to receive the bandwidth it requires.

Many routers are capable of making the "right" allocation of bandwidth, but they have to know what that allocation is.

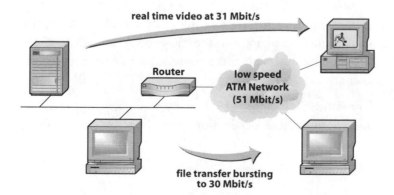

◀ **Figure 9.2**

If the network tries to support both the video stream and other traffic simultaneously, there may not be enough bandwidth to go around.

That is where resource reservation comes in. With resource reservation, an application gives advance notice of the network resources that it requires. The video transfer, for example, could reserve 31 Mbit/s of network bandwidth. By granting the reservation, the affected hosts and routers commit to providing those resources. If, in the example, the router knows the video flow's requirements, it could limit the file transfer to 20 Mbit/s.

Resource reservation can also indicate when the necessary resources are not available. Suppose, for example, that the real-time video required 62 Mbit/s of bandwidth. The network, with its 51 Mbit/s ATM link, clearly cannot support that requirement. When the video application attempted to reserve the resources it needs, the routers would have a chance to refuse the reservation. The application finds out right away that the network cannot support it; it does not have to resort to a costly trial-and-error approach.

RSVP Operation

Two key concepts that underlie RSVP are flows and reservations. This section considers each in turn, as well as other key aspects of RSVP operation.

Flows

When RSVP reserves resources, it reserves them for a *flow*. Flows are traffic streams from a sender to one or more receivers. Figure 9.3 shows a sample flow through a network. Datagrams belonging to the flow originate at the video server, travel through three routers, and arrive at the video client.

Normally, RSVP identifies a flow by its destination IP address and, optionally, a destination port. Specific source IP addresses or source ports may further refine RSVP's definition of

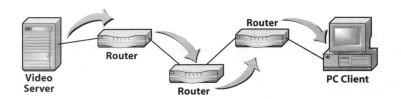

◀ **Figure 9.3**

A flow consists of traffic for a particular destination following a specific path through the network.

a flow. In the context of MPLS, a flow is a particular label switched path.

Along with the traffic that makes up a flow, RSVP identifies the particular quality of service that the flow requires. This quality of service determines the network resources the flow requires. The Resource Reservation Protocol itself does not actually understand this *flowspec*, as it is known; it simply passes it from the application to hosts and routers along the flow's path. Those systems can examine the flowspec to see if they can accept the reservation, and once it is accepted, they use the flowspec to actually reserve the required resources.

Reservations

Unlike some resource reservation protocols (including CR-LDP), RSVP expects traffic receivers to make the actual reservations. At first, this approach may seem backward. After all, the system that generates traffic ought to know more about the resources its traffic requires. Indeed, in the simplest cases, this is often true; RSVP, however, supports more than the simplest cases. Having receivers make the reservations gives the protocol greater flexibility for handling multicast flows, particularly those that are diverse or dynamic.

Figure 9.4 presents a situation that benefits from the flexibility of receiver-initiated reservations. In the figure, the server sends a flow to a multicast destination. Two clients belong to that multicast group and reside at different places in the network. The bottom client has a fast Ethernet and an ATM network between it and the server. The slowest link on that path is the Ethernet LAN, so throughput is limited to 100

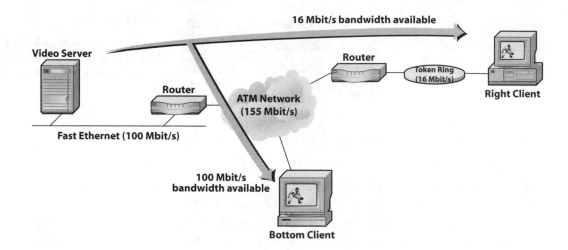

Figure 9.4 ▲

As this example illustrates, an application relying on multicast will likely encounter different paths to different receivers, and the network resources available to those paths may differ as well.

MBit/s. The right client. on the other hand, has a Token Ring LAN in its path. This Token Ring network limits the throughput to 16 Mbit/s.

If the standard video stream requires 31 Mbit/s of bandwidth, then the right client is not on a fast enough path to receive the flow. Some video encoding methods, however, can sacrifice quality for bandwidth. As a simple example, the right client might find that processing only 15 frames per second still provides acceptable video quality, and that rate requires only 15 Mbit/s of bandwidth. The client could achieve that rate by accepting only every other video frame.

This approach suggests that the two clients might need different resources reserved for the flow. The bottom client uses the full 31 Mbit/s, while the right client makes do with 15 Mbit/s. If the server were the system making the reservation, it would have to know the characteristics of all possible receivers and structure its reservation accordingly. When the receivers reserve resources, however, things are much simpler. Each receiver need understand only its own capabilities and requirements.

Receiver-based reservations also easily support a dynamic environment. New receivers can join the flow, and existing ones can drop out, all without bothering the sender.

There are two complications with RSVP's receiver orientation. One question is how does a receiver know to make a reservation in the first place. In most cases, RSVP expects the application to handle this problem. Typically, applications announce the flow in advance, periodically during the flow's lifetime, or both. Even though they may go to the same destination, these announcements themselves should not require reserved resources. They are not time-critical and can travel across the network without RSVP's assistance.

Path Messages

A trickier problem is how the receiver knows which path the flow will take. Receivers must know this path so they can reserve the appropriate resources. Suppose, for example, that the video clients know of an upcoming video broadcast for which they must reserve resources. They know the source of the broadcast, but they are unaware of the path that the broadcast will take.

At first glance, the dilemma may seem trivial to resolve. After all, the path from the server to any client would seem to be just the reverse of the path from that client to the server. Figure 9.5 shows an example of why this reasoning may be wrong. There, a network has two parallel wide area network technologies. All of the network's routers are connected via satellite and frame relay. The satellite links suffer long delay, and so they are not ideal for most traffic. In general, the routers prefer to use the frame relay network. But satellite transmission is inherently a broadcast medium, and the satellite links provide a very cost-effective way to distribute multicast traffic. For multicast video traffic, therefore, the routers will employ satellite instead of frame relay.

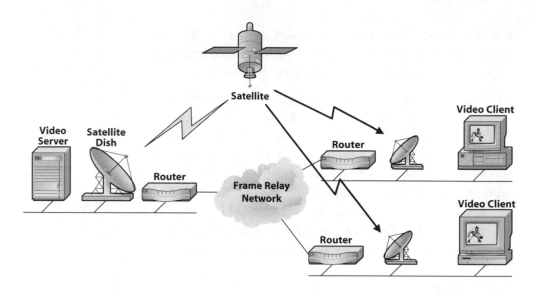

Figure 9.5 ▲

This network shows why the path from a sender to a receiver may not be the same as the reverse of the path from the receiver to the sender. Datagrams *from* the video server can take advantage of the high bandwidth satellite link. But that link only works in one direction, so return traffic uses the relatively low bandwidth frame relay network.

The problem with receiver reservations is evident in this example. If the clients simply send reservation messages to the server, those messages will travel across the frame relay network. In this case, however, there is no reason to reserve resources along that path.

To make sure that resources are reserved along the correct path, RSVP uses special *path* messages. Unlike reservation requests, path messages come from the flow's sender and travel in the same direction (on the same path) as the flow itself.

A path message primes the routers in the flow's path. It identifies the flow and tells the routers to expect reservation requests. To ensure that the path message follows the same path as the flow itself, it is sent to the same destination address as the flow. At each hop, the router inserts its own IP address as the message's last hop.

As the message travels through the network, each router can look at the last hop field to learn where the flow came from. Should it later receive a reservation request for the flow, this last hop information tells it where to send the reservation request next. Figure 9.6 shows a path message winding its way through a network.

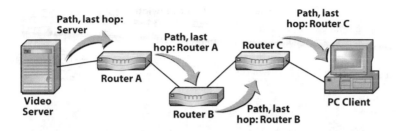

Because path messages start at the flow's source and precede reservation messages, they give the sender an opportunity to describe the flow to its receivers. As long as that description is not too complex, RSVP provides room in the path messages for it. (If the flow description won't fit in a path message, the application must transfer it through some other means.)

Merging Reservation Requests

When a flow has a multicast destination, different destination systems may require different reserved resources. Refer back to figure 9.4 for an example of this situation. When it arises, intermediate routers may be asked to merge multiple reservations for the same flow. Figure 9.7 shows this process.

In the figure, the left router receives two reservation requests for the flow. The first request requires only 15 Mbit/s of network bandwidth. (Recall that the right client has reduced its requirements because of the capabilities of the intervening Token Ring LAN.) The second request, from the bottom client, asks for 31 Mbit/s of network bandwidth. The router must combine these requests intelligently before forwarding a further request toward the video server. In this case, the intelligent way to combine the requests is to take the maximum of the two. The router does this in step 3 of the figure. Different resources may require different treatment. If the reservation specified a required delay limit, for example, the intermediate router would take the minimum of multiple requests. Other resources might require the sum of individual values.

◀ **Figure 9.6**

So that the client will know the path traffic from the server is taking, the RSVP path message has each hop insert its own IP address in the message. When the message arrives at the client, the client knows that the previous hop was router C, who knows that the hop before it was router B, and so on. This information lets the routers reconstruct the forward path for the flow when they process reservation requests coming from the destination.

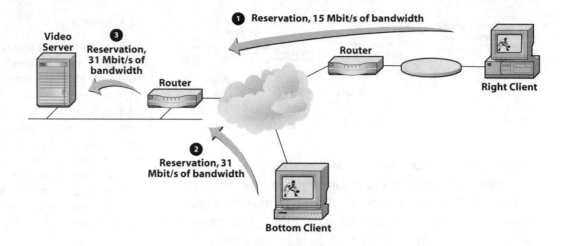

Figure 9.7 ▲

In this example the left router receives two different reservations for the same multicast flow. Because the flow is multicast, the router doesn't have to pass each request separately upstream. Instead, it simply takes whichever request asks for the most bandwidth and passes that upstream. The lower bandwidth request piggybacks on the higher bandwidth request.

Reservation Styles

So far, this chapter has described an effective, though somewhat limited, style of reservation, one that requires receivers to explicitly reserve resources for each flow they can accept. The Resource Reservation Protocol actually provides more flexibility than this limited approach by defining different reservation styles. Table 9.1 lists the styles defined by the current protocol specifications, although RSVP anticipates that network designers will add more styles in future revisions.

Table 9.1 RSVP Reservation Styles

Abbreviation	Style	Use
FF	Fixed Filter	Reserve resources for one particular flow.
SE	Shared Explicit	Reserve resources for several specific flows at once, allowing those different flows to share the reserved resources.
WF	Wildcard Filter	Reserve resources for a general type of flow without specifying the flow precisely; all flows of this type share the reserved resources.

All the previous examples assumed the straightforward, *fixed filter* style where each flow needs its own reservation. Figure 9.8 shows an example that benefits from a different reservation style. In it, five personal computers are participating in an audio conference. All but one of the PCs resides on the same Ethernet LAN. That fifth PC requires two routers and a point-to-point link to connect it with the other participants. The example concentrates on the link between the two routers, and it focuses on traffic flowing from the Ethernet to the Token Ring.

Because there are four PCs on the Ethernet side of the link, there will be four separate flows that cross it. If fixed filter reservations were in use, separate reservations would be needed for each flow. Assuming that an audio transmission requires 16 Kbit/s of bandwidth, these reservations would consume 64 Kbit/s of the link's resources.

Audio conferences have a special property, however. Not all parties speak at once. (Well, if they do, understanding is probably lost, so it makes little sense for the network to go out of its way to accommodate that behavior.) In the most polite conferences, all the application really needs is 16 Kbit/s of bandwidth. More realistically, it would be preferable to reserve about 32 Kbit/s of bandwidth so that some extra bandwidth is available to handle momentary outbursts.

To reserve this bandwidth, the application can have RSVP make either *shared explicit* or *wildcard filter* reservations.

▼ **Figure 9.8**

In this example, there are potentially four flows crossing the link between the routers, one for each of the PCs on the left. But not everyone will speak at the same time, so it's okay to reserve somewhat less bandwidth than all the flows together might theoretically need. All four flows can then share that reservation. Only active flows would actually use the reserved bandwidth at any one time.

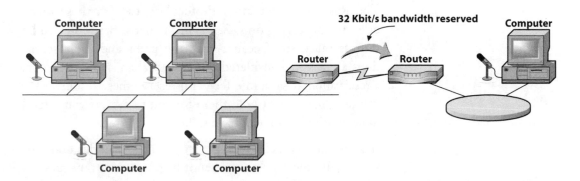

Each of these styles reserves a network resource (in this case 32 kbit/s of bandwidth) and shares that resource among multiple flows. The four flows sharing the bandwidth are the transmissions from the four PCs.

The difference between the two styles is how tightly the application must specify the flows that share the resource. With a shared explicit reservation, the application must explicitly identify every participating sender. In the example of figure 9.8, the right PC would have to explicitly list the source addresses of participants 1 through 4.

The wildcard filter style lets an application share a resource without identifying every sender. Any flow that matches the reservation's specification may use the resource, regardless of its sender. The right PC, for example, could reserve the resources for any traffic that has a destination port of 5004. Such a reservation assumes that no other traffic will use the same port, either accidentally or deliberately. Wildcard filters offer convenience in exchange for control and security.

RSVP and Dynamic Networks

In some ways, reserving network resources seems to conflict with the very nature of IP networks. The Internet Protocol, after all, was designed for dynamic networks. What good is a reservation when one of its supporting routers fails? And how does RSVP adapt when a new, more efficient route suddenly becomes available?

The Resource Reservation Protocol copes with these kinds of events by relying on *soft state* in the network's routers. The state is called soft because both the paths and the reservations are always considered tentative. When a router accepts a reservation, it says, in effect, "I'll reserve these resources for you now, but I won't hold them for you forever; if you intend to keep using them, you have to keep telling me."

Indeed, this is exactly how RSVP operates. A sender does not send a path message only when it begins a new transmission.

Instead, it continues to send path messages for the life of the flow. If the network experiences no changes, these subsequent path messages merely refresh the existing path. If a new route appears, however, the path messages will introduce the flow to routers along that new path. Reservations work the same way. Receivers periodically send reservation requests. These requests may refresh existing reservations, or they may let a new router know what is required of it.

The next four figures show how a new client can join a video multicast already in progress. As they illustrate, such an operation requires the services of several different protocols. Figure 9.9 shows the situation before the new client appears. Two clients are receiving the video. As the figure points out, the sender periodically generates new path messages, and the receivers periodically refresh their reservations.

In figure 9.10 a new client wishes to receive the video. The client starts this process by joining the appropriate multicast group. To do this, it sends an IGMP group membership report message on its local Ethernet (step 1). The local router receives this message and updates its own record of who belongs to the group. To update the rest of the network, the router builds an OSPF link state advertisement and floods it through the network (step 2). Once all routers are updated,

▼ **Figure 9.9**

Once a flow is in progress, the sender periodically resends path messages and receivers periodically refresh their reservations. This behavior allows RSVP to respond automatically to changes in the network.

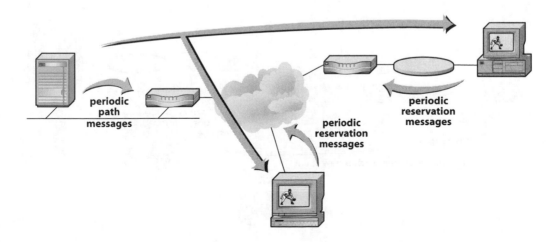

periodic path messages

periodic reservation messages

periodic reservation messages

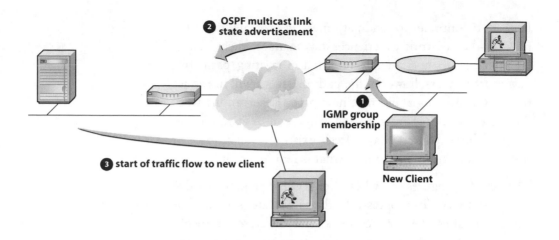

Figure 9.10 ▲

To receive multicast traffic, a new client must first join the multicast group.

Figure 9.11 ▼

Once the client has joined the group, it begins receiving the sender's path messages. With the path information, the client can place its reservation.

multicast traffic begins to flow to the new client (step 3). So far, no reservations have been placed. Without reserved resources, the traffic flow to the new client may not be suitable for the video transmission.

The Resource Reservation Protocol gets involved in figure 9.11. Now that multicast traffic reaches the new client, path messages for the flow can reach it as well. In step 4, a periodic path message from the sender does reach the new client. With this path message in hand, the client can identify the flow and place its own reservations (step 5).

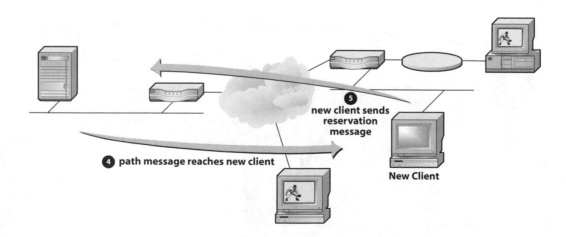

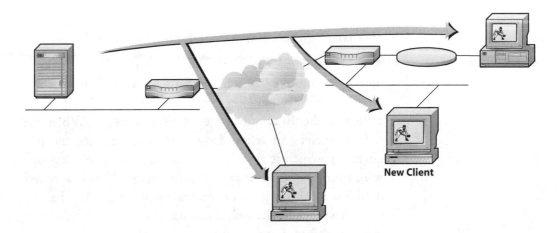

Figure 9.12 shows the results of this reservation. The video transmission continues with all three clients participating, each with the required resources reserved. The server continues sending its periodic path messages, and now all three clients periodically refresh their reservations.

Optimizing RSVP Performance

Although its soft state operation makes RSVP responsive to dynamic networks, not all environments require this flexibility. Particularly in the case of label switched paths, the network path and its associated resource requirements may be static, stable, and built on reliable networks. In those environments, the constant path and reservation refreshes are unnecessary, and processing the messages can become a burden on the RSVP-capable routers maintaining the flow. Internet engineers have developed several extensions to the basic RSVP protocol to optimize its performance in static and stable environments.

The simplest extension is the *bundle* message. A bundle message is, quite simply, a collection of several different RSVP messages bundled together and sent as a single message. Combining individual messages reduces the number of RSVP messages flowing through the network. Bundles minimize

▲ Figure 9.12

With its reservation complete, the new client participates in the application assured that the network has reserved for it the necessary resources.

bandwidth that RSVP itself uses, and they reduce the number of separate packets that each router has to process.

Another extension to RSVP adds an optional, and unique, message identifier to each standard message. The message identifier permits two key optimizations. First, it lets a recipient explicitly acknowledge an RSVP message. When the sender receives an acknowledgment, it can reduce the frequency at which it refreshes the message. A second key optimization is the *summary refresh* message. When a router needs to refresh a path or reservation message that has already been acknowledged, it can use the summary refresh to indicate the message identifier being refreshed. As long as nothing about the path or the reservation has changed, the message identifier serves as a convenient abbreviation for the full message.

Extensions for Traffic Engineering

It is clear that the normal operation of RSVP very closely resembles the operation of CR-LDP. Where CR-LDP uses a label mapping request message, RSVP has a path message. And CR-LDP's label mapping message has a function very similar to the RSVP reservation message. Support for traffic engineering through label distribution, therefore, is a natural extension for RSVP. These extensions are usually abbreviated RSVP-TE.

As the name suggests, the RSVP extensions are primarily intended for traffic engineering. As such, they correspond much more to CR-LDP than to basic LDP. For example, RSVP-TE assumes a downstream-on-demand advertising discipline; it does not support downstream unsolicited advertising.

In order to support traffic engineering, RSVP-TE makes a few additions to traditional RSVP. First, it expands the definition of traffic flows to include label switched paths. That lets an RSVP-capable router assign traffic to RSVP flows based on their MPLS label. Second, RSVP-TE modifies the protocol rules so path and reservation messages can travel between

RSVP-TE Status

Just as is the case for CR-LDP, the RSVP-TE specifications were, at the time of this writing, still only works in progress. Although the general principles in this section are firmly established, details such as message formats may change before the work becomes a proposed IETF standard. Implementers are strongly encouraged to consult the latest IETF specifications for an up-to-date status of the RSVP-TE protocol.

ingress and egress routers. As figure 9.13 shows, this is slightly different from standard RSVP, where path and reservation messages travel between the flows' original source and ultimate destination.

In the RSVP messages themselves, RSVP-TE adds fields that let path messages request label mappings and reservation messages return label values. The RSVP-TE extensions also allow an ingress router to specify an explicit route for the flow, much the same way as CR-LDP. Finally, RSVP-TE makes the actual resource reservation optional. With this flexibility, routers can use RSVP-TE to distribute labels even when the paths do not need reserved network resources.

RSVP Message Formats

As a control protocol like ICMP, RSVP places its message in the payload of IP datagrams. The IP next header value for RSVP is 46. It is also possible to carry RSVP within UDP datagrams; however, that encapsulation is primarily for older host systems that force all applications to use either TCP or UDP.

Each RSVP message begins with a common RSVP header. As figure 9.14 shows, the header contains eight defined fields, plus two reserved areas. The RSVP message begins with a version number. The current version of RSVP is 1. The next four bits, labeled *flags*, indicate optional capabilities of the sender. Currently only the least significant bit is defined; if it is set, the sender supports refresh reduction.

▼ **Figure 9.13**

When RSVP supports traffic engineering, path and reservation messages originate at the ingress and egress routers, not the source and destinations for the flows.

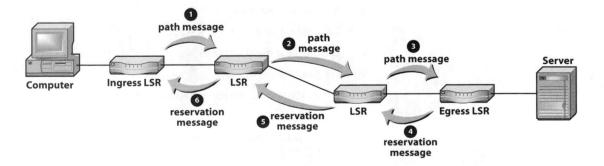

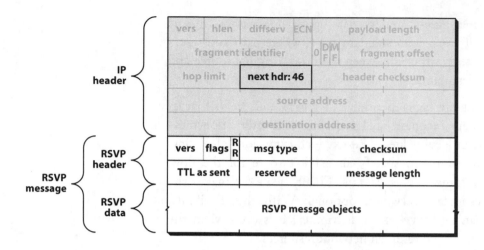

IP header				
vers	hlen	diffserv ECN		payload length
fragment identifier		0 D F M F		fragment offset
hop limit		next hdr: 46		header checksum
source address				
destination address				

RSVP message

RSVP header				
vers	flags R R	msg type		checksum
TTL as sent		reserved		message length

RSVP data	
RSVP messge objects	

Figure 9.14 ▲

RSVP messages are carried directly in IP datagrams. The consist of a header and RSVP data.

The RSVP *type* byte identifies the particular type of RSVP message. The chapter has discussed the two primary message types, path messages and reservation messages. In addition, RSVP defines messages to report or diagnose errors, terminate paths and reservations, and confirm reservations. Table 9.2 lists the values that the type byte may take.

Table 9.2 RSVP Message Types

Value	Message Type
1	Path message
2	Reservation message
3	Path error message
4	Reservation error message
5	Path teardown message
6	Reservation teardown message
7	Reservation confirmation message
8	Diagnostic request message
9	Diagnostic reply message
10	Reservation teardown confirmation message
12	Bundle message
13	Bundle acknowledgement message

Table 9.2 continued

Value	Message Type
15	Summary refresh message
20	Hello message
25	Integrity challenge message
26	Integrity response message
66	Designated subnetwork bandwidth manager offer message
67	Designated subnetwork bandwidth manager claim message

Integrity Message Types

RFC 2747 specifies that the integrity challenge and integrity response have message types of 11 and 12, respectively. Those values were assigned in error, however, as type 12 identifies a bundle message. RFC 3097 lists the correct values.

The *checksum* field contains the standard TCP/IP one's complement checksum of the entire message. It protects against the message being corrupted in transit.

The *TTL as sent* field in the RSVP header is a slightly tricky mechanism to detect non-RSVP routers in the path. When a router sends a path message, it sets the value of this field in the RSVP header to match the value of the IP header's hop limit field. Figure 9.15 shows such a message leaving the left router. If the next hop doesn't understand RSVP, it merely decrements the IP hop limit field and forwards the datagram. When the message arrives at the right router, that router compares the received IP hop limit field with the RSVP send TTL field. If, as in the figure's example, they differ, then there must be a non-RSVP router in the path.

▼ **Figure 9.15**

The TTL-as-sent field lets RSVP routers detect the presence of a non-RSVP router between them. The non-RSVP router will decrement the IP hop limit, but it won't know to update the RSVP message header.

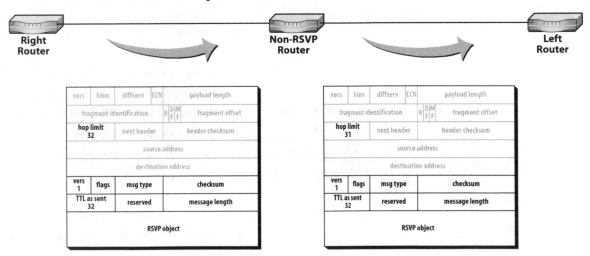

Figure 9.16 ▶

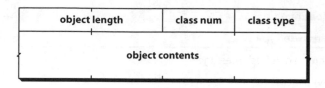

Figure 9.16 ▶

RSVP data consists of one or more
RSVP objects. All objects have the
same general format.

The last two bytes of the common RSVP header contain the
length of the whole RSVP message.

The remainder of every RSVP message consists of a series of
objects. These objects are figure 9.14's message body. Each
object has the same basic format, shown in figure 9.16. The
object length indicates the size of the object, while the class
number and class type distinguish different object types.
There are currently 38 different object types defined; table 9.3
lists their class numbers and types.

Table 9.3 RSVP Objects

Num	Object	Type	Description
0	NULL		Ignored by recipient.
1	SESSION	1	Traffic flow defined by IPv4 destination.
		2	Traffic flow defined by IPv6 destination.
		3	Traffic flow defined by encrypted IPv4 destination.
		4	Traffic flow defined by encrypted IPv6 destination.
		7	Traffic flow defined by IPv4 label switched path.
		8	Traffic flow defined by IPv6 label switched path.
3	RSVP_HOP	1	IPv4 previous or next hop address.
		2	IPv6 previous or next hop address.
4	INTEGRITY	1	Keyed MD5 authentication data.
5	TIME_VALUES	1	Frequency of path or reservation refreshes.
6	ERROR_SPEC	1	Error information from an IPv4 system.
		2	Error information from an IPv6 system.

Table 9.3 continued

Num	Object	Type	Description
7	SCOPE	1	List of IPv4 hosts to which wildcard style reservation refresh messages apply.
		2	List of IPv6 hosts to which wildcard style reservation refresh messages apply.
8	STYLE	1	Style of reservation.
9	FLOWSPEC	2	Flow specification qualities.
		3	Flow specification class of service.
10	FILTER_SPEC	1	IPv4-based filter to apply to flow.
		2	IPv6-based filter using source port values.
		3	IPv6-based filter using flow label values.
		4	Encrypted IPv4-based filter.
		5	Encrypted IPv6-based filter.
		7	IPv4-based filter using label switched path.
		8	IPv6-based filter using label switched path.
11	SENDER_ TEMPLATE	1	IPv4-based description of flow sender is generating.
		2	IPv6-based description of sender's flow.
		3	IPv6 flow label sender is generating.
		4	Encrypted IPv4-based description.
		5	Encrypted IPv6-based description.
		7	IPv4-based LSP sender is generating.
		8	IPv6-based LSP sender is generating.
12	SENDER_ TSPEC	1	Traffic specification.
		2	Traffic class of service.
13	ADSPEC	2	Sender's advertised information for flow.
14	POLICY_DATA	1	Policy information for flow.
15	RESV_ CONFIRM	1	IPv4 reservation confirmation.
		2	IPv6 reservation confirmation.

continues…

Table 9.3 RSVP Objects (continued)

Num	Object	Type	Description
16	RSVP_LABEL	1	MPLS label.
17	HOP_COUNT	1	IPv4 hop count.
19	LABEL_REQUEST	1	Generic MPLS label request.
		2	ATM label request.
		3	Frame relay label request.
20	EXPLICIT_ROUTE	1	Explicit route for LSP.
21	ROUTE_RECORD	1	Recording of LSP route.
22	HELLO	1	Neighbor greeting request.
		2	Neighbor greeting acknowledgment.
23	MESSAGE_ID	1	RSVP message identifier.
24	MESSAGE_ID_ACK	1	Message identifier acknowledgment.
		2	Message identifier rejection.
25	MESSAGE_ID_LIST	1	Message identifier list.
		2	IPv4 message identifier source list.
		3	IPv6 message identifier source list.
		4	IPv4 message identifier multicast list.
		5	IPv6 message identifier multicast list.
30	DIAGNOSTIC	1	IPv4 diagnostic.
		2	IPv6 diagnostic.
31	ROUTE	1	IPv4 route.
		2	IPv6 route.
32	DIAG_RESPONSE	1	IPv4 diagnostic response.
		2	IPv6 diagnostic response.
33	DIAG_SELECT	1	Diagnostic selection.
42	DSBM_IP_ADDRESS	1	IPv4 designated subnetwork bandwidth manager.
		2	IPv6 designated subnetwork bandwidth manager.

Table 9.3 continued

Num	Object	Type	Description
43	SBM_PRIORITY	1	Subnetwork bandwidth manager priority.
44	DSBM_TIMER_INTERVALS	1	Designated subnetwork bandwidth manager timer intervals.
45	SBM_INFO	1	Media type.
64	CHALLENGE	1	Authentication challenge value.
161	RSVP_HOP_L2	1	IEEE (MAC) address of RSVP hop.
162	LAN_NHOP_L2	1	IEEE (MAC) address of next hop.
163	LAN_NHOP_L3	1	IPv4 address of next hop.
		2	IPv6 address of next hop.
164	LAN_LOOPBACK	1	IPv4 loopback.
		2	IPv6 loopback.
207	SESSION_ATTRIBUTE	7	LSP tunnel attribute.

Path Messages

The RSVP specifications contain precise descriptions of path messages, including the objects that they may contain and the order in which those objects must appear in the message. A full path message, however, can be lengthy and complex; this section, therefore, considers a typical path message as shown in figure 9.17.

Following the common RSVP header, the message contains four different objects; these objects identify the destination, the message's previous hop, the frequency at which it will be refreshed, and the flow itself. Most of the objects' values are straightforward and require no discussion. Some fields, on the other hand, are not obvious. The SESSION object, for example, includes its own flags field. Currently, only the least significant bit of this field is defined.

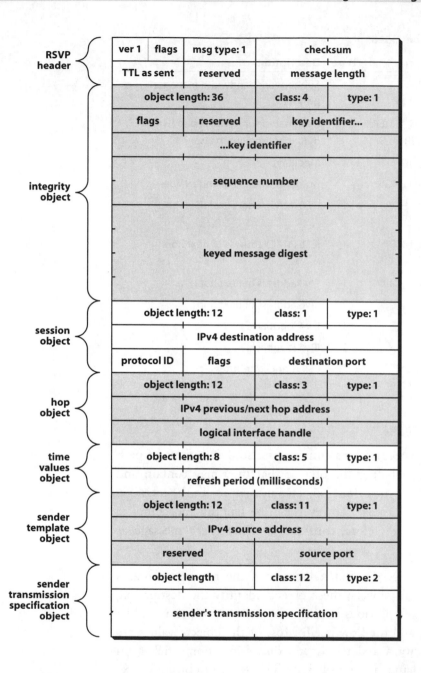

Figure 9.17 ▲

This example shows a typical RSVP
path message.

The source of a flow starts by setting this flag bit in its path
messages. As the path messages travel through the network,
each router determines if it is capable of limiting the traffic

for the flows. By limiting traffic, a router makes sure that the flow uses no more bandwidth than has been reserved. Exercising such a limit is known as *traffic policing*. The first system that is capable of traffic policing clears this bit in the path messages, and the bit remains clear as the messages travel to their destinations.

The RSVP_HOP object includes a logical interface handle. A router sets this field to help identify the flow. Any reservation requests from downstream systems include this value.

The TIME_VALUES object announces the frequency at which the source will refresh path information. The first field tells how often the sending router will itself refresh the path. For example, if the refresh period is 100, then the router claims that it will send new path messages every 100 milliseconds. The second field allows downstream systems to refresh less often, but it specifies an upper limit. A value of 500 would allow downstream routers to go as long as 500 milliseconds between new path messages.

Path messages are addressed to the same destination as the flow itself. Unlike data flow, though, routers along the path must examine the contents of each message. Figure 9.18 illustrates this process by showing a path message traversing a network. As the figure shows, each router modifies the message by inserting its own address in the RSVP_HOP field. To make it easy for routers to distinguish RSVP messages that need this type of special treatment, the messages include the router alert option in the IP header.

If a path message travels through a router that does not understand RSVP, that router passes the message like any other traffic, oblivious to its contents. Of course, a router that doesn't understand RSVP won't reserve resources for an RSVP flow, but it won't block the flow either. This behavior makes it possible to introduce RSVP support into a network gracefully, without having to upgrade all the network's routers at the same time.

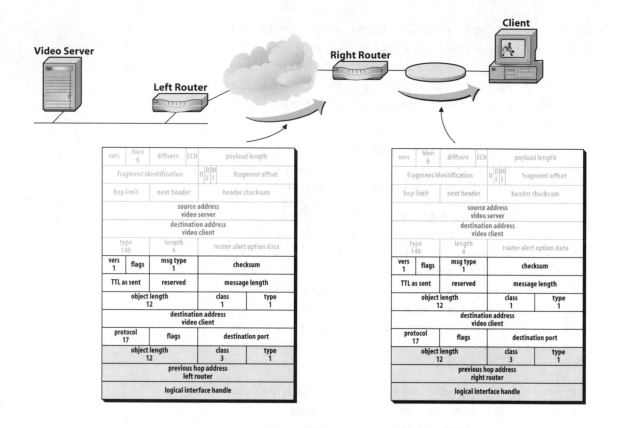

Figure 9.18 ▲

As this example indicates, RSVP path messages are addressed to the flow's destination, even though intermediate routers are expected to examine and modify the message. Each router, for example, places its own IP address in the RSVP previous hop object.

Reservation Requests

Like path messages, reservation requests have a prescribed set of objects and order for those objects, and the resulting messages can be rather complicated. Figure 9.19 presents a typical reservation request with a few key objects. The SESSION object describes the destination address and, optionally, the destination port for the flow being reserved. The RSVP_HOP object identifies the last system to handle the reservation request. Because the reservation travels in the opposite direction of the flow itself, this object also identifies the system that will be the next hop for the flow.

The TIME_VALUES object serves the same purpose here as in an RSVP path message. It tells how often the sender (of the

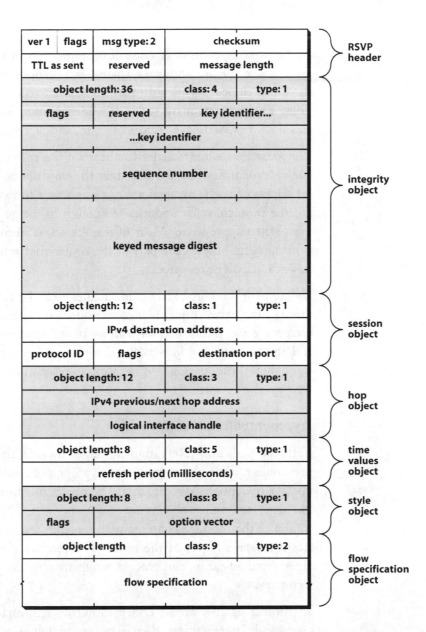

ver 1	flags	msg type: 2	checksum		RSVP header

The figure shows an RSVP reservation message with the following structure:

ver 1	flags	msg type: 2	checksum
TTL as sent	reserved	message length	

RSVP header

object length: 36		class: 4	type: 1
flags	reserved	key identifier...	
...key identifier			
sequence number			
keyed message digest			

integrity object

object length: 12		class: 1	type: 1
IPv4 destination address			
protocol ID	flags	destination port	

session object

object length: 12		class: 3	type: 1
IPv4 previous/next hop address			
logical interface handle			

hop object

object length: 8		class: 5	type: 1
refresh period (milliseconds)			

time values object

object length: 8		class: 8	type: 1
flags	option vector		

style object

object length		class: 9	type: 2
flow specification			

flow specification object

reservation request, not the flow) will refresh its reservation and how long upstream systems may go between refreshes.

The next object, STYLE, indicates the reservation style. The *option vector* part of this object identifies the style. Its first 19

▲ **Figure 9.19**

This example shows a typical RSVP reservation message.

bits are currently not used. The next two bits identify the type of sharing control. A value of 01_2 represents distinct reservations while 10_2 indicates shared reservations. The last three bits indicate wildcard (001_2) or explicit (010_2) reservations. The three standard styles of wildcard filter, fixed filter, and shared explicit have vectors of 17, 10, and 18, respectively.

The FLOWSPEC object carries the heart of the reservation request. It identifies the resources that the flow needs. The exact details of the FLOWSPEC are not important to RSVP itself, but the protocol must understand enough to merge reservations when appropriate. Most of the FLOWSPEC information is meaningful only to the part of the router that actually reserves and assigns resources.

Unlike path messages, reservation requests can be forwarded through the network just like conventional IP datagrams. At each stage the IP destination address is the upstream router and the IP source address is the downstream router. Figure 9.20 shows the passage of a sample reservation request through the network.

Cryptographic Authentication

Both the path and reservation messages include an INTEGRITY object. This object provides cryptographic authentication for the entire RSVP message. The object functions much the same as similar objects for OSPF and RIP. The sender combines the message contents with a secret key and generates a message digest of the result. The receiver checks the digest by duplicating the process, using its own copy of the secret key.

To protect against an adversary capturing legitimate messages and later reusing them inappropriately (an exploit known generally as a *replay attack*), the INTEGRITY object includes a sequence number that must continually increment with each new message.

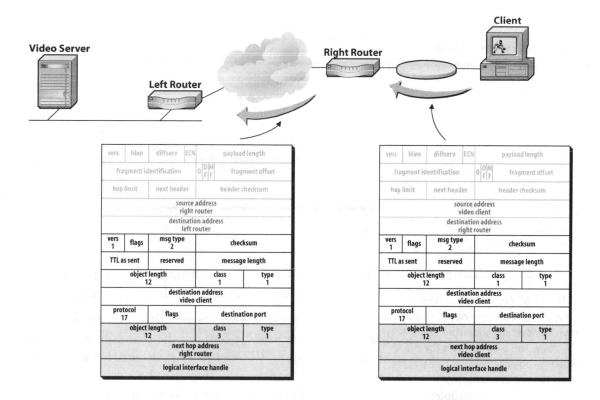

The size of the message digest depends on the particular digest algorithm. For the commonly used MD5 algorithm, the digest is 16 bytes, which is what figure 9.21 shows.

There are also two additional message types—integrity challenge and integrity response—that let one system pick up where it left off after a restart or reinitialization. This function is optional, however, and may be vetoed by either party. The handshake flag in the INTEGRITY object indicates a sender's willingness to use handshake messages.

Figure 9.22 shows an integrity challenge message. It carries just one object, a CHALLENGE object. This object identifies the key that the recipient should use, and it provides some data for which the recipient should create a digest. One way

▲ **Figure 9.20**

Unlike path messages, reservation requests have intermediate routers as their explicit destination.

Figure 9.21 ▶

This example shows a message
integrity object. RSVP routers use
this object to prove they know the
secret key.

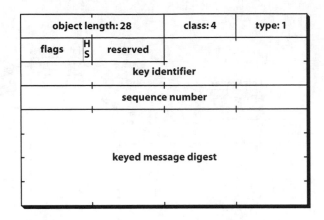

Figure 9.22 ▼

The RSVP integrity challenge
message asks a peer router to
prove it knows the shared secret
key. The only object is the
challenge object. The peer must
respond with a keyed hash of the
cookie in this object.

to generate this data is to perform an MD5 message digest of
the time of day a and secret known only to the sender.

The receiver responds with an integrity response message
like that of figure 9.23. It contains the challenge object and
an integrity object. When the original sender verifies its
message digest (and verifies that the challenge cookie was
not altered), it knows that the peer shares the same key.

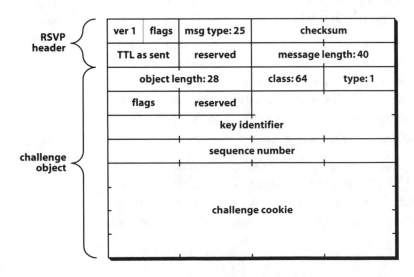

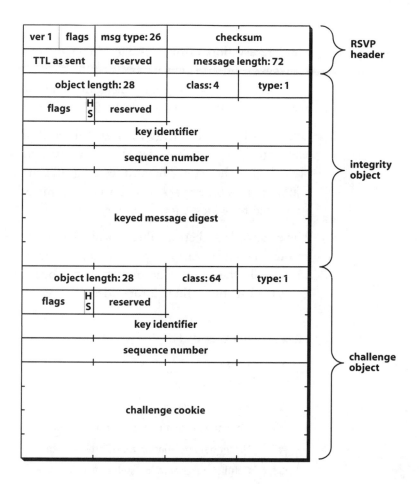

ver 1	flags	msg type: 26	checksum		RSVP

The figure shows the following fields:

- ver 1 | flags | msg type: 26 | checksum — RSVP header
- TTL as sent | reserved | message length: 72 — RSVP header
- object length: 28 | class: 4 | type: 1 — integrity object
- flags | H S | reserved
- key identifier
- sequence number
- keyed message digest
- object length: 28 | class: 64 | type: 1 — challenge object
- flags | H S | reserved
- key identifier
- sequence number
- challenge cookie

Error Messages

Path messages and reservation requests may encounter errors, and RSVP defines a separate error message for each. When a system detects an error, it usually sends the error report along the reverse path of the original message. This procedure allows systems that previously accepted the message to release any resources they had reserved on the assumption that the reservation would succeed.

In general, each error message includes enough objects to identify the RSVP message that caused the error. Path error

▲ Figure 9.23

The RSVP integrity challenge response message returns the challenge object and an integrity object with the results of the keyed hash.

messages contain SESSION and SENDER_TEMPLATE objects, while reservation error messages include SESSION, STYLE, FLOWSPEC, and FILTER_SPEC objects. Both types of messages also include an ERROR_SPEC object that indicates the error encountered. Figure 9.24 shows the format of this object.

Only two bits of the flags field are currently defined. The least significant bit indicates that a reservation remains in place despite the error. The next least significant bit indicates that a reservation error occurred because some other receiver attempted to request more resources.

The error code and error value provide details of the problem encountered. The error code normally indicates a specific error, while the error value provides additional information. Table 9.4 lists the defined error codes.

Table 9.4 RSVP Error Codes

Code	Cause
1	Admission control failure
2	Policy control failure
3	No path information for this reservation
4	No sender information for this reservation
5	Conflicting reservation styles
6	Unknown reservation style
7	Conflicting destination ports
8	Conflicting sender ports
12	Service preempted
13	Unknown object class
14	Unknown object type
21	Traffic control error
22	Traffic control system error
23	RSVP system error

object length: 12		class: 6	type: 1
IPv4 address of system that detected the error			
flags	error code	error value	

◀ **Figure 9.24**

The ERROR_SPEC object identifies a particular error and the router that detected it.

Diagnostic Messages

The standard RSVP error messages provide information when a path or reservation fails, but there are many occasions other than complete failure when network administrators could use information about the state of RSVP flows. To provide that information, RSVP has two special message types—a diagnostic request and a diagnostic reply.

Figure 9.25 shows how these messages can be used in a network. The workstation in the figure needs to diagnose the real-time flow between the server and client. It sends a diagnostic request to the last hop for the flow, the right router. That router adds its soft state information, including interface addresses, hop counts, merge state, and timer values, and forwards the request to the next hop upstream, the left router. The left router adds its information and forwards the request upstream to the video server. When the flow's source receives the request, it adds its own information and returns the reply to the workstation. At that point the workstation has collected complete RSVP state information for the flow.

▼ **Figure 9.25**

This example shows how an RSVP diagnostic exchange collects information about an active flow. The flow's destination begins the exchange with a diagnostic request. The request travels hop by hop until it reaches the flow's source. The source then returns a diagnostic reply.

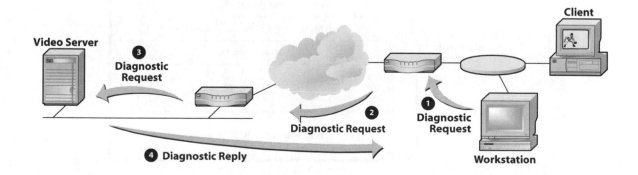

Both diagnostic requests and diagnostic replies share the same message format. Figure 9.26 shows its structure. The message type is 8 for requests and 9 for replies. The new object in the figure is a DIAGNOSTIC object. It contains a hop count limit and a hop count. If the limit is nonzero, it provides a limit to the number of RSVP hops the message can traverse. Intermediate routers increment the hop count until it reaches the maximum value, at which point they return an error message. This behavior allows a router sending diagnostic messages to perform an expanding hop count search for an intermediate router causing problems with diagnostic messages. The path MTU, fragment offset, and MF (more fragments) fields let routers fragment diagnostic messages if necessary.

Figure 9.26 ▼

This example shows a typical diagnostic request or reply message.

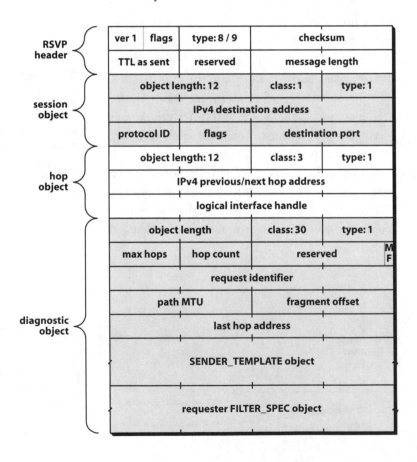

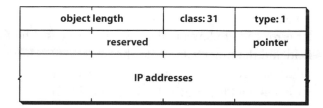

object length	class: 31	type: 1
reserved		pointer
IP addresses		

The ROUTE object lets diagnostic exchanges trace the path of a flow. As diagnostic requests travel upstream, each router adds its own address to this object.

If the system generating a diagnostic request wants to record the RSVP path of a diagnostic exchange, it does so with the ROUTE object of figure 9.27. As the request travels through the network, each hop adds its own address to the object and increments the pointer. When the reply returns, it follows the same path in reverse. Routers don't alter the address list in the reply, but they do decrement the pointer so that it always points to the next destination for the reply.

Figure 9.28 shows the actual diagnostic information returned in the reply; it's contained in a DIAG_RESPONSE object. The object notes the time the diagnostic request arrived, the incoming and outgoing interfaces for the flow (which will be opposite from the interfaces of the diagnostic request), and the previous RSVP hop. The DIAG_RESPONSE object also carries the number of IP hops between the current router and the last RSVP router to handle the request. The next field is a

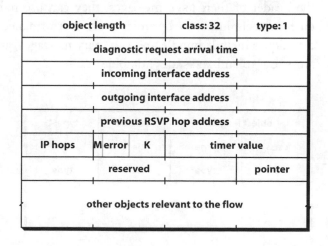

object length		class: 32	type: 1
diagnostic request arrival time			
incoming interface address			
outgoing interface address			
previous RSVP hop address			
IP hops	M error K	timer value	
reserved			pointer
other objects relevant to the flow			

◀ **Figure 9.28**

The diagnostic reply message returns a DIAG_RESPONSE object. The object carries summary information about the flow.

single-bit flag set to 1 if the reservation is merged. A three-bit error code follows; table 9.5 lists its values. The four-bit κ field and the timer value hold the router's refresh time. The κ value is used to (slightly) randomize the timing of refresh messages, and the time value is rounded to seconds.

Table 9.5 Diagnostic Response Errors

Value	Error
000	No error
001	No path statistics
010	Packet too big
100	Route object too big

The DIAG_RESPONSE object concludes by embedding other objects relevant to the flow. By default, these other objects are the SENDER_TSPEC object, the FILTER_SPEC object, the FLOWSPEC object, and the STYLE object. If the system that creates the diagnostic request message wants a different set of objects for the flow, it can list them in a DIAG_SELECT object. As figure 9.29 shows, this object consists solely of a list of class and type values.

Refresh Reduction

If two routers both set the refresh reduction capable flag in the header of their RSVP messages, they can use refresh reduction techniques to optimize RSVP performance. These techniques include bundle and summary messages, as well as MESSAGE_ID and MESSAGE_ACK objects.

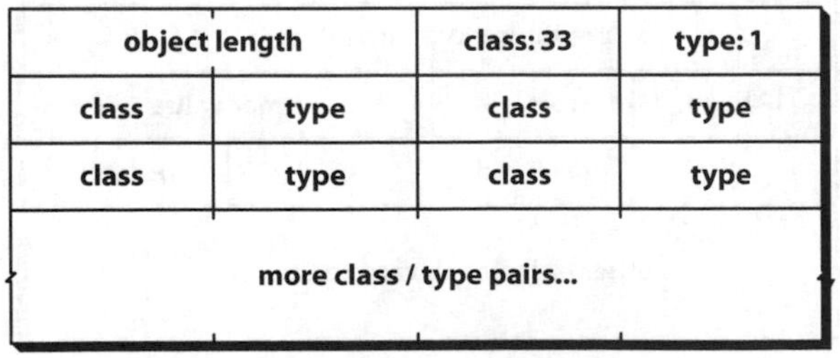

Figure 9.29 ▶

The DIAG_SELECT object lets a system generating a diagnostic request specify which objects (by class and type) it wants included in the DIAG_RESPONSE object.

object length		class: 33	type: 1
class	type	class	type
class	type	class	type
more class / type pairs...			

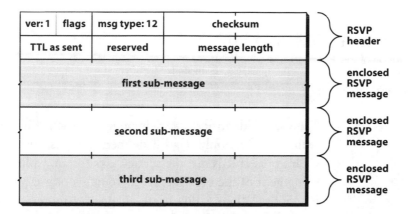

The bundle message simply combines other RSVP messages into one, reducing the number of separate messages that the routers must process. Figure 9.30 shows an example. After the common RSVP header, individual messages—or sub-messages—follow, one after the other.

The MESSAGE_ID object can simplify the processing of reservation and path messages. When a router first generates either message, it assigns that message a unique identifier. Later, when it needs to refresh the state by resending the same RSVP message, it includes the same message identifier. The receiving router can recognize that the message identifier hasn't changed, so it knows to simply refresh the existing state. No new information is present, so the receiving router can avoid parsing and processing the entire message. Of course, once the flow state changes, the sending router has to generate a new message identifier.

Figure 9.31 shows a MESSAGE_ID object. The epoch value is a random number generated each time the router restarts; the

▲ **Figure 9.30**

The bundle message is a convenient way to combine many individual RSVP messages into one. Doing so can reduce network and processing overhead.

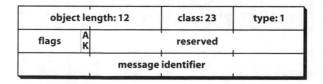

◀ **Figure 9.31**

The MESSAGE_ID object uniquely identifies a specific RSVP message so it can be referenced later by other messages.

Figure 9.32 ▶

The MESSAGE_ID_ACK object acknowledges reception of the message identified by the included message ID.

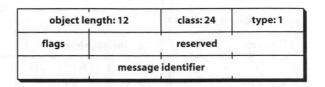

object length: 12	class: 24	type: 1
flags	reserved	
message identifier		

message identifier itself increments each time the state changes. The only flag bit defined so far is the least significant one. If it is set, the sender asks for an explicit acknowledgment of the message. It lets routers optimize their refresh periods. When a flow state changes, a router can send the new reservation or path message with this bit set, and it can resend the message very frequently. When its peer acknowledges the message, the router falls back to a more lengthy refresh period. This procedure reduces network traffic and the routers' processing burdens, but it still allows the network to respond rapidly and robustly to changes.

To acknowledge a message the peer includes a MESSAGE_ID_ACK object, shown in figure 9.32. No flags are defined for this object. Here is also a MESSAGE_ID_NAK object to indicate a message did not arrive. It has the same format as in figure 9.32, except the object type value is 2. If the receiving router doesn't have a convenient message in which to include its acknowledgment, it can use the special acknowledgment message of figure 9.33.

Figure 9.33 ▼

The acknowledgment message can carry MESSAGE_ID_ACK or MESSAGE_ID_NAK objects if the sender doesn't have any other convenient message in which to include them.

The MESSAGE_ID object can save processing time in routers that receive reservation or path messages, and it can help reduce the frequency of those messages. The object alone

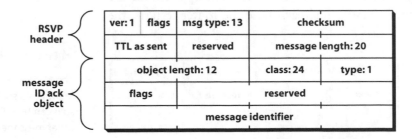

RSVP header

message ID ack object

ver: 1	flags	msg type: 13	checksum	
TTL as sent	reserved	message length: 20		
object length: 12		class: 24	type: 1	
flags	reserved			
message identifier				

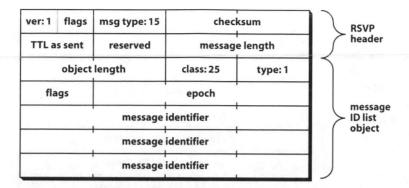

ver: 1	flags	msg type: 15	checksum	
TTL as sent		reserved	message length	
object length			class: 25	type: 1
flags		epoch		
message identifier				
message identifier				
message identifier				

doesn't reduce the size of the messages, though; the path and reservation messages still must include all their normal objects. If the sending router knows the receiving router understands message identifiers, however, it ought to be able to omit those other objects entirely. To remain compatible with RSVP routers that don't support refresh reduction, the extra objects can't be eliminated from the path and reservation messages themselves. Instead, a new message type—the summary message—provides that optimization. Figure 9.34 shows a simple summary refresh. The only object in its example contains a list of message identifiers, along with the epoch associated with all of them.

For multicast flows, two other objects summarize their message identifiers. Figure 9.35 shows a MESSAGE_ID_SRC_LIST

▲ **Figure 9.34**

The summary refresh message is a shorthand way to refresh previous path or reservation messages. It indicates the specific messages it is refreshing by their message identifiers.

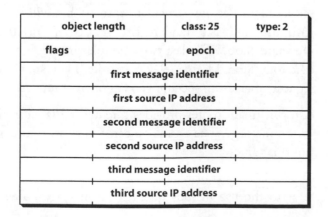

object length		class: 25	type: 2
flags		epoch	
first message identifier			
first source IP address			
second message identifier			
second source IP address			
third message identifier			
third source IP address			

◀ **Figure 9.35**

The MESSAGE_ID_SRC_LIST object can summarize multicast flows that may have the same message identifier used by multiple senders. The object explicitly includes the sender's IP address to distinguish those messages.

Figure 9.36 ▶

The MESSAGE_ID_MCAST_LIST object also summarizes multicast flow messages. In addition to the message identifier and sender's IP address, it includes the flow destination.

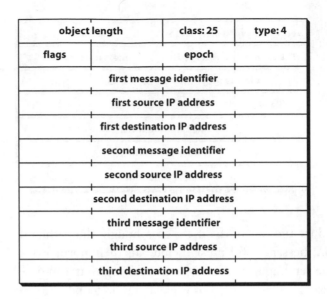

object length		class: 25	type: 4
flags		epoch	
first message identifier			
first source IP address			
first destination IP address			
second message identifier			
second source IP address			
second destination IP address			
third message identifier			
third source IP address			
third destination IP address			

object, which includes the sender's IP address along with the message identifier. The MESSAGE_ID_MCAST_LIST object, shown in figure 9.36, adds the destination multicast address.

Traffic Engineering Extensions

The RSVP extensions to support MPLS traffic engineering are relatively straightforward. To begin the label distribution process by requesting a label, upstream routers add a LA-BEL_REQUEST object to their path messages. Figure 9.37 shows several examples of this object. In all three cases the sender identifies the particular protocol that will be using the path; this value is a standard Ethernet type, so IP traffic uses the value 0800_{16}. The last two examples in the figure are specific to ATM and frame relay networks. They allow routers to request labels from specific VPI/VCI or DLCI ranges.

A downstream router provides a requested label in its reservation message. The LABEL object, shown in figure 9.38, carries this value.

Once a label is available for a label switched path, routers can refer to the LSP in subsequent RSVP messages. These paths,

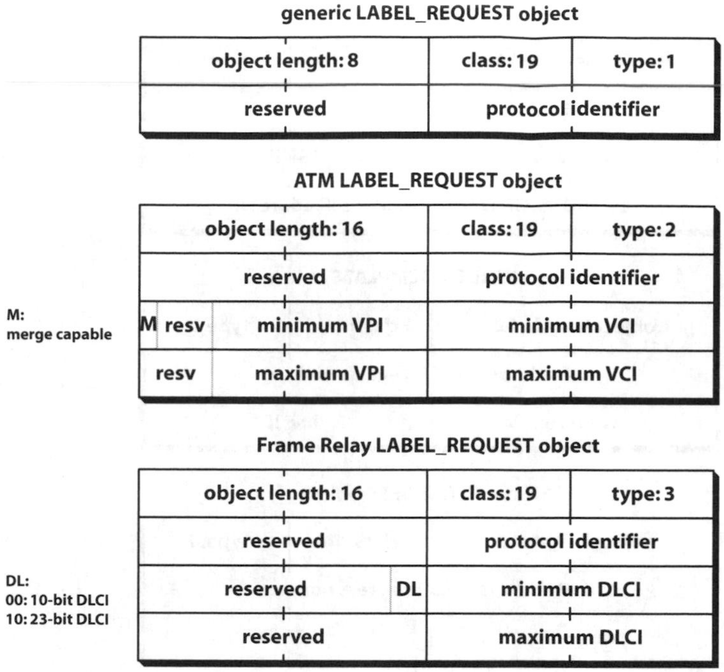

generic LABEL_REQUEST object

object length: 8	class: 19	type: 1
reserved	protocol identifier	

ATM LABEL_REQUEST object

object length: 16	class: 19	type: 2
reserved	protocol identifier		
M	resv	minimum VPI	minimum VCI
resv	maximum VPI	maximum VCI	

M:
merge capable

Frame Relay LABEL_REQUEST object

object length: 16	class: 19	type: 3
reserved	protocol identifier		
reserved	DL	minimum DLCI	
reserved	maximum DLCI		

DL:
00: 10-bit DLCI
10: 23-bit DLCI

◀ **Figure 9.37**

The LABEL_REQUEST object lets RSVP routers request an MPLS label. The label can be a generic label, or it can be an ATM VPI/VCI or frame relay DLCI.

which RSVP calls *tunnels*, can appear as SESSION objects, as SENDER_TEMPLATE objects, or as FILTER_SPEC objects. Figure 9.39 shows all three forms. The extended LSP identifier of the SESSION object is normally zero, but the sender can set it to its own IP address if it wants to ensure the session has an unambiguously unique identity.

For constraint-based routing, the EXPLICIT_ROUTE object lets an ingress router specify the full path for an LSP. As figure 9.40 illustrates, the object contains a series of subobjects, each representing a subsequent hop for the path. As a message travels through a network, each hop removes the first subobject in the list. That way, the first subobject always refers to the message's next hop. The most significant bit of

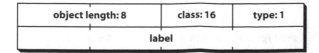

object length: 8	class: 16	type: 1
label		

◀ **Figure 9.38**

A LABEL object carries MPLS labels.

Figure 9.39 ▶

RSVP can reference an MPLS label in SESSION, SENDER_TEMPLATE, and FILTER_SPEC objects.

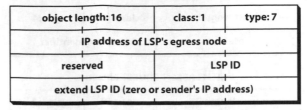

LSP as a SESSION object

object length: 16	class: 1	type: 7
IP address of LSP's egress node		
reserved	LSP ID	
extend LSP ID (zero or sender's IP address)		

LSP as a SENDER_TEMPLATE object

object length: 12	class: 11	type: 7
IP address of LSP's egress node		
reserved	LSP ID	

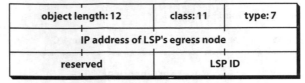

LSP as a FILTER_SPEC object

object length: 12	class: 10	type: 7
IP address of LSP's egress node		
reserved	LSP ID	

each subobject, shown as *L* in the figure, is set if the next hop is *loose*. Loose hops don't have to be the immediate next hop for the path; the path only has to reach them eventually. The figure includes both of the two subobjects so far defined as next hops for IPv4 networks—an IP address prefix and an autonomous system number.

Because the EXPLICIT_ROUTE object allows loose hops, it does not provide complete protection against request loops. That responsibility falls to the RECORD_ROUTE object. Figure 9.41 shows the situation RECORD_ROUTE can prevent. In the

Figure 9.40 ▼

The EXPLICIT_ROUTE object can define a full path through the network. Routers use this object to specify a complete label switched path for traffic engineering.

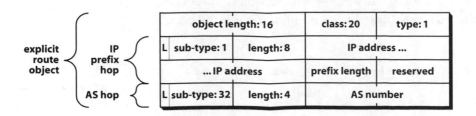

	object length: 16		class: 20	type: 1
L	sub-type: 1	length: 8	IP address ...	
	...IP address		prefix length	reserved
L	sub-type: 32	length: 4	AS number	

explicit route object — IP prefix hop / AS hop

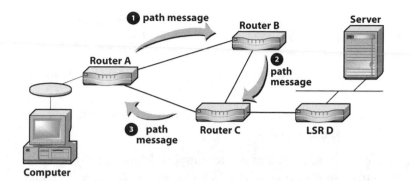

◀ **Figure 9.41**

When routers use RSVP to request a label, an error may cause the path message to loop endlessly.

figure, router C mistakenly sends the path message back to router A rather than the more appropriate next hop router D. Without knowing any better, router A could treat the message the same as it did the first time and forward it on to router B. The request could loop this way forever. To combat this error, RECORD_ROUTE tracks the routers through which a message passes. When the request reaches router A the second time, router A sees its identity already recorded in the option. Router A detects the loop and reports an error.

▼ **Figure 9.42**

The RECORD_ROUTE object records the hops through which a path message travels; it allows routers to detect indefinite looping.

The format of the RECORD_ROUTE object, shown in figure 9.42, is similar to EXPLICIT_ROUTE. A router that processes a message with this option records its IP address using the IPV4

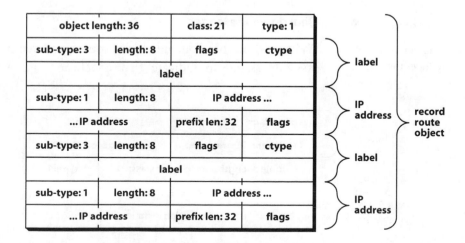

prefix construction with a length of 32 bits. A router may also record the label to which it will forward the message, if it is sending the message on an LSP. A flag in the SESSION object indicates whether label recording is desired. Note that each hop adds its information to the front of the object. At any point, therefore, the first subobject in the list is the last hop the message visited.

The last RSVP extension to support label distribution and traffic engineering is the hello message. Routers exchange RSVP hello messages with their immediate neighbors to assure each other that they're still functioning. Hello messages are especially useful if two neighboring routers are not supporting an active flow but want to maintain contact in case a new flow appears or in case an existing flow needs to be rerouted. The hello message can be used either as a request or a response. A request looks like figure 9.43; it has a HELLO_REQUEST object. The response carries a HELLO_ACK object instead. The only difference between the two is that HELLO_ACK has an object type value of 2 rather than 1. Both objects include *instance* values for both the sender and its peer. These values are random quantities that change whenever a router restarts or loses communication with a peer. When a router reports a new instance value, its peer can reset any state information associated with it.

Teardown Messages

Figure 9.43 ▼

The RSVP hello message gives routers a way to meet their peers.

When a flow has concluded, the source and receivers send RSVP messages to indicate that conclusion. A reservation

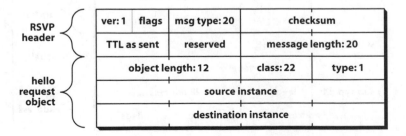

teardown, sent by flow recipients, tells the network that the reserved resources are no longer needed. Like reservation messages, these packets are addressed hop by hop. Figure 9.44 shows an example.

▼ **Figure 9.44**

This example shows a typical RSVP reservation teardown message, which indicates that a reservation is no longer needed.

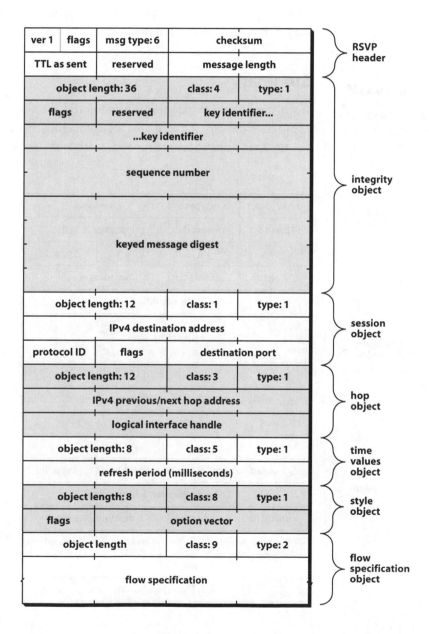

The path teardown, which the flow's sender generates, allows systems to disregard any information they have been maintaining for the flow. These messages follow the same forwarding rules as path messages. They have the same destination address as the flow itself, but intervening routers eavesdrop on the payload to detect and process them. Figure 9.45 illustrates a path teardown.

Figure 9.45 ▼

Sources use a path teardown message to indicate that a flow is no longer active.

Summary

Both the Label Distribution Protocol and the Resource Reservation Protocol are capable of managing label switched paths; their differences are more a matter of perspective than

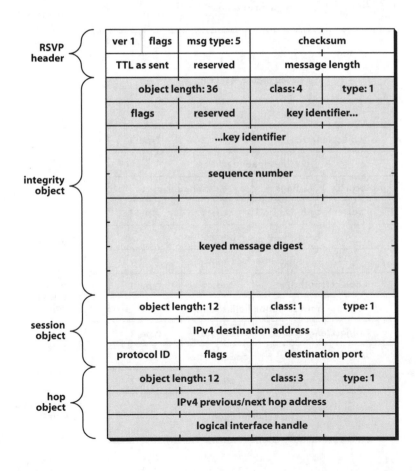

different functionality. While LDP began as a simple label exchange protocol that added resource reservations through its CR-LDP extensions, RSVP started out as a resource reservation protocol that, with the RSVP-TE features, added support for label distribution.

The key difference between the two protocols is how each handles state management in the label switched routers. The Label Distribution Protocol is a hard state protocol. Once two LSRs have exchanged information, each assumes the other retains that information indefinitely, unless it hears otherwise. In contrast, RSVP is a soft state protocol. When two LSRs exchange information with RSVP, they don't assume that the information is stored indefinitely. Rather, the routers periodically refresh the information by resending. Soft state requires more network bandwidth for its refresh messages, which may be costly for particularly large networks, but soft state can be much easier to implement in routers, and it allows the network to adapt more dynamically to changes in the network or the application.

GLOSSARY

Abstract Node   A hop in a path specified by a CR-LDP message.

Acknowledgment   A message that indicates to a peer that data it has transmitted has been successfully received.

Active Connection Request   When an application indicates to its local TCP implementation that it wants to establish a connection with a remote system; also known as a *call*.

Address   A value that uniquely identifies a system or some aspect of a system such as a network interface. Also, an LDP message that a label switched router uses to indicate the IP addresses associated with its interface.

Address Prefix   An IP address in which only some of the most significant bits are relevant; address prefixes often represent subnetworks.

Address Withdraw   An LDP message that a label switched routers uses to indicate IP addresses no longer associated with its interfaces.

Application   A specific function provided to an end user of a network; applications include Web browsing, file transfer, and electronic mail exchange.

Application Layer   The protocol layer that implements the actual application, such as Web browsing, file transfer, and electronic mail.

Area   An administratively defined subdivision of an autonomous system.

Area Border Router   A router that connects different areas within an autonomous system.

AS Boundary Router   A router that connects to a larger network beyond an autonomous system.

Asynchronous Transfer Mode (ATM)   A wide area network technology.

Authentication   The process of verifying the identity of a peer.

Autonomous System   A network of hosts and routers operating under the same administrative domain.

Backbone   A special routing area to which all other areas connect.

Backbone Router   A router within the backbone area.

Backup Designated Router   A router that offers to serve as a designated router should the network's primary designated router fail.

Border Gateway Protocol (BGP)   A path vector routing protocol that supports policy based routing, most often used to coordinate the operation of routers belonging to different network administrations.

Broadcast   Communications intended for all systems on a subnetwork; also, an address used as the destination address for such communications.

Bundle   An RSVP message that combines multiple RSVP messages into one to improve efficiency.

Call   When an application indicates to its local TCP implementation that it wants to establish a connection with a remote system; also known as an *active connection request*.

Checksum   A simple arithmetic calculation performed on a protocol message and included in the message. Recipients can repeat the calculation; if the results differ, the message has encountered an error in transmission.

Confederation   An autonomous system that has been divided into islands known as member autonomous systems. The confederation uses IBGP to exchange routing information among these islands.

Connectionless   A mode of communication in which the network treats each message independently and delivers it to its destination; the communicating parties must themselves provide the context for their message exchange.

Connection-Oriented   A mode of communication in which the network creates an association between the communicating parties and provides a context for their message exchange.

Conservative Label Retention   LDP operation in which paths are only maintained when traffic actively uses them. See also *Liberal Label Retention*.

Constraint-Based Routing   Using additional information to determine the path on which to route traffic. The additional information may include routing policy, current network loading, and other traffic engineering constraints.

Constraint-Based Routing Label Distribution Protocol (CR-LDP)   Extensions to the basic Label Distribution Protocol that allow it to perform constraint-based routing.

Counting to Infinity   A problem with distance vector protocols that can cause a delay in discovery of the correct network topology after a change.

Data Link Connection Identifier (DLCI)   The value that frame relay uses to distinguish different connections. MPLS can use DLCI values as labels.

Database Description Packet   An OSPF message that a router uses to summarize the contents of its link state database.

Datagram   A single packet or message carried by a connectionless protocol such as IP or UDP.

Demand Networks   A network that incurs expenses whenever it is active, even if no useful traffic travels across it. OSPF has special mechanisms to limit the amount of time demand networks must be active.

Designated Router   A fictitious router that acts as a neighbor to all real routers on a broadcast or multi-access network; the designated router is a bookkeeping mechanism that simplifies the link state database and shortest path first algorithm.

Destination   The system for whom a message is intended.

Destination Unreachable   An ICMP message that indicates a particular destination cannot be reached.

Diameter   The maximum number of hops that any destination in a network may be from any source.

Differentiated Service (Diffserv)   Distinguishing classes of traffic and providing different grades of service to different traffic classes.

Diffserv Codepoint (DSCP)   A specific value used to indicate with grade of service a datagram should receive.

Dijkstra's Algorithm   A specific algorithm that takes a link state database and efficiently calculates the paths to all destinations in a network; also known as the *Shortest Path First Algorithm*.

Distance Vector Routing   An approach to routing in which each router periodically advertises to its neighbors the destinations it can reach and the distance to get there. RIP relies on distance vector routing. See also *Link State Routing* and *Path Vector Routing*.

Don't Fragment   A flag in the IP header that prohibits routers from fragmenting a datagram.

Dotted Decimal   A convention for representing IP addresses in text; each byte of the address is expressed as a decimal number, and the bytes are separated by periods.

Downstream On Demand Label Distribution   An exchange of MPLS label information initiated on request of an upstream router; the label information, however, comes from the downstream router.

Downstream Unsolicited Label Distribution   An exchange of MPLS label information initiated by the downstream router in a path.

Echo Reply   An ICMP message sent expressly as a response to an echo request.

Echo Request   An ICMP message that asks a system to respond if it is able.

Ethernet   A high-speed local area network technology.

Expiration Timer   The longest amount of time a RIP router will accept a path as valid after ceasing to here of that path.

Explicit Congestion Notification (ECN)   A technique in which routers mark datagrams that are passing through links that are, or are nearing, congestion. The marking suggests to the application that they should reduce the rate that they insert traffic into the network.

Extension Headers   Optional IP version 6 headers that follow the basic IP header and precede its payload.

Exterior Gateway Protocol (EGP)   A routing protocol that operates between autonomous systems; BGP is an exterior gateway protocol.

External Link State Advertisement   A link state advertisement that carries information about destinations outside of an autonomous system.

Fixed Filter Style   A reservation style in which resources are dedicated to a single flow.

Flooding   The technique of disseminating a link state advertisement throughout a network of routers. A router that receives the advertisement sends a copy to all links except the one on which it arrived.

Flow   A series of messages belonging to the same application.

Flow Control   The process of controlling the rate at which a peer system transmits data so as to avoid overwhelming the destination.

Flow Label   A header field in IP version 6 datagrams that explicitly indicates the traffic flow to which a datagram belongs.

Flowspec   The specification of a flow used by RSVP.

Forwarding   The process of examining a message's destination address to decide where to send it next so that it moves one step closer to its destination; see also *Switching*.

Forwarding Equivalence Class (FEC)   The description of traffic which can use a specific MPLS path.

Fragment Identification   An IP header field that identifies the original datagram from which several fragments may have been created; all fragments from the same source with the same fragment identification belong to the same original datagram.

Fragment Offset   A field in the IP header that identifies where in the original datagram the current fragment belongs.

Fragmentation   Dividing a large datagram into smaller pieces so that the pieces are small enough to travel across a particular subnetwork.

Frame Check Sequence   A more sophisticated version of a checksum used by some network technologies. Specific mathematical algorithms used for the frame check sequence include cyclic redundancy checks (CRCs).

Garbage Collection Timer   The amount of time a RIP router retains information about a path it considers expired before it discards the information completely.

Hello   A message in several protocol (OSPF, LDP, RSVP) that systems use to introduce themselves.

Hierarchy   The technique of dividing information into successively smaller subdivisions so that each subdivision can operate somewhat autonomously; IP addresses and IP networks may be organized in hierarchies.

Hop Limit   A field in the IP header that limits the number of routers through which a datagram may travel; this field was originally called the time-to-live field.

Host   A system that acts as the original source or ultimate destination for a message; see also *Router*.

Hypertext Transfer Protocol (HTTP)   The application protocol used for Web browsing.

Independent Label Distribution Control   LDP operation in which each hop in a path exchanges label information independently of other hops in the path. See also *Ordered Label Distribution Control*.

Initialization   An LDP message that a label switched router uses to establish a session with a peer.

Interior BGP (IBGP)   The Border Gateway Protocol when used within an autonomous system.

Interior Gateway Protocol (IGP)   A routing protocol that operates within an autonomous system; OSPF and RIP are interior gateway protocols.

Interior Router   A router whose interfaces are all part of the same area.

Internet   The global data communications network based on Internet Protocol technology.

Internet Control Message Protocol (ICMP)   A special protocol that works with IP to control address assignments, report errors, and diagnose network problems.

Internet Group Management Protocol (IGMP)   A special protocol that works with IP to manage membership in multicast groups.

Internet Protocol (IP)   The unifying protocol of the Internet that allows the combination of many different network technologies and many different network applications.

Internetwork Layer   The protocol layer that ensures messages are delivered to the appropriate destination.

Internetwork   A larger communications network consisting of multiple, interconnected subnetworks.

KEEPALIVE   A BGP message that keeps a TCP connection between peer routers active.

KeepAlive   An LDP message that a label switched router uses to reassure its peer that it is still active.

Label   A value that MPLS associates with a packet that identifies that path that packet will take through the MPLS network.

Label Abort Request   An LDP message that indicates a label request is no longer needed.

Label Distribution Protocol (LDP)   A communications protocol for exchanging MPLS labels between routers.

Label Mapping   An LDP message that indicates a new label is available.

Label Release   An LDP message that indicates a label is no longer needed.

Label Request   An LDP message that a label switched router uses to request a label mapping.

Label Stack   The nesting of MPLS paths within each other.

Label Switched Path (LSP)   A path through an MPLS network associated with a specific label.

Label Switched Router (LSR)   A router that supports MPLS.

Label Withdraw   An LDP message that indicates a label is no longer available.

Layer   Part of a network architecture that combines many different communications protocols; layers usually have specific and well-defined responsibilities that can be satisfied by particular protocols.

Liberal Label Retention   LDP operation in which label switched paths may be maintained even when no traffic is actively using them. See also *Conservative Label Retention*.

Link State Acknowledgment Packet   An OSPF message that a router uses to acknowledge receipt of link state information.

Link State Advertisement (LSA)   A message of a link state routing protocol (such as OSPF) that identifies the links to which a router connects.

Link State Database   The list of links to which all link state routers in a network are connected; it holds the complete topology of the network.

Link State Request Packet   An OSPF message by which a router requests link state information from its neighbor.

Link State Routing   An approach for sharing information among routers and calculating paths to network destinations. Link state routing distributes the entire topology of the network to all participating routers, and those routers use special algorithms to calculate paths from the topology. OSPF relies on link state routing. See also *Distance Vector Routing* and *Path Vector Routing*.

Link State Update Packet   An OSPF message that a router uses to advertise its link state information.

Listen   When an application indicates to its local TCP implementation that it is willing to accept a connection; also known as a *passive connection request*.

Loop Detection   Techniques to prevent or detect routing loops or similar problems in related protocols.

Loose Source Routing   When the source of a message lists some of the hops through with a message must travel on the way to its destination; the message may pass through other, unlisted intermediate hops as well.

Maximum Transmission Unit (MTU)   The size of the largest protocol message that a specific subnetwork can carry.

Member Autonomous System   An artificial division of an autonomous system that allows efficient use of IBGP.

Membership Query   An IGMP message that asks for members of a particular multicast group to announce themselves.

Membership Report   An IGMP message by which a system announces it has joined a multicast group.

Membership Termination   An IGMP message by which a system announces it has left a multicast group.

Merging   The process of combining reservation requests from multiple destination systems before passing the reservation further upstream.

More Fragments   A flag in the IP header that indicates the specific datagram is not the final fragment.

Multicast   Communications that has a set of systems as its destination; also, an address used as the destination address for such communications.

Multicast Routing   Sharing information and calculating paths for multicast traffic.

Multi-Exit Discriminator (MED)   A path attribute that BGP routers use to express a preference among different links, all of which connect to the next hop of a destination.

Multi-Protocol Label Switching (MPLS)   A technique for establishing paths through a network and very efficiently forwarding messages along those paths.

Network Link   A special OSPF link that connects a real router to a designated router.

Next Header   A field in the IP header that identifies the higher layer protocol whose message is carried in the datagram's payload; this field was originally called the protocol field.

Non-Broadcast Multi-Access (NBMA)   Network architectures that allow multiple systems to communicate directly, but don't have native support for broadcast or multicast transmission. Example NBMA networks include ATM and frame relay wide area networks.

Not So Stubby Area (NSSA)   A routing area that permits limited propagation of routing information for destinations beyond it.

NOTIFICATION   A BGP message that reports errors.

Notification   An LDP message that reports an error.

Opaque Link State Advertisement   A link state advertisement whose contents are currently unspecified; the LSA is defined now to allow for graceful introduction of new features in the future.

Open Shortest Path First (OSPF) Protocol   A link state routing protocol most commonly used to coordinate routers within a medium or large-scale network.

OPEN   A BGP message that establishes a session between peer routers.

Ordered Label Distribution Control   LDP operation in which all hops in a path coordinate the exchange of label information. See also *Independent Label Distribution Control*.

Padding   Arbitrary information added to a protocol message to force that message to be a specific length, often because cryptographic functions require the specific length.

Parameter Problem   An ICMP message that reports a problem with a previous datagram.

Passive Connection Request When an application indicates to its local TCP implementation that it is willing to accept a connection; also known as a *listen*.

Path Attribute   Information that BGP associates with the path to a destination.

Path Vector Routing   An approach to routing in which each router periodically advertises to its neighbors the destinations it can reach and the path it would use to reach them. BGP relies on path vector routing. See also *Link State Routing* and *Distance Vector Routing*.

Path   An RSVP message that indicates the path a flow is taking.

Payload   The content of a packet or protocol message, not counting any protocol headers.

Penultimate Hop Popping   Removing an MPLS label one hop earlier than expected to improve forwarding efficiency.

Ping   A user command on UNIX and Windows systems that initiates an ICMP echo request and reply exchange; it's often used as a quick check to make sure that a remote system remains functioning.

Poison Reverse   A more aggressive variant of split horizon in which distance vector routers advertise the distance to destination learned from a neighbor as infinity in updates returned to that neighbor.

Policy-Based Routing   Using administrative policy to influence network routing decisions.

Port   A value that distinguishes different applications operating in the same system; transport protocols UDP and TCP have source and destination port fields in their headers.

Privileged Port   A port value that some operating systems (e.g. UNIX) limit to only those application programs with special privileges.

Protocol Data Unit (PDU)   A protocol message or packet.

Pseudo Header   An imaginary protocol header that systems use in calculating checksums and other authentication data.

Redirect   An ICMP message that suggests a better next hop to use for a particular destination.

Refresh Reduction   A enhancement to RSVP that allows routers to reduce the amount of traffic needed solely to refresh soft state.

Reliable Delivery   The responsibility of some transport protocols to ensure that data is delivered to its destination in order, without errors, and without duplication.

Reservation   A request for network resources to be dedicated to a one or more flows.

Reservation Style   How a reservation is associated with one or more flows.

Resource Reservation Protocol (RSVP)   A protocol that allows systems to reserve network resources for particular applications.

Resource Reservation Protocol for Traffic Engineering (RSVP-TE)   Extensions to the basic Resource Reservation Protocol that allow it to support traffic engineering objectives.

Route Aggregation   Combining multiple destinations that share a common IP address prefix and advertising that address prefix as a single destination.

Route Pinning   Preventing the exact label switched path from changing during its lifetime.

Route Reflector   A special IBGP router that re-advertises routing information learned from some peers to other peers.

Router   An intermediate system in between the source and destination of a message; routers move the message one step closer to its destination.

Router Advertisement   An ICMP message that routers use to announce their presence.

Router Link   A normal OSPF link between two routers.

Router Solicitation   An ICMP message that hosts use to query for routers on the subnetwork.

ROUTE-REFRESH   A BGP message to request full routing information from a peer router.

Routing Information Protocol (RIP)   A distance vector routing protocol most commonly used to coordinate routers within a small to medium-scale network.

Routing Loop   An error in the exchange of routing information that causes datagrams to loop endlessly within a network instead of reaching their destination.

Routing Protocol   A communication protocol that coordinates the operation of routers on a network, generally by providing a way for routers to exchange network topology information.

Routing   The process of exchanging network topology information so that routers can determine how to deliver messages appropriately; informally, the term is often used to mean forwarding.

Segment   A single TCP message carried in an IP datagram.

Shared Explicit Style   A reservation style in which resources are reserved for multiple flows and shared by those flows.

Shortest Path First Algorithm   A specific algorithm that takes a link state database and efficiently calculates the paths to all destinations in a network; also known as *Dijkstra's algorithm* after its inventor.

Socket   The combination of an IP address and a port.

Soft State   Said of a protocol in which all information is considered tentative and must be periodically refreshed. RSVP is a soft state protocol; LDP is not.

Source   The system that transmits a message.

Source Routing   When the source of a message selects the path that the message should follow through the network; strict source routing requires the source identify every intermediate hop explicitly, while loose source routing only lists some of the intermediate hops.

Split Horizon   A refinement to distance vector routing that has routers omit destinations learned from a neighbor in its own advertisements to that neighbor.

Stream Control Transmission Protocol (SCTP)   A relatively new transport protocol that offers increased reliability and greater performance for some applications.

Strict Source Routing   When the source of a message explicitly specifies every intermediate hop through which the message must travel on the way to its destination.

Stub Area   A routing area that has only one connection into or out of it.

Subnet   A collection of communicating systems relying on a common network technology (such as an Ethernet Local Area Network); also the IP address prefix that refers to such a network. Same as *Subnetwork*.

Subnet Mask   A convention for denoting the number of relevant bits in an IP address prefix; the mask is expressed in dotted decimal notation with relevant bits set to one and other bits set to zero.

Subnetwork   A collection of communicating systems relying on a common network technology (such as an Ethernet Local Area Network); also the IP address prefix that refers to such a network. Same as *Subnet*.

Summary Link State Advertisement   A link state advertisement that carries information summarizing destinations beyond an area.

Switching   The process of moving a message onto its next hop in a prearranged path without looking at its destination address; see also *Forwarding*.

Three-Way Handshake   The first three TCP messages that systems use to establish a TCP connection.

Time Exceeded   An ICMP message that indicates one of two problems: Either a message exceeded its hop limit, or a message could not be reassembled in a timely manner by the its destination.

Time-to-Live   The original name for the hop limit field in the IP header.

Token Ring   A local area network technology.

Traceroute   A user command on UNIX systems (the Windows equivalent is *tracert*) that uses a series of messages and ICMP responses to discover the network path to a destination.

Traffic Engineering   Tailoring the flow of traffic through a network in order to optimize the network's performance or reliability.

Transmission Control Protocol (TCP)   A transport protocol that establishes connections and provides reliable delivery.

Transport Layer   The protocol layer that provides whatever reliability is appropriate for a communications.

Triggered Update   A refinement to distance vector routing that has routers send updated routing information as soon as they become aware of it rather than waiting for its normally scheduled transmission.

Tunnel   How RSVP-TE refers to label switched paths.

Unicast   Communications that has a single system as its destination; also, an address used as the destination address for such communications.

UPDATE   A BGP message that exchanges routing information.

Urgent Data   Information that is especially critical for the peer in a communications exchange.

User Datagram Protocol (UDP)   A transport protocol that does not provide reliable delivery.

Vendor Identifier   A special value added to non-standard LDP messages and parameters that indicates the manufacturer that is uses it.

Virtual Circuit Identifier (VCI)   One of two values (the other is the virtual path identifier) that ATM uses to distinguish different connections. MPLS can use VCI values as labels.

Virtual Path Identifier (VPI)   One of two values (the other is the virtual circuit identifier) that ATM uses to distinguish different connections. MPLS can use VPI values as labels.

Well-Known Port   A special port value dedicated to a particular application.

Wildcard Filter Style   A reservation style in which resources are reserved for a general type of flow.

Withdrawn Routes   Destinations in a BGP UPDATE message that the sender can no longer reach.

INDEX